THEORY
AND
PRACTICE OF
NON VIOLENCE

THEORY AND PRACTICE OF NON VIOLENCE

Edited By
S. R. Sharma
Director Education

COSMO PUBLICATIONS
2001 INDIA

THEORY AND PRACTICE OF NON VIOLENCE
First COSMO Print 2001

ISBN 81-7755-137-x

Published by
MRS. RANI KAPOOR
for COSMO PUBLICATIONS Div. of
GENESIS PUBLISHING PVT. LTD.
24-B, Ansari Road, Darya Ganj,
New Delhi-110 002, INDIA

Composed at
Cosmo Publications

Printed at
Mehra Offset Press

CONTENTS

Chapter-1

Introduction to Theories of Nonviolence

A. Paul Hare

Chapter-1

Over the the Years several approaches have been taken in the study of nonviolence. The earlier analyses tend to focus on the values held by a nonviolent actors, or to describe the behaviour of other actors and the response of their oppoentns. More recent articles discuss the motivation of Negro participants in the sit-ins and demonstrations in the U.S. South, the relationship between nonviolent activity and attitude change, and phases in the development of nonviolent activity considered as a social movement. After first abstracting an article by Gene Sharp which gives an overview of the types of principled nonviolent activity, I will review each of the articles in turn, approximately in chronological order subdivided into early analyses and current perspectives.

Early Analyses

Gene Sharp is currently at the Center of International Affairs at Harvard Unviersity where he is just completing a book on nonviolence which will summarize the work he has been doing over number of years. During this time he has produced several different classifications of nonviolent action. In the most recent he limits his discussion to action by persons who rejects violence on principle. He describes six types as follows:

1. *Nonresistance.* Nonresistant groups, such as the Mennonites or Amish, are concerned with being true to their beliefs and maintaing their own integrity, rather than with attempts at social reconstruction. They refuse to resist, even with nonviolent techniques, attacks or encroachments on their way of life.

2. *Active reconciliation.* This type, represented by the Religious Society of Friends (Quakers), favors using active goodwill and reconciliation to bring about social change. Some of the members of these groups do not believe in the use of nonviolent

direct action or strategy.

3. *Moral resistance.* Peace societies in New England in the nineteenth century are representative of those who believed that evil should be resisted, but only by peaceful and moralmeans. Their activities included both refusal to participate in war or holding of slaves and a moral imperative to do something actively such as speaking, writing, or preaching. Nonviolent resistance was not ruled out although the major emphasis was usually placed on education, persuasion, and individual example.

4. *Selective nonviolence.* Groups of this type, such as the International Socialists, especially during World War I, and the Jehovah's Witnesses, refuse to participate in *particular* violent conflicts, usually international wars. In certain other situations the same groups might be willing to use violence to accomplish the desired ends.

5. *Satyagraha.* The believer in *satyagraha,* which was practiced in India by followers of Gandhi, seeks truth through love and right action. He attempts to convert his opponents through sympathy, patience, truthfulness, and self-suffering. He tries to build a new social and economic order through voluntary constructive work. The principle is combined with a variety of techniques and strategies of resistance.

6. *Nonviolent revolution.* As a recent ideology, nonviolent revolution is still a developing trend of thought and action rather than a movement with a fixed program. Persons of this type believe that the major social problems of the world have their origins at the roots of individual and social life and can be solved only by revolutionary change. This revolution, however, is tobe brought about the nonviolent, cooperative, and egalitarian methods rather than by exploitation, oppression, and war.

In another version of his typology Sharp adds three types of nonviolence which are not necessarily based on principle: passive resistance, peaceful resistance, and nonviolent direct action. These forms he places between selective nonviolence and satyagraha along his continuum from least to most revolutionary. Of the three types, the nonviolent direct action is of the most interest since most of the case material cited in analyses of nonviolence would seem to fall into this category. Sharp describes this type as follows:

Nonviolent direct action. This is a method of producing of thwarting social change by intervention aimed at establishing new patterns or policies or disrupting actives regarded as evil. The motivation of the activists may vary from belief in nonviolence as a moral principle to adherence to a temporary nonviolent discipline as a practical method to achieve a particular objective. As in satyagraha, the direct action may be preceded by investigation of the facts, discussions with those responsible for the policy found objectionable, negotiations, public appeals, publicity about the grievance, or prayer, fasting, and other racts of "self-purification." As an example of this type Sharp cited one of Gandhi's campaigns in India. Other examples are the demonstrations by members of CORE (Congress of Racial Equality) in their attempts to combat racial discrimination in the United States.

Another person who has concentrated on Gandhi's methods in Joan Bondurant, a political scientist, who first became interested in Gandhi during her residence in India in 1944-1946 and returned in subsequent years for further study. Her book. *Conquest of Violence: The Gandhian Philosophy of Conflict,* is a classic on this subject and provides the most systematic outline of Gandhi's major campaigns.

In a chapter in which she discusses the basic precepts of satyagraha, Bondurant develops the meaning of the Indian word *ahimsa* which she feels to be central to the concept of nonviolence. This gives further insight into the values which lie behind the actions of the nonviolent protestor. *Ahimsa* means "action based on the refusal to do harm."Gandhi equated *ahimsa* with love and as a result required a positive program of action from his followers. He said: "It does not mean meek submission to the will of the evil-doer, but it means the putting of one's whole soul against the will of the tyrant." This theme, which is a version of the Christian tradition, appears again in the ideology of Martin Luther King and other leaders in the early phases of the American civil lights movement. It still provides the basic philosophy of nonviolence for those who act on principle rather than use non-violence only as a strategy for the moment.

Clarence Case was a pastor in the Society of Friends and a university professor of sociology. In 1923 be published a book on *Nonviolent Coercion* which is probably thefirst academic treatment of the subject. He examines a number of historical accounts of nonviolence as examples of socializing influence.

One of his cases concerns an Archbishop in England who was set upon by a highwayman. The Archbishop asks what his problem is and on learning that he is desperately in debt, offers to give him the money he needs. Presumably this indicates that "a soft answer turneth away wrath," although in this instance money was proffered. Case notes that this should also work for any individual confronting a hostile aggressor, "provided that it does not degenerate into object submission, but takes on the noble aggressiveness of an exalted moral and religious character."' It would seem that the nonviolent actor must be of equal or higher status compared with his opponent. Then the 'unexpected' act of kindness" would have high value for the opponent, and the nonviolent actor might expect a return of love for love. This idea will be developed in more detail below after a review of the other theories of nonviolent confrontation.

Another early theorist who was attracted to Gandhis method of handing conflict is Richard Gregg, an attorney who worked in labor-management relation before going to India to live with Gandhi and learn from turn over a period of four years. His first insights into the method came from two sources, one a book on Japanese jiujitsu wrestling and the other an article on military strategy. On his return to the United States in 1929, he searched the libraries for psychological literature which would help him explain the process of nonviolence. The result was a book, first published in 1935, on *The Power of Nonviolence,* which has been revised and reprinted several times. A key idea in his book is that nonviolence is a form of "moral jiujitsu."

If a person is attacked and hits back, the attacker's morale is sustained and his sense of values is vindicated. That is, the attacker knows that the person is willing to fight on his term. But if theperson has a look and posture which shows not fear but courage and his steady resistance of will reveals no subserviance, then the attacker looses his moral support. Again we note that the actor must not appear submissive if he is to obtain a loving response.

Gregg offers a number of psychological observations explain the fact that the attacker seems to be thrown off guard as if the person had used "jijujitsu" The prolonged anger of the attacker presumably leads to psychological exhaustion, he has mixed feelings which work against each other, and be experiences curiosity and wonder; which "tends to exclude repugnance, disgust, and contempt, in relation to its object."

If an audience is present the attacker begins to feel "brutal" since the person's willingness to suffer attests his sincere belief and his respect shown (or the attacker (in front of the audience) puts the attacker to shame. As we shall see, the presence of a third party, or audience, is often important for die nonviolent actor since it facilitates a kind of "alter-casting." Playing to the audience, the person can make the attacker (alter) appeal to be unjustified in his hostile reaction. This effect would be especially strong if the attacker has high regard for the opinion of the audience.

Pitirim Sorokin, who died in 1968, had a long and distinguished career as a sociologist. Born in Russia in 1889, he came to the United States in 1922. He founded the Department of Sociology at Harvard University and in his later years established a Research Center in Creative Altruism. One of the books written at the Center was *The Ways and Power of Love Types Factors and Techniques of Moral Transformation, in* which he provides evidence that love begets love and hate begets hate" He cites research in mental hospitals, with college students, and with children in which individuals tend to respond to positive acts with positive reactions and to aggressive acts with aggressive reactions.

Like his colleagues who did research before the mass desegregation activities in the United States in the early 1960's. Sorokin had relatively few published accounts of case material or rearch to draw on for analysis and interpretation, other than the campaigns of Gandhi. The situation was different for the remaining authors whose work is reviewed under "current perspectives." Most of these social scientists wrote against a background of personal experience with the civil rights movement in the United States, sometimes basing their generalizations on their own participant observation, sometimes using interviews or questionnaires, but in almost all cases playing some part in the collection of their data. Part of this change used result of new methods and new theory in social science authors such as Sharp, Gregg, and Bondurant may have had first-hand experience with Gandhi and India, but they generally worked within their own theoretical frameworks. In the later research were see much more convergence of findings and a greater awareness of the relationship between nonviolent activity and, more general forms of social behavior.

Current Perspectives

In addition to teaching at Negro Colleges in the U.S. South, James Vander Zanden has published several sociology texts on race relations. This experience is reflected in his, analysis of the nonviolent resistance movement among Southern Negroes The use of nonviolence is seen as an attempt to mediate between the conflicting roles of the traditional accommodating Negro and the new militant Negro. Guilt feelings over the militant and aggressive acts are countered by an emphasis on suffering. The themes of "love your enemies" and "suffer" were emphasized in the speeches of Martin Luther King at rallies in the South. They are part of the Christian tradition, which asserts that suffering is redemptive in that it purchases good things here and in the other world, and they are also part of the Gandhian approach. Thus from Vander Zanden's analysis we see that the nonviolent movement in the United States began with the same general ideology that had been used effectively in

India.

Botn Jacob Fishman and Fredric Solomon were psychiatrists in the Medical School at Howard University in Washington D.C., during the early 1960's. This gave them ample opportunity to observe and interview white and Negro students who participated in the sit-ins and other demonstrations. They were especially interested in the motivations of the adolescents who participated in the demonstrations.

The typical Negro participant came from a background in which the Negro male was degraded and deprecated and could not serve as an adequate ego ideal or model for identification for his children. Thus the adolescent search for identity and recognition as an adult was interwoven with the struggle of Southern Negroes as a social group for recognition as mature human beings. "The Negro students would act out through the sit-ins, their early childhood frustrations and parental conflicts and wishes Fishman and Solomon call this John of acting-out prosocial in contrast to the *anti-social* behavior of delinquents.They provide a case study of a student who feels that he is doing what his parents and the nation really want him to do but are afraid to recommend openly."

By taking a passive, submissive role, the Negro demonstrators provide for white extremists the opportunity to act out for them the very anger and resentment that they (the Negroes) have themselves felt. The anger and violence, however, have been externalized and projected onto the "aggressor" so that students feel guiltless and even exhilarated in their justifiable indignation (Again we see the use of alter-casting.) The nonviolent stance of the demonstrator also helps to win the sympathy of the observing public and reduces fears of whites that Negroes intend to retaliate violently for past suppression. As in the analysis of Sorokin, they indicate their willingness to trade love for love.

Although Christian tradition and Gandhi and King are incorporated in the student ideology, Fishman and Solomon feel that the students are generally not pacifists. Rather, their nonviolence was consistent with the traditional passive and submissive role in the face of white domination and potential retaliation.

However, the fact that they were able to engage in direct action was related to developing a new sense of identity. Fishman and Solomon suggest:

> A young person feels most free or independent only after having done something active and aggressive to win that independence. In this context perhaps an "independent" identity can never be freely given—it must be at least partially *taken* by adolescents and possibly by young nations as well.

George Lakey, a sociologist, has been involved in nonviolent direct action both as a participant and as an observer. He collaborated with Martin Oppenheimer on *A Manual for Direct Action,* has written several articles, and recently joined the crew of the *Phoenix* in an attempt to take medical supplies to North and South Vietnam. In a pamphlet on the "Mechanisms of Nonviolent Action" be describes three ways in which nonviolent action seems to work.

The first of these "mechanisms" is *coercion.* This was used by the Roman peasants in the fifth century B.C. when they withdrew to the mons sacra and would not return until they were given a share in the government and the common lands." The second is *conversion.* As an example of this type Lakey cites the success of Portuguese soldiers in Brazil in 1531 in winning over the Chavante Indians by approaching them without guns. The Indians called them a tribe of white Indians." Here it is possible that the effect was not so much *conversion* as persuading the Indians to treat the soldiers as they would other Indians rather than as members of an "out group." As Erikson notes in his paper to be discussed below, nations, tribes, and other human collectivities have traditionally assumed that only the members of their own groups were "human" and mat others who were non-human should be kept at bay. Thus, as long as the Portuguese respected their hunting rights and did not come armed, the Indians were willing to treat them as brothers. Lakey says that the principle at work is "identification" and quites Freud on this subject: the effects of identification are founds in "a person limiting his aggressiveness towards those with whom he has identified himself, and in his sparing them, and giving them help."

The third type of nonviolent mechanism, mentioned by Lakey is *persuasion.* Here the example is the salt satyagraha of Gandhi where the British gave in to the Indians demands although they presumably were not convinced,

Like Lakey with whom he coauthored the *Manual for Direct Action,* Martin Oppenheimer has combined teaching and research in sociology with social action with the AFSC, CORE, and other race relations and peace groups. In a paper called "Towards a Sociological Understanding of Nonviolence" he lists seven tenets of the nonviolent ideology and six variables which will affect the results of nonviolent action, which together form a review of some of the prior research."

The seven tenets of the ideology are:

1. Action based on "truth-force" or love.
2. A need to communicate with an opponent to bring a change of heart.
3. Never attempting to overcome evil with evil, only with good.
4. Enduring unmerited suffering.
5. The search for truth in which it is not for man to judge man irrevocably by killing him or using physical violence.
6. Respect for the individual.
7. Religious feeling, because the resister needs this kind of .security when his life is at stake.

The six factors which effect the outcome of nonvioleot demonstrations are taken in part from Kuper's discussion of *Passive Resistance in South Africa.* They are:

1. The relative size of the opposing groups, since larger groups are more threatening.
2. Differences in culture, since subordinate groups can .be seen as non-human.

3. Differences between leaders and followers in ideology, since leaders cannot use techniques which appear too strange.
4. The "threshold of resistance" of the dominant group, since the subordinate group may not be able to suffer long enough to make an impact. This factor would be com pounded if the public did not know about the suffering.
5. Attack versus defense. Negroes in the U.S. South were on the 'attack' to change customs whereas Bantu in South Africa were on the "defense" to maintain the status quo. Those on the defense, are more likely to be seen as inher ently weak.
6. Psychological differentials. People to some cultures may be more ready for nonviolence! as a result of childhood training.

Unfortunately Oppeneimner does not cite evi dence to support this last point, since before the mass civil rights demonstrations in the United States it used to be argued that nonviolence might have worked in India against the British because of their particular ideologies, but its would never work in America. All of the other authors discussed here adduce social or psychological principles which are assumed to operate across cultures and do not deal with individual or group differences, although I would agree with, Oppenheimer that they probably exist.

As a result of discussions in a college course on attitude change, Sidney Perloe, David Olton, and David Yaffe wrote a paper on "Attitudes and Nonviolent Action" in which they reviewed the literature on attitude change, and applied it to an analysis of the effects of nonviolent demonstraitons. At, present Perloe is a professor of social psychology and Olton and Yaffe are both graduate students in psychology.

Attitudes have cognitive, affective, and behavioral components. To bring about attitude change: one must disturb the equilibrium of one or more of these components. There are three phases in attitude changer unfreezing changing, and refreezing.

Attitudes have three functions in social behavior: they facilitate object orientation, that is, they allow a person to identify objects which, are capable of directly rewarding or harming him; they serve as ego-supports since they can earn approval for a person from significant reference groups; and they can be used in ego-defense to reduce anxiety caused by unconscious conflicts

Projection is one method of ego-defense. "If the frigtening impulse is aggression against respected authorities or institutions, projection leads the individual to attribute the impulse to other persons and allows him to aggress against those other persons, thereby giving some indirect expression to the troublesome motive," One wonders if some members of the police force might not be drawn into their occupation by a concern about aggression against respected authorities and thus be prone to project violence into the actions of non-violent demonstrators.

Perloe *et al.* give an example of a father who has high regard for his son but a low regard for civil rights demonstrations in which the son has taken part to illustrate an individuals need for cognitive consistency. In such a situation the father may try to bring his attitudes into balance by changing the attitude which required the least effort, since balance would be obtained if the father had a high (or low) regard for both the son and his activities. Another possibility in this case would be to differentiate the civil rights demonstration into several parts and assume that the son participated only in the "good" part.

Another way of interpreting this situation is to say that the individual tries to reduce the dissonance between conflicting attitudes Following this theory one can understand why, when the coercive form to change attitudes is great, a person may not be converted, since the knowledge of the force being applied to him is a third variable. That is, the individual may give the appearance of change to satisfy the person applying the coercive force, but covertly maintain his former attitude.

Although targets of nonviolent demonstrations and audiences may be "immunized" by accounts in newspapers, the first confrontation with nonviolent action may still have an "unfreezing" impact and lead to a change in "object-oriented" attitudes. Members of the audience in turn may attempt to deny the dissonance created by seeing presumably "satisfied" Negroes demonstrating for their rights. The audience may blame the disturbance on "outside' agitators. This would be easier to do if the demonstrators appear hostile or defiant.

Changing ego-supportive attitudes by changing the relative salience of reference groups is probably the most powerful technique available to facilitate the acceptance of nonviolent action." That is, the actors should try to have some important person or group endorse their activity. At the very least, they should arrange for police protection since it would indicate the legal status of the protest.

The most difficult to change would be ego-defensive attitudes since a demonstration usually carries, with it some element of threat which would only serve to nake others more defensive. The defensive distortion of events could be minimized if the demonstrators would help; keep paths clear, cooperate with legitimate police requests, and perform other helpful acts.

Perloe *et al.* observe that the pressures on the target, a lunch counter operator, for example, are coercive pressures rawer than attitude change pressures and are not covered by this theory. However, if a lunch counter owner desegregates under protest, he may not change his attitudes, but white customers using the using the desegregated facilities may. The same would be true of the effects of new legislation. Here again we see a difference in the affects nonviolent demonstration on the target and on the audience or others who may participate in a less direct way.

As a final prescription for attitude change Peroloe *et al.* suggest that "it is probably best for the protestors concentrate on coercing behavior change in a way which used as little force as possible to ensure the desired *changes* and to focus on changing attitudes only when me information needed to apply attitude change theories is available". It is quite apparent in this paper, and probably true for, the authors cited here, that the persons who do research nonviolence are not indifferent to the outcome of nonviolent demonstrations. They want them to succeed, but. they also hope that the actors will attempt to understand the social-psychological principles at work.

The next three authors deal more with nonviolence as a social movement than with face-to-face encounters of demonstrators or attitude change. Judith Stiehm is a political scientist, Victor Lidz a sociologist, and Herbert Blumberg a psychologist.

Stiehm observes that there are two sets of values that are intermingled in the nonviolent social movements in the United States. These two schools are "conscientious" and "pragmatic" nonviolence. The goal of the person practicing "conscientious" nonviolence is conversion. Coercion is ruled out. This form has an individualist orientation, each individual is to avoid wrong doing, and its followers believe that it would be best to have no government at all.

In contrast, "pragmatic" nonviolence is usually practiced by a group rather than an individual. The group may conduct a highly organized campaign which brings up a problem of leadership. Followers are more concerned to avoid being wronged than they are to avoid doing wrong. They feel that a democratic form of government is best.

In a comment on this article Lidz suggests that the two schools are really two stages in the development of any social movement. The conscientious form precedes the pragmatic. In addition, the money to support the social movement usually comes from conscientious appeals.

Based on interviews with participants, businessmen, and political figures who were involved in a 1963 nonviolent mass demonstration for civil rights at Durham, N.C., Blumberg develops a model to account for the personnel involved, the site, and the form of such a protest." He shows that a protest in any one city is related to the history of negotiation and protest in that city and the timing and relevance of protests in other cities. The processes involved in his model include evolution, contagion, and reinforcement.

1. *Evolution* The evolution of the movement fullows from a series of encounters between demonstrators and oppenents from which the "fittest" forms survive.

2. *Contagion* the will to participaate and the form of the protest is passed from one person to another. The spread of information follows the communication network in the city.

3. *Reinforcement* The selection of a protest site depends on a sequence of rewards (positive and negative) provided by a series of encounters at a given site.

Blumberg's utility model does not deal directly with the outcome of the movement. He suggests that people do what seems to be most rewarding and that the outcome follows a series of complicated interactions in which the variables are those indicated by Oppenheimer and Perloe *et al.*

Erik Erikson brings to his analysis of "Problems of Identity, Hatred, and Nonviolence" a rich background of training and practice in psychoanalysis, especially with children. His published works deal mainly with problems of personality development, especially with the problem of identity. At the time that be wrote the present article he was gathering material for a book in which he hoped to be able to interpret the events surrounding Gandhis adoption of the philosophy and practice of nonviolence. He begins his article with some historical background of Gandhi's life. then summarizes Lorenz's work on aggmsion in animal, and finally discusses the similarities and differences between aggressive and non-aggressive behavior in animals and men.

In contrast to folk belief, Lorenz discovered that animal are not just "naturally" violent. Within their own species, ritualized threatening behavior in animals often *prevents* murder. Only rarely does it escalate into injurious attack.

Although man also has instinctual drives, these are shaped by the process of socialization. Man in his long childhood has a minimum of instinctive pattern and maximum of free instinctual energy available for investmented a growing variety of basic psychosocial encounters which will, if he is lucky, bind his energy in patterns of mutuality, reliability, and competence.

Sociogenic evolution has split mankind into pseudo-species, into tribes, nations, religions, castes, and classes which bind their members into a pattern of individual and collective identity. However, they reinforce the pattern by a mortal fear of and a murderous hatred for other pseudo-species. The other species are models for "negative identity." Aa history changes, these images change their values, and only positive historical change can rebind them into a new and wider identity promising a sense of inner freedom.

The most powerful historical example of a negative identity attempting to become positive is that of the highly educated German nation, despised by the world after World War I, turning to a mystical Aryanism to bind up its shattered identity fragments. In such a cultural regression one can recognize a specific rage which is aroused whenever identity development loses the promise of a traditionally assured wholeness. This latent rage, in turn, is easily exploited by fanatic and psychopathic leaders.

Negative identities can be converted into positive ones by participating in a more inclusive identity. The Roman Empire is an example in that it provided a more inclusive identity which helped an era bind up the fears, the anxieties and the dread of existence. Erikson suggests that

> in all parts of the world, the struggle is now for the *anticipatory development of more inclusive identities*, whether they comprise the communality of the peasant-and-worker, or of all nonwhites, the joint interests of common markets and of technological expansion, or the mutual trusteeship of nations. The goal of imaginative and psychologically intuitive leadership, m each case, is the setting free of untold new forces; the price of default of such leadership [is] malaise, delinquency and riot. In this sense, some of our activist youth today attempt to confront us with more inclusive images, in which old hatreds must wither away; and we are stunned to see how much we have ignored and have left to them who seem to sense that the species is the only identity inclusive

enough.

Erikson goes on to contrast Gandhi creating an all-India identity and also including -the British through their sense of fair play, with Hitler creating an identity 'based on totalistic exclusion of the Jews. Gaodhi in a satyagraha campaign moved in on the mill owners. He employed engagement at close range. Then, when his followers began ,to feel that he was not suffering enough, he began his first fast. The acceptance of suffering and death which was so basic to his "truth force" constitutes an actn e choice without submission to anyone. It is the highest affirmation of individualism in the service of humanity. It is at once a declaration of non-intent to harm others, and the Erikson feels the parallel to Lorenz's study is most striking) an expression of a faith in the If opponent's inability to persist in harming others beyond a certain point, provided, of course, that he is convinced that neither his identity nor his rightful power is in real danger. The mood of this event is pervaded by a spirit of giving the opponent the courage to change even -as the challenger changes with the events.

At such a period in his life Gandhi was possessed of a Franciscan gaiety and of a capacity to reduce situations to their naked essentials, thus helping other discard costly defenses and denials and to realize hidden potentials of good will god energetic deeds. Gandhi emerges as a man possessing that quality of supreme presence which can give to the finite moment a sense of infinite meaning for it is tuned both to the "inner voice" and to historical actuality, that is, to the potentialities for a higher synthesis other individuals or in the masses.

The final selection in this review of research on nonviolence is an article on "Nonviolent Action from a Social-Psychological Perspective" which I wrote after collecting most of the case materials for the book on Nonviolent Direct Action mentioned above. Because of my interest the study of small groups, I wanted to account for the various forms of interaction which take place when a nonviolent actor comes face-to-face with an opponent or an audience. According to the ideology of nonviolence, he should be able to exchange love for love and win the opponent to his side. However, only three of the dozen incidents of nonviolent action which we collected were free from major physical violence. Thus it was clear that the actual interaction did not usually proceed according to plan. Why want this so? After giving a brief account of three cases: Gandhi's satyagraha against the Rowlatt Bills in India in 1919, a protest at a United States missile base in 1959, and an integrated walk for peace through the U.S. South in 1963, I attempt to explain the course of the interaction using the "exchange" theory of Homans and the two- and three-dimensional approaches to the study of interaction proposed by Leary and Bales.

Following Homans, social behavior is seen as an exchange of activity, tangible or intangible, and more or less rewarding or costly, between at least two persons. In general, a person tries to maximize his profit, that is the reward minus the cost Exchanges can be made with activities (such as help) or sentiments (such as approval). The nonviolent actor would like to exchange love for love; often, however, he seems to receive dominance and hostility in return for his actions. To understand why this might be so we turn to the three-dimensional theory of Bales which is based on the work of Leary and others.

All interpersonal behavior can be described by using three dimensions which are presumably the same ones that people use implicitly in everyday life. The three dimensions are: dominance vs. submission (up or down), negate vs. positive (left or right), and task oriented conforming vs. deviant or advocating change (forward or backward). On the first dimension individuals tend to exchange dominance for submission and vice versa, while on the other two dimensions exchanges tend to be made at the same end of the continuum, i.e., love for love, or work for work. Bales goes on to show how his categories for Interaction Process Analysis can be used to identify different interactional patterns. These patterns, 26 in all, can be used independency of Bales' categories as representations of types of behavior which combine one, two, or three dimensions.

The nonviolence actors usually intend to play a submissive, positive, deviant role as they confront others, especially those in authority. When they can maintain' this role they seem to be able to "pull" a dominant-positive response which may lead to social change. However, if then become negative or appear to be negative, they will pull a hostile response. The moost positive exchange seems to occur between demonstrators and others who are of equal status.

Summary and Conclusions

To completely understand social behavior one needs to have information about the social system at several different levels. Beginning with the human biological organism, one moves to the level of individual personality, then to the group, the society, and finally the culture which provides the goals and standards which guide behavior. In the articles reviewed here, factors relating to the practice and effect of nonviolent action have own discussed at all levels, although most of the analysis has centered on the group level which includes face-to-face interaction, and nonviolence as a social movement.

At the level of the biological organism, Erikson gives evidence that man cannot simply explain the use of aggression as part of his "animal nature," since animals generally avoid excesses of aggression, especially within species. At the next level, the components and functions of attitudes, and the, processes of attitude change discussed by Perloe, Olton and. Yaffe, and Lakey deal with one aspect of the personaltiy structure of the individual as well as with aspects of the interactional system at the group level which might lead attitude change. The problem of developing a sense of identity is also an aspect of the personality system. Both Fishman and Solomon and Erikson discuss this process in relation to the values of the culture or subculture in which adolescents find themselves Negro youth act out in a *prosocial* manner the values which they feel their parents really hold. Youth and adult leaders such as Gandhi strive to find more inclusive identities which will allow them to behave towards others in a more loving fashion.

At the group level the interaction between the nonviolent

actor, his opponents, and the audience has been discussed by case who observed that "a soft answer turneth away wrath," by Gregg who proposes the principle of "moral jiujitsu," by Sorokin who notes that love is usually exchanged for love, and by Hare who provides an analysis of nonviolent behavior using the three dimensions of dominance-submission, positive-negative, and task oriented-deviant.

Another type of group which has as its goal a change m the organisation of society is the social movement. At various times nonviolence has been clearly associated with social movements under the leadership of Gandhi, King, or others in CORE, SNCC and other civil rights organizations. Nonviolence also has been practiced by individuals acting more or less alone, or by small groups. Sharp, Bondurant, Vander Zanden, Oppenheimer, and Stiehm have discussed the types of social movements and their distinctive values. Lidz adds that two of these types, the "conscientious" and the "pragmatic," actually represent stages in the development of any social movement, and Blumberg suggests that the processes of evolution, contagion, and reinforcement are important determinants of the form the social movement will take.

In this review of the literature there has been relatively little discussion of the two highest system levels of society and culture since this would have taken us into other areas of sociology, economics, political science, and anthropology while the range of articles was intentionally limited to social psychology.

Since the major source of aggression today is international conflict, it would seem that the aggression of business is to create more inclusive identities of that men may act towards each other as number of the same pseudo-species. Next the residual interpersonal hostility which can occur within a speties would have to be understood and controlled, prevented, or worked out in non-lethalsubstitute behavior. One current approach to this problem through psychotherapy and sensitivity training groups, both the international and the interpersonal level alternate ways of solving conflicts will need to be found and used such as courts and arbitration. In the short run, and for unmanageable cases at any time, new tranquilizing weapons could be used in order temporarily to halt an aggressor, before harm can be done. The precedent set by the use of tranquilizing drugs for violent mental patients could be followed here. Until the day when all defenses can be internalized people will need to have some external defense against the frightening activities of other people.

Six Suggestions for Reading the Contributions

1. For those who are not familiar with the meaning of nonviolence. Gene Sharp's essay provides as description of different forms of nonviolent action, their, objectives, and possible results.

2. Read one or tho of the selections, such as those by Proudfoot and Merwin, uncritically, trying to get the flavor of nonviolent action.

3. *Use Bondurant's outline* in order to compare different encounters. Joan Bondurant has provided an extremely useful way of organizing and interpreting the facts of an incident.

4 There suggestions were prepared by Herbet H. Blumberg.

The content is arranged according to universal headings which help prevent the possibility of overlooking important information and facilitate comparisons between different encounters.

While the other cases are not explicitly organized in this fashion, familiarity with the outline will help one to form crucial questions such as. Do the antagonists in different cues react in essentially the same way? If not, are the differences attributable to the locale? To the nature of the action? And so forth. By suggesting a standard set of essential features of a nonviolent encounter, the outline provides a start in comparing encounters.

4. *Note in what way an encounter moves people*—look for ways to predict this movement. One form of understanding results from the ability to use the background informaticn of an encounter for accurately predicting the results of the encounter on the basis of specifiable reasons, not just intuition. This abil-

ity may follow from regarding nonviolent action as a force that will move people from one set of behaviors and attitudes to another. This new set (not necessarily the one desired by the nonviolent participants) may lead to further nonviolent action, then to further changes in the people reacting to it. until some balance is reached. Scrutiny of the background and results of known uncover some of the variables which predict a person's initial position and reaction he is likely to have to a given encounter.

In comparisons of different cities, variations in required effort may be due to location (deep South vs. border state), size larger cities may be easier to desegregate. What "intermediate variables" are relevant?), incomparable targets (a Northern barber shop may be more firm than a Southern lunch counter), other variables, and chance.

Within a given city, which targets of nonviolent action are most resistant? What variables best predict degree of resistance? A possible variable is "degree of social closeness among patrons of a target." An independent measure of "social closeness" might reveal that one is closer to others in a swimming pool than to others at a lunch counter. Another relevant variable might be socioeconomic class. Working class people at an amusement park might be more extreme segregationists than patrons of a legitimate theater. One can make particularly well-controlled observations when evidently equivalent agencies, e.g., different variety store lunch counters in the same city, are not equally ready to yield to a nonviolent protect. What types of managers are more ready to change their attitudes? ... their policies?

Prediction will at first probably be based on guessed variables, with reised estimates following wrong predictions. One will soon be able to assign tentative weights to selected variables and then perfect one's knowledge by revising the weights and the list content and by drawing general conclusions. (This procedure is similar to calculating multiple correlations.) Further understanding of a reasonably accurate predictive system may be had by seeking variables that are more basic. For example, why might working classes be more resistant than middle classes to nonviolentaction for desegregation? Perhaps economic security is a more basic variable. Then, are working class people having job tenure quicker to favor equal employment opportunities than are equally well-paid working class people without tenure?

For many questions the available cases will not provide sufficient answers (e.g., do many people react to a nonviolent campaign in a given way simply because their attitudes change when those of their friends do?), be best one can do is to make reasonable guesses (the selection, by than and June Robbins suggests some social forecasting ;upon those who react to a nonviolent campaign by describing the hostility directed against someone reacting untraditionally check relevant experimental literature (a study by Berelson and others shows that political behavior can be accounted for partly on the basis of attitudes of family and friends), or carry out specially designed experiments.

5. Estimate the likelihood of alternative outcomes of *campaigns;* test for systematic causes of alternative outcomes. Certain difficulties for carrying out such estimates and tests arise and can be partly surmounted The available information for testing what "really" happens in an encounter may beworse than insufficient, it may be misleading. Not all events are reported Not .ill details of reported events are available. Most of the case studies in this book were not written with the intent of providing sourer material for a study such as this and the might not present all the ideas which detract from tin objectives or the technique of the nonviolent participants. The careful student of nonviolence needs to examine even important type of encounter and to know whether the reactions described in examined encounters are typical.

From Peck's account of the freedom rides one could start by counting the number of stops along a specified bus route in a given year that react (1) violent, (2) indifferently, and (3) sympathetically. Peck himself compares the "intermediate South" of 1947 with that of 1961, his readers could go on to compare the "intermediate South" of 1947 with the deep South of 1961 and ask how they do—and how they do not—represent equivalent points on a course of desegregation brought about by nonviolent action.

Out of the pacifist voyages which have taken place in recent years, two are described in the case studies (accounts by Bigelow and Merwin). One can therefore probably get a fair idea of the reaction to such an encounter. In general, the cases selected provide an approximate notion of the likelihood of different reactions to a nonviolent encounter, although there is no complete tabulation of reactions to nonviolence.

A few of the authors suggest what determines a reaction. Peck (freedom rides) indicates that the militance of the state governor and the quality of protection by local police determine whether nonviolent campaigns for desegregation in the deep South will engender mob action. One can enlarge and refine the list of "determiners."

6. *Ask key questions* of the reading. Here is a sample set of questions some suggested by Bondurant's outline.

(a) What forms does nonviolence action take? Rather than simply being listed, the techniques should be seen in context. Why for instance, are sit-ins carried out in some encounters demonstrations in others and boycotts in still others? Is there an ordered progression of techniques in a situation, with some reserved until others fail? What does and what should influence the choice of a particular technique?

(b) How thoroughly planned are campaigns? The demonstrators in sympathy with Everyman discuss what action they would take in a variety of circumstances, yet they are called upon to make specific decisions on the spot.

(c) What are the objectives of a protest? By Lakey's classification, how much were the sit-ins designed to: (1) change attitudes, (2) change behavior by eliciting sympathy, and (3) change behavior through coercion? Does the distribution of actual change in these three categories mirror intended ratios? Are official intentions likely to mirror private hopes? The objectives stated in the selections may not be the most immediate ones. Such protests as those described by Albert Bigelow, and by Wilmer Young, copuld not realistically be said to have the immediate purpose of achieving a significant change in the policy of this United States Government. The immediate objective these cases might be eliciting public opinion in favor of the change being sought or it might be carrying out an ineffective protest rather than doing nothing at all Authors including James Peck, Jhan and June Robbins, and Merrill Proudfoot describe cases where they claim nonviolent action changed the consciences of individuals. In none of these three particular cases was the protest aimed primarily at such a goal. One who is trying to relate nonviolent action to its objectives should remember that for some participants nonviolence may be adopted as an efficient tactic, while for others it is a moral imperative without other choices.

(d) What theories best explain the facts of an encounter? A statistical theory would simply state that specific reactions to nonviolence have predictable probabilities under given circumstances. More analytic theories will be found among the social-psychological analyses. These theories must be evaluated. One of the simplest statements is by Sorokin: Love begets love, hate begets hate. How much data does this "theoretical model" account for? It explains Eddie's behavior in the selection by Than and June Robbins but does not immediately account for the actions of other hecklers. Are the available theories trying to explain different forms of nonviolence? Do they contradict each other? Do they contradict data from the American case materials? Can one formulate plausible theories other than those described?

Chapter-2

Attitudes And Nonviolent Action

Sidney I. Perloe, David S. Olton
and David L. Yaffe

Chapter-2

Describing the present attempt to relate nonviolent action to experimental examinations of attitude change, Dr. Perloe writes:

> *The paper grew out of a discussion of an early set of the case study material in my attitude-change course . . . One part of the course attempts to apply theories of attitude change, which have been developed mainly in the lab, to actual social phenomena involving attitude change. I do this because I believe that one of the functions of social science is to help in the understanding and control of social processes in vivo. The application of lab-inspired concepts to field phenomena gives us information on what we are overlooking as the result of our reliance on controlled situations. It points up ambiguities in our concepts and at times uncovers unsuspected sources of strength. As we note in the paper, the payoff is often small for the person who has problems requiring immediate solution. In the present case I think that we may have helped by making some distinctions that seem to have been overlooked and by raising questions that the practitioner must ask before he can make use of attitude-change theory. Indeed, some of the question might be useful apart from the context of the application of theory.*
>
> *As is often the case, the application of existing theory results in more prescriptions should not stand in the way of actions that seem desirable on other grounds. We do not know enough to be able to say with confidence that a given course of action will surely fail. Rather, the prescriptions might be used as guides in planning the action and in evaulting its outcome. In this way the probability of success might be increased and our understanding of our theories deepened. The latter been fit can only be gained if there is an attempt to conduct a rigorous evaluation of the outcome. This often means diverting resources from the action and putting aside one's hopes, in the interest of gaining objective information.*

In the long run this should pay off with increased effectiveness of social action.

Sideney Perloe was born in 1932, received a Ph.D. in Social Psychology from the University of Michigan, has taught at Yale University, and is currently Associate Professor of Psychology at Haverford College. Born in 1943 in Baltimore, David Yaffe received a B.A. from Haverford College in 1964, has since studied in Germany on a Fulbright grant, and received a B.A. from Haverfored College in 1964 He has received an M.A. from the University of Michigan, where he is currently a graduate student specializing in physiological psychology.

ALTHOUGH there has been much discussion of nonviolent social action, there has been little attention paid to the processes responsible for its effects. Thus far, most theoretical analyses of nonviolence have emphasized the philosophical rationale behind the technique rather than thc conditions required for its success. While such analyses are probably useful in maintaing the convictions and morale of the members of nonviolent movements, they may not provide a sound basis for the tactica planning of nonviolent actions. They also do not add to the body of social science, which ultimately must provide the knowledge needed for the development of a just and humanitarian society. It therefore seems desirable that an attempt be made to bridge the gap between the practice and philosophy of nonviolence on the one hand and social science theories of behavior and attitude change on the other. The present chapter is directed toward establishing this connection.

It must be realized at the outset that the social science bank, upon which one end of our structure will be grounded, is not very solid. Our theories leave much to be desired in the way of precision and empirical support. Furthermore, we lack much of the detailed information about nonviolent action needed to project behind our foundation toward the concerns of the nonviolent actors and planners. Nevertheless, a start can be made. The social science theories will help in uncovering the assumptions made about behaviour and attitudes by the practitioners of nonviolence, in addition, they will point to situations in which these assumptions are likely to be incorrect. Most importantly they will raise questions which must be answered if reliable predictions about the effects of nonviolent actions are tobe made.

The consequences of Nonviolent Social Protest

Attitude Change Versus Behavior Change

Nonviolence is often used to a tool for altering the *status quo*. Such alterations always require changes in the behaviours of at least some of the people involved. It may or may not make a difference to those engaged in nonviolence whether the change is in behavior only or whether it stems from a change in people's feelings and ideas, i.e., a change in their attitudes. Many desegregation demonstrations in the United States appear to aim primarily at behavior change, namely, providing Negroes with access to facilities regardless of whether the whites involved accept the justice of the integration. Anti-war demonstrations, on the other hand, usually aim at attitudes rather than behavior. Although the two ends are often not incompatible, important tactical decisions should be made differently depending upon the relative importance of attitudes and behavior to the agents of nonviolent social change.

Lakey has described three points on the continuum between the attitude- and behavior-change consequences of non-violent social action. He calls the first *coercion.* Here there is no need for opinions to change. The target of the demonstration is obliged to comply with the demands of the protesters because he is less powerful than they are. A peaceful labor union strike is an example of nonviolent coercion. The second type, *persuasion,* is effective because the target has changed his views of the demonstrators, though not of the action they advocate. He has come to believe that the demonstrators are good people even though he disagrees with their aims. His compliance is based on his positive evaluation of the participants; although he could continue to resist their demands for change in his behavior, he complies. *Convesion,* the third type described by Lakey, brings the target into wholehearted agreement with his former adversaries. The distinction between the attitude- and behavior-change results of demonstrations indicates a limit in the range of application of the propositions discussed below. Attitude change is the subject of our treatment, and only those aspects of nonviolent social action involving attitude change fall within the area we cover.

Targets and Audiences of Demonstrations

Lakey's discussion, like most others, does not distinguish between several possible groups affected by a demonstration. Although the target of a sit-in might be a realtor and the aim might be to get him to adopt an open 'housing policy, it is clear that many more people are touched by the nonviolent action. There are people who happen to be at the office during the protest; there are people nearby who might come to the demonstration site as a result of hiring reports of the action. There are people connected with the news media and others who get their information from these sources. There are government, party, business, and religious leaders in the immediate community, etc. It is important to recognize the diversity of audiences potentially involved because the goals of the demonstration with respect to one audience may differ from the goals with respect to another. Furthermore, the tactics appropriate to one group may not be appropriate to another.

Theories of Attitude formation and Change

We will begin building our bridge between theory and practice at the theory end on the assumption that the reader can use his familiarity with nonviolence to *see* the relevance of our effort.

The Coponents of Attitudes

Attitudes may be thought of as having three components: cognitive, affective, and behavioral. The cognitive component consists of beliefs concerning the event, group, or abstraction about which the attitude is held. The term attitude object is often used to denote the focus of the attidue. The *affective* component of an attitude is the evaluation of the attitude object. It refers to how good or bad, pleasant or unpleasant a person feels the attitude direct is. The third component is the *behavioral* component and consists of tendencies to act in certain ways toward the attitude object.

Fro example, he might believe that civil disobedience involves resisting arrest by sitting down so that on would have to be carried off bodily by police, that it is against the law, that it is currently used by civil rights or anti-war demonstrators, and that Gandhi made great use of it in his successful campaign for Indian independence. The attitude's affective component could be an evaluation of civil disobedience as morally right and a great force for good, or as morally wrong and thoroughly disreputable, or anything in between including indifference. The behavioural component might include a tendency to read or to skip over newspaper articles on civil disobedience to encourage civil disobedience and suggest it use, or to deplore it publicly and attack those engaged in it. It should be noted that behaviour itself is not considered part of the attitude, which is merely the predisposition to behave in certain ways that forms part of the attitude.

As a final point we should nate that although the three components of an attitude are generally consistent, they may disagree with one another. For instance, mone may believe that smoking causes lung cancer and possibly other diseases (cognitive component) and yet may continue to like smoking (affective component) or be disposed to smoke (behvairoal tendency). Similarly one might feel that a desegregation of public facilities is good, but be disposed to avoid buying a house in an integrated neighbourhood.

The Prerequistites of Attitude Change

Attitude are affected by two sets of forces. One set arises from the desires, impulses, and drives that motivate human behaviour; the other from the tendency toward consistency and equilibrium that characterizes human thought. Attitudes inequilibrium also are not involved in contradictions among themselves or with an individual's beliefs and perceptions.

In order for lasting attitude change to occur, old equilibria must be destroyed and new ones must be estabished. Edger Schein, in his book *Coercive Persuasion,* describes tree phases in the production of lasting attitude change. In the first phase, called *unfreezing,* the old euqilibrium is broken. This is accomplished either by detracting from the attitude's usefulness inhelping an individual reach his goals or by creating an inconsistency involing the attitude. The disturbance of the original equilibrium creates an unstable state in which attitudes are susceptible to change. It is to this susceptibility that Richard Gregg refers in *The Power of Nonviolence* when he speaks of the highly "suggestible" condition of an opponent against whom nonviolence has been employed.

In the next phase, called *chaing,* a direction must be indicated leading to a new condition of balance in which an individual's atttidues are once again consistent and are able to satisfy his needs Un development or other pressure, people may come to realize the indelicacy of their old ways of thinking, but if they lack guidance to any better positions, they may return to their old attitudes unless the pressure is irresistible, in which case they may flounded runcomfortably in the "unforzen" state unable to pass through the changing stage. Finally the change must pass into the third phase, called *refreezing.* Here a new equilibrium is established involving the new attitude. Without the establishment of the new equilibrium, the attitude remains susceptible to change back towards its old form.

The Functional basis of Attitudes

The specific processes of attitude change are best understood by starting with the functions that attitudes serve for people. This is so because interference with these functions is a major method of unfreezing old attitudes and establishment of new functions is a major way of refreezing changed attitudes. We shall examine three classes of functions: object orientation, ego-support, and ego-defense.

Object Orientation. Human action is purposive or motivated. For this reason it is important that individuals be able to recognize objects which are capable of directly rewarding or harming them. It is also important for them to recognize the instrumental value of objects which, though having no intrinsically rewarding or punishing properties, serve to bring the individuals into desirable or undesirable situations. Much of human learning is directed at discovering intrinsic or instrumental motivational values of objects. The outcome of such learning may be conceived of as the establishment of attitudes. For example, a person may learn that certain foods are pleasant to taste and thereby form positive attitudes toward such foods, that is, he attributes qualities to the food which are relevant to its gratifying character. He also evaluates the food positively and prepares himself to eat the food when the attitude is aroused. If he also learn that restaurants run by members of a given ethnic group are likely to serve these foods, he is likely to form a positive attitude toward these restaurants as well as toward the food.

In the example given above, the attitudes were formed on the basis of direct contact with the attitude objects. This need not always be so, especially where instrumentality valued social objects are concerned. When we examine attitudes toward social groups and institutions, we often find that much of the information upon which these attitudes are based does not arise from direct contact with relevant objects. Indeed, there are often no objective yardsticks which a person can use in establishing the validity of the cognitive components of such attitudes. For example, most individuals cannot get access to objective information about whether white children attending schools with large proportions of Negro children get a poorer education than those attending all-white schools. A thermometer can tell person whether his child should be kept home from school, because of a fever, but he has no comparable information on which to base his decision about whether to keep his child 'home in protest against school integration. Because the issue is an important one, he cannot merely suspend decision. He therefore relies upon "social reality." i.e., the ideas and opinions of others in the absence of an objective source of information.

Regardless of the directness of the information on which they were based, attitudes help a person to organize the world he perceives. They direct his attention toward aspects of objects which are relevant to his goals. Ambiguous information about an attitude object is simplified so that it becomes consistent with the attributes included in the cognitive component of the attitude. The selective effect attitudes upon the way a person takes in information and the subsequent directive effect upon his tendencies to, behave are essential for his survival. Every situation a person encounters confronts him with an enormous amount of information, occurring in a combination which is not quite the same as any combination he has previously met. His attitudesallow him to sift out what is relevant and to ignore what is irrelevant. If a person saw every new event or every new person he encountered as unique, he would be doomed to live a world that could never become familiar, a chaotic worlds in which there could be no precedent to guide his reactions to new situations. There could be no learning in such as world; children and adults would be alike in their ignorant bewilderment.

Adjustive processes which help useful maintain stability in the face of environmental variation may also function male adoptively. In the case of attitudes this is particularly likely when cognitive components are established on the basis of limited, unrepresentative contact with a class of attitude objects or when our beliefs about attitude objects rest upon in valid, mediated information, e.g., stereotypes transmitted by word of mouth or the mass media. Under these circumstances attitudes serve to select irrelevant information and to distort ambiguous information. A classic example of the latter is given by Allport and Postman. In their study, subjects were shown a complicated picture of a scene which contained, among other things, the figures of a well-dressed Negro and a shabbily dressed white man, with the latter bolding an open razor. The two figures were facing each other. Not infrequently, this scene was reported as one in which a shabbily dressed Negro, holding a razor, was threatening a well-dressed white man. The more complicated and fast-moving the situation, and the more intense the purpose or motive aroused, the more likely it is that the cognitive aspects of relevant attitudes will result in selection and distortion of information. In the current context, the attitudes that spectators hold toward the participants in a demonstration or toward the goals of the demonstration will affect the information the spectators carry away with them.

The foregoing material may appear to present a paradox. We started by stressing the way in which attitudes serve to adapt individuals to the rewarding and punishing aspects of the situations they face. But we ended with a situation in which attitudes led to a gross error in the perception of significant aspects of an important situation. The paradox can be resolved by recognizing that there are several conditions which permit maladaptive errors to continue. Not all attitudes function merely to orient individuals toward potentially rewarding and punishing objects. There are other functions which outweigh the orientation function and cause the individual to resort to defensive stratagems designed to maintain his attitude in the face of contradictory information. These other functions will be considered below. However, even when the orientation function is paramount, social attitudes incorporating incorrect beliefs continue to be held. This is so because the prolonged direct contact with the attitude object, needed to overcome the initial resistance to contradictory information, does not occur. To cite an extreme example, few Americans have ever seen a nonviolent demonstrator face to face, to say nothing of having had conversations and in tractions with him. In part this is because there are so few demonstrators and so many Americans. But it is also due to the fact that initially negative attitudes lead people to avoid contact with attitude objects and thereby prevent them from coming into contact with the information needed to invalidate their beleifs.

Still another reason for the persistence of incorrect beliefs is the fact that the firsthand information an dividual has about a class of attitude objects is often unrepresentative the class as it actually exists or as it might exist under changed conditions. The attitudes of lower class whites toward Negroes may persist in large part due to this factor. Voder these circumstances and the ones described in the previous paragraph, attitudes with incorrect or unrepresentative cognitive components persist because, from the point of view of the persons who bold them, they continue to provide valid guides for goal-directed behavior. Given the information to which the individual is exposed or to which he allows himself to be exposed, the attitudes are quite rational and function all.

There are several ways to prevent an attitude from performing its object-orienting function and thereby unfreeze it. Considering instrumentality functional social attitudes, we might try to change the goals of a person so that the function previously performed by the attitude is no longer necessary. Direct as it may be, this is not a promising route to attitude change; the goals toward which important attitude objects are instrumental are not easily changed. White people, who, are against integrated schools because,thy see integration as leading to lowered academic standards, sexual or aggressive assaults upon their children, etc., are unlikely to give up their attitude because they no longer care about high academic standards or the safety of their children

When the old goal cannot be changed, it may be possible to change the attitude by showing that the attitude object does not in fact have the instrumental effects attributed to it. Reports indicating that when other things are held equal, property values do not decline when Negroes move into previously white neighborhoods, are aimed at this method of decreasing the functional value of negative attitudes toward selling houses in white areas to Negroes. Nonviolent actions by Negro demonstrators may also weaken the instrumental link that an observer believes to exist between Negroes and violence.

Still another method of changing the real or imagined instrumental value of an object is to make environmental changes which would prevent the instrumental effect of the attitude object from occurring For example, if integrated schools were to be liberally supplied with excellent teachers, with especially fine facilities for upgrading under-educated children, and with visible increases in steps to prevent aggressive and other disruptive behavior, e.g., more counseling and corrective facilities for disturbed or delinquent youths, the opposition to integrated schools would have little functional support left.

The fact that people have a way of resisting information that indicates that their attitudes are based on invalid beliefs or that their behavior tendencies are not appropriate in the light of their goals, has important implications for attitude-change programs. Generally, public and private agencies restrict their attitude-change attempts to educational programs, which are the ones most easily discounted by those toward whom the information is directed. To the extent that nonviolent demonstrations serve to break through the barriers designed to protect attitudes against invalidating information, they may effectively unfreeze attitudes. However, there must be some direct, easily understood connection between attitude components one wishes to change and the demonstration in order for the latter to accomplish the unsettling of old attitudes. While school boycotts segregated lunch facilities may force people to give up the belief that Negroes are by and large satisfied with their place in our society, they will not necessarily affect beliefs about the negative consequence school integration, referred to above

There is one more route to attitude change that makes use of the object-orientation functions. Here we establish new instrumental relations between attitudes objects having one value and goals having another." Negatively evaluated objects may be linked with positive positive goals as, for example, a militant civil rights group carrying out a large cleanup-fixup program in a blighted residential area. 'More will be said about this technique of attitude change later.

Despite the fact that many organizations oriented toward social change, believe their programs show the pubic that old attitudes are not functional in the object orientation sense, it is unlikely that the successes the organizations have can be accounted for by this route. Our society is too large and the social action groups are too small to be sure of getting their information attended to and believed by people they wish to reach. Even when they get through, the instability resulting from the new information is likely to be short-lived. It may be easily overcome by many of the other factors we will discuss below.

Ego-Support. Although all attitudes refer to attitude objects, they do not necessarily perform their primary service to an individual by helping him to act adoptively with' respect to these objects Some attitudes function to help an individual maintain an image of himself which is favourably evaluated by groups or people with whom he wishes to affiliate. They help him adapt to groups rather than to attitude objects per se.

The maintenance of a favorable self-image is a central human motive. The formation of a person's self-image is always dependent, to some degree, upon the way others evaluate him. As he grows he develops an image which is acceptable to the persons whose approval he needs. An important component of this image, and therefore an important determinant or whether or not he gains the approval be desires, is his collection of social attitudes. Approval is contingent upon his holding attitudes deemed proper by those whose approbation is sought. Another important component of his self-identity is his group affiliations. For example, when individuals are asked to name characteristics which they consider most important in describing themselves, they usually list some of their group memberships, e.g., religious and ethnic group membership. The importance of group identity as a means of supporting one's individual identity varies from one adult to another. The more uncertain a person is about his worth as an individual, the more likely he is to try to bolster his feelings of being worthwhile by emphasizing his membership in groups he values.

Acceptance by a group, like acceptance by significant others, is often contingent upon holding the attitudes prescribed by the group. Groups which affect an individuals attitudes in the manner described above are known as reference groups. They are probably the most important single determinant of social attitudes. The more strongly attracted an individual is to a reference group and the more he depends upon his membership as a means of supporting a favorable image of himself, the more powerful are the effects of the group's expectations concerning the attitudes he should and should not hold.

The standard behavioral component of an ego-supportive attitude is the tendency to express it before appropriate audiences, thereby showing them, and oneself, that one is a proper kind of person. Comparing the object-orienting and ego-supporting functions, we see that with the former it is some aspect of the attitude object itself that aids or hinders the individual in attaining his goals. With the latter it the expression of the attitude which aids or hinders him. The holder of an ego-support attitude need never come into contact or relationship with the attitude object for his attitude to fulfill its function.

Attitude's which function primarily support an image a person wishes to create of himself are relatively unaffected by information about attitude objects, even when this information is accepted by the individual. Instead such attitudes must be unfrozen by interfering directly with their ego-supporting functions. For example, one might lead a person to recognize that he was mistaken inbelieving that one of his important reference groups expected him to hold some attitude. This may be accomplished by having the leaders or influential members of the group speak of behave in a manner which indicates that the either do notched the attitude in question or that they accept members who do not hold the attitude.

When an individual perception of the attitudes required by one of his important reference groups is, correct, one might try to unfreeze his attitude by chaning the reference group's expectations. Reference group norms may be changed by coercing, persuading, or converting the leaders, as when political leaders or civic leaders are led to wake public pronouncements and acts indicating that old patterns of his crimination and prejudice are no longer appropriate. Attitude-change effects focused on such leaders may be multiplied by the effect these leaders have on reference group norms and expectations.15 If reference group norms that support attitudes we wish to change cannot themselves be changed we must try to get the individual to disassociate himself from the group in question. This might be accomplished by discrediting the group or by supplanting it with a group which can provide even more ego-support than the one whose influence we wish to remove. The latter is illustrated by trying to supplant a person's identification of himself as a white Southerner" with the identification of himself as a good Christian" or a "good American." The use of a target's identic as in American is likely to be much more useful to the civil rights demonstration than to the peace demonstration. Equality among citizens is clearly part of the norms carried along by the American identity; anti-militarism is not. Although the effects of reference groups upon attitudes can be amply documented, much less is known about bow to change reference groups identifications. To a great extent people are born into the reference groups that affect their attitudes.

Sometimes attitudes, which are based on reference group norms, may be changed by taking advantage of the fact that , on some issues individuals are often affected by more than one reference group. A person's business friends and church associates may have opposite expectations concerning attitudes toward desegregation or the anti-war movement. When his ties to both groups are equal in strength, his attitude in a given situation will depend upon which of the two groups is most salient for him at the time. Nonviolent demonstrations may have the effect of altering the relative salience of opposed reference groups and as a result change attitudes. Unfortunately, this effect may continue only as long as the demonstration continues or is prominent in the minds of the affected persons.

Changing reference group norms or changing the reference groups with which an individual identifies are very potent types of attitude change methods. They not only unfreeze and direct the attitude change, but they insure support for the new attitude and insulate it against further change.

The Ego-Defensive Function. Some attitudes help individuals defend themselves against anxiety caused by unconscious conflicts. These attitudes often involve the use of the projection defense mechanism through which an individual disposes of a wish or impulse of which he is ashamed or afraid. He remains conscious of the impulse but attributes it to someone else. This protects him against the anxiety he would experience if he recognized the true source of the wish. Often the projection also allows the individual to give some behavioral expression to the anxiety arousing impulse by perceiving his response as required by the characteristic he has projected onto another person. If the frightening impulse is aggression against respected authorities or institutions, projection leads the individual to attribute the impulse to other persons and allows him to aggress against these other persons, thereby giving some indirect expression to the troublesome motive.

Ego-defensive attitudes are undoubtedly the most difficult to change. To do so, a person's defensive structure most be altered, either by substituting a new defense, e.g. getting him to hate Communists instead of Negroes or by trying to resolve the conflict which gives rise to the defense. ;The forever method is not likely to be useful in establishing the attitudes desired by me participants in nonviolent protest movements. The latter method does not always succeed, even when prolonged individual psychotherapy is used, a means certainly beyond the reach of any social action movement. It is encouraging that studies by Katz and his colleagues have shown that ego-defensive attitudes may be changed using less costly methods designed to provide an individual with insight into the defensive nature of scene attitudes.

The tendency toward cognitive consistency

In the previous section we were concerned with the operation of forces growing out of 'people's purposes, wishes, and impulses. Here we deal with forest stemming from the structure of attitudes, that is, from the relationships among the cognitive, affective, and behavioral components of an attitude and among the many attitudes held by a person. Our analysis will be a bit more abstract and microscopic than it was above. To some extent we will be dealing with the cognitive processes set in motion by some or the situations leading to attitude change already described.

When an individuals's actions toward an attitude object are not consistent with his beliefs and evaluations concerning the object, or when there are inconsistencies among the beliefs and evaluations themselves, an unstable situation exists. The consistency referred to here is not necessarily logical, instead we must conceive of a "psychologic" in which object evoking the same emotion, objects to which similar labels have been learned, or objects which have occurred together in the past are seen as equivalent and as demanding similar attitudes. Several psychologists have offered interpretations of the problem of cognitive consistency and conflict between attitudes. We shall consider those of Milton Rosenberg and Robert Abelson, and of Leon Festinger.

The Balance Model. Rosenberg and Abelson's model is a structural one which deals with elements and their interrelationships. The elements are conceptions of attitude objects. Two elements may have any one of three kinds of relationships with each other. They may be positively related, negatively related, or unrelated. Each of the elements may also be positively or negatively evaluated. A balanced or consistent structure exists when attitude elements with the same evaluation are positively related or when elements with opposite evaluations are negatively related. Imbalance, on the other hand, exists when oppositely evaluated elements are positively related or similarly evaluated elements are negatively related. Structures may vary in complexity from one containing only two elements with a single relation between them to ones containing many elements and interrelationships.

As an example of how the model might be applied, consider the case of a man who heartily disapproves of civil rights demonstrations but who finds that his son has participated in one. Here we have two objects, the son having a strong positive evaluation, and the demonstration with a negative evaluation, connected by a positive bond. According to Rosenberg and Abelson's formulation, there are three possible paths for the father to follow to reach attitudinal balance. He may revene the evaluation attached to his son, the evaluation of the demonstration, or the sign of the bond connecting them. To reverse his 'opinion of his on create great difficulties, for the son is positively related to numerous other positively valued objects: the home the family's reputation, many happy experiences and very importantly, the man's own ego or self-image, including his picture of himself as a good father. The sign of the bond between son and demonstration would be difficult to reverse if there were dear and direct evidence that the boy was really involved. Beliefs baled on direct or nearly direct experience are most difficult to change because the fame information will simply enter again and again to disrupt the structure of beliefs. The evaluation of the demonstration is also difficult to reverse, since the demonstration is positively bonded to so many negatively valued objects: danger, disrepute, possible arrest, the bad opinion of friends and neighbors. In short, each change toward consistency produces inconsistencies elsewhere in the pattern. Rosenberg and Abelson propose a principle of least effort to predict that the means chosen will be the one which renders the *whole structure* consistent while making the fewest possible total changes in attitude elements or in relation ship bonds.

A second way to regain consistency is known *differentiation*. Instead of reversing the evaluation of an attitude object, one partitions it into two separate attitude which one recognizes as relatively independent and to which one assigns opposite evaluations. Thus, oar hypothetical father might decide that his son's civil rights activities (a newly created, negatively valued attitude object) have little to do with his son as a member of the family (the other part of the former undifferentiated "son" attitude object). Or if the situation lent itself, he might consider those aspects of the demonstration m which his son participated separately from the rest of the demonstration. Differentiation is surely one of the most important mechanisms in maintaining a consistent attitude structure. However, it often involves some distortion and may force the person to avoid or distort further in order to maintain the separation of the cognitions.

There is one relationship in the attitude structure that merits special mention. This is the one perceived between an attitude object and the ego, which is probably the most important attitude object within the entire structure. As a result, other attitude objects which are related to the ego will be very difficult to alter; the stronger the bond, the greater will be the difficulty in changing either the sign of the relationship or of the attitude object. Thus, any attempt to predict the outcome of an unbalanced structure must take as one of its prime considerations the degree to which each attitude has become "ego involved." The greater the extent to which a person's ego is involved with an attitude object, the more likely that this particular attitude object will remain unchanged in an unbalanced situation, and that other, less ego-involved attitudes will be altered to restore balance.

The Dissonance Model Similar attitude situations are discussed by Festinger in his theory of cognitive dissonance. The elements involved in the relationships he considers are not limited to attitude objects. They can be ideas, beliefs, evaluative judgments, a person's perception or his own action, etc. Any item of knowledge can become an element to a dissonant relationship. Dissonance between elements is said to exist if the negation of one element is consistent with another element, that is, if "not A' is psychologically consistent with "B," then A and B are dissonant. If the dissonance is great enough to exceed an individual's tolerance for inconsistency, the situation becomes unstable, and dissonance reduction must take place. The amount of dissonance generated in any situation depends upon the number of inconsistent elements relative to the number of consistent elements and also upon the relative importance of the elements. In consistency between important elements creates more dissonance than inconsistency between unimportant elements.

One area to which Festinger has applied these ideas is to the attractiveness of attitude objects and their association with the self, either through their having been chosen or through forced association with them. The first case is that of post-decision dissonance. When an individual chooses the more highly preferred of two alternatives, the situation being such that he cannot have them both, the negative qualities of the chosen alternative and me positive qualities of the unchosen one are dissonant with his knowledge of the choice he has made. The common path of dissonant reduction to this case is to play up the positive qualities of the chosen alternative and play down its faults while playing up the faults and playing down the virtues of top unchosen one. As a result, the evaluation of the chosen alternative is more favourable after choice than before, and that of the unchosen one less favorable. Obviously, the closer in value the two objects were before choice, the more dissonance there will be to reduce and the more attitude change there will have to be after the choice if consonance is to be regained.

In a second type of application of theory, a subject's attitude on some issue is measured, and he is then pressured into some action in opposition to his attitude, such as a public disavowal of his attitude or public support for opponents of his position. He thus experiences dissonance between his belief and his knowledge that he has made a statement contradicting it. Under some conditions, dissonance is reduced here by his altering his real opinion in the direction of the one expressed. This finding adds a point of interest to Lakey's typology of behaviour change, namely, that through dissonance reduction, persuasion or coercion may become conversion. That is, a person led to act against his convictions may alter his convictions. Therefore, nonviolent action aiming ultimately at conversion might rest content with persuasion or coercion as an immediate goal, knowing that in time conversion might follow.

Coerced expression of performance which is contradictory to a person's attitudes does not always produce dissonance. The major determinant of whether or not dissonance is created is the amount of force applied in coercing the action. Knowledge of this amount becomes a third element added to the person's knowledge of his action and the relevant attitude. If the reward for the action is very great or the punishment for not performing is very great, the knowledge of the action and the knowledge of the reward or punishment are quite consonant. This consonance may be strong enough to outweigh the dissonance between the attitude and action elements, thereby reducing or eliminating the pressure for change. For example, if a store owner is faced with financial ruin if he does not accede to the demands of demonstrators to hire Negroes, his compliance may not affect his opinion concerning the advisability of hiring Negroes. On the other hand, if the pressure is just great enough to get him to comply, but not any greater, the compliance would create the maximum amount of pressure toward change.

The implications for attitude change of the amount of pressure exerted to coerce conformity to the demands of demonstration is related to a theoretical point made by Brehm and Cohen. According to these theorists, dissonance between a person's opinions and his knowledge of his actions occurs only when he feels he was relatively free to decide whether or not to act as he did. The greater the perceived freedom, me more the individual see the act as a consequence of his own volition and me more dissonance is aroused by an act which is inconsistent with his opinions. From mispoint of view, me less pressure used in getting a person to comply with a request, the more likely he is to feild that his commitment was the result of his own volition and thedissonance will be created if me action is inconsistent with his attitude. This point is related to the one made in connection with Abelson and Rosenberg's theory concerning the importance of the relation between attitude objects and the self.

The relation between the amount of pressure brought to bear in coercion and the amount of dissonance created is further complicated in situations where me- pressure is great, but not great enough to get compliance. Here the store owner's action and belief elements are consonant but the action element is dissonant with me knowledge that business will be lost because of the refusal to comply. Under these circumstances, dissonance may be reduced by increasing the importance of the attitude against hiring Negroes and thereby increasing the amount of consonance between the attitude and the action. Successful resistance in the face of pressure increases the likelihood of even greater resistance in the future.

One other situation in which dissonance reduction takes place is of particular interest. When neither a person's attitude nor his knowledge of dissonant information can be changed and when he is also unable to push the dissonant elements out of his awareness, he may resort to the stratagem of finding social support for his attitude. Every time her perceives that another person agrees with his point of view, an element consonant with his attitude is added. If enough agrees can be found, the person might be able to swamp the stubborn dissonance between his attitude and his other knowledge with consonance between his attitude and the knowledge that many people agree with him.

Summary

Our brief survey of theories of attitude formation and change has presented the major factors influencing the cognitive, evaluative, and behavioral components of attitudes, with major emphasis placed on the first aspect. Lasting attitude change was said to pass through three phases: unfreezing, changing proper, and refreezing. In order to enter the first phase of changing an individual's attitude, we saw that we must either interfere with a function the attitude performs for the individual or introduce some inconsistency into the relations among the components of the attitude or between the attitude components and other cognitions. The three functions we discussed were: (a) object-orientation, in which attitudes direct a person's attention and prepare him to respond adoptively toward motivationally relevant aspects of his environment; (b) ego-support, in which the mere holding of an attitude helps a person to maintain a self-image which he desires and which is also acceptable to his reference groups, and (c) ego-defense, in which attitudes protect an individual against anxiety resulting from recognition of taboo impulses.

Object-orientation functions were shown to be hindered by changing a person's goals or by changing his perception of the instrumental value of an object in helping him get to his goals. Ego-support functions were said to be blocked by changing the norms of the reference group relevant to the attitude, or by changing the particular reference group upon which the individual relied in evaluating the validity of his attitude. It was suggested that ego-defensive functions were very resistant to interference, but that they might be affected if the threat they protected the individual against were removed or if the individual were given insight into the general process of ego-defensive attitudes.

Two theories concerning the development of inconsistencies were discussed. One focused on the development of imbalance among the conceptions and evaluations of sets of attitude objects. Imbalance was said to exist if two similarly evaluayed objects were seen to be negatively related or if two dissimilarly evaluated objects were seen to be positively related. It was proposed that imbalance led to changes designed to restore balance. These were as follow: (a) changes in the evaluation of the aattiude objects; (b) changes in the direction of the relations among the attitude objects and (c) the differentiation of attitude objects into separate aspects, each of which was in balance with related cognitions.

The second theory treated inconsistencies between a broad range of cognitions. Two cognitions were said to be dissonant if the negation of one was psychologically consistent with the other. Like imbalance, dissonance was seen to create pressure toward change. The pressure could be reduced by: (a) changing one or more of the elements in the dissonant set so that they were no longer inconsistent; (b) by decreasing the importance of the elements; (c) by adding new elements which were consistent with some of the elements already present; and (d) by avoiding thinking about or perceiving information relevant to one or more of the dissonant elements,

Although they were discussed separately the changes brought about by interference with the functions of attitudes and those achieved by creating inconsistency are often synonymous. This is particularly true when we interfere with the object-onenting function of attitudes.

The Susceptibility of Attitudes to Nonviolent Pressures Tword Change

The previous section was intended primarily as an exposition of theories relevant to attitude change in response to non-violent change attempts. In this section we will focus on the consequences our theories lead us to expect from the practice of nonviolence. As is often the case, consideration of concrete social events provides both too much and too little information relevant to the application of our theories. On the one band, there are more processes taking place than our attitude theories can describe or explain. On the other hand, there are gaps in the specific data we need in order to use our theories. For these reasons, we will be able to discuss only some aspects of the consequences of nonviolent action and our discussion will be couched in terms of what might happen, rather than what would happen.

The Novelty of Nonviolence

We shall start by examining how a nonviolent demonstration exerts pressures toward change on the initial attitudes held by targets and onlookers; how, in Scheurn's terms, the "unfreezing" process begins. A striking fact of great importance in unfreezing is that nonviolent action takes place in societies that are not nonviolent. Despite lip service to the precept of turning the other cheek, mod individuals are taught to fight back when they are attacked. Armed forces are believed to be very important and consume large shares of national budgets. Approval is widely given when these forces are employed to protect or advance the interests of a country. As a remit of the importance and prominence of violence, most citizens have learned to interpret and react to violence in ways which preserve their attitudinal equilibria. Generally, equilibrium maintenance involves justification of violence either in terms of self-defense or in terms of the moral or patriotic ends to be achieved through the use of violence.

When a segment of the population resorts to nonviolent tactics, many of the conditions justifying a violent response are absent. Other types of responses may not be known so that the citizen confronted with nonviolence may become uncertain of what to believe and what to do. This uncertainty can serve as the first step in the process of unfreezing old attitudes. It should be recognized, nowever, that nonviolent protests have become frequent enough so that most people have learned of them through me mass media. The mass media contact with nonviolence may allow time for citizens to create adjustive responses which allow them to resist the pressures toward change. The weakened exposure to the protest through the mass media may function to immunize people against me stronger they would experience as a result of direct contact with a nonviolent protest. On the other hand, it may be that whent he protest argets and bystanders are in face contact with non violence for the first time, the intensity of nonviolent impact may overwhelm the barrier created by immunization. The failure of immunization is likely to be greater when the mass media have presented very distorted descriptions of nonviolent protests. In this case the targets and bystanders are unable to defend themselves against the unsettling effects of unexpected aspects of the protest situations.

The susceptibility to unfreezing is not only a function of prior knowledge about nonviolence. It is also quite dependent upon the functional basis of the attitudes relevant to the protest. We will therefore examine the nature of the effects nonviolence is likely to have on attitudes serving one or another of the three basic functions described in the first part of the chapter.

Nonviolence and Object-Oriented Attitudes

To the extent that the information a person receives about a nonviolent demonstration is inconsistent with his object-oriented attitudes, his attitudinal equilibrium will be upset. For example, a person holding negative 'stereotypes concerning Negroes might be considerably affected by a nonviolent demonstration which included well-dressed, dignified, peaceful Negroes, who were clearly dissatisfed with their lot but who accepted many of the values of the whites. Both dissonance theory and the Abelson-Rosenberg balance theory would assert that these inconsistencies create a disequilibrium, which would motivate attempts to change some of the elements in or re-establish a balance between attitudes and information. Probably the first tendency of the unsettled person would be to try to discount the information. Perhaps the Negroes are outsiders or perhaps there were agitators who stirred up the Negro community. If there are white participants, who are also well-dressed, etc., they might be seen as communist agitators. All of these are attempts to deny the relevance of the information received from the demonstration to the person's attitudes about Negroes. If the protest is to be successful, steps must be taken to seal off the avenues of escape from the uncomfortable inconsistency. When the demonstrators hold their ground and remain peaceful in the face of verbal and physical assault, they make escape difficult. Their tenacity and willingness to suffer establishes their sincerity and increases the credibility of their message.

The spectator's task of rejecting the impact of what he sees is made considerably easier if the demonstrators behave in ways which he believes are wrong or evil. For example, a slovenly, unkempt appearance in many of the demonstrators, frivolous behaviour, the shouting of angry slogans, or the use of signs carrying such slogans all work against the unfreezing of object-oriented attitudes. Let us assume that the observer in question places a negative evaluation on the demonstration and its goals and that the imbalance if caused by links between the demonstrators and valued ideals or characteristics. Providing him with links between the demonstration and negatively valued elements compensates for the imbalance and may outweigh it. If there are enough bonds established between the demonstration and undesirable elements, then the path of least resistance toward the re-establishment of the equilibrium would be to change the links between the demonstration and the positive elements, i.e., to deny that the participants really were well-dressed, polite, etc., or to attribute their apparent conformity to acceptable behaviour standards to an intent to deceive. In terms of dissonance theory, the observer might simply place greater weight on the unfavorable elements in the situation which are consonant with his previous views than on the dissonant favourable elements. Dissonance or consonance created by important elements contributes more to the overall level dissonance so that in the present example the overall state of the onlooker might not be dissonant at all.

The person who learns of the action through the mass media may have a still easier time of protecting his attitudes. The mass media are likely to play up elements consonant with local beliefs, e.g., printing pictures of a considerably greater proportion of unkempt participants than of well-dressed participants, even though the latter were more numerous. Pictures may also concentrate on other acts likely to be evaluated negatively, e.g. Negro males and white females walking arm in arm in the protest.

Object-oriented attitudes are probably the most susceptible to change by nonviolent action. Despite manoeuvres aimed at protecting old attitudes, persistent disconfirmation of old beliefs by actions which vary in style and location (so as to remain novel and noteworthy) may finally break through. If the breakthrough is tot occur,' the nature of 'the belied to be invalidated should be 'known by the actors and the action should be designed to refute as many of them as possible. Care must also be taken to avoid providing negative elements which would outweigh the positive ones. This requires knowledge of the belief' systems possessed by the targets and onlookers. It also requires a willingness to forego a defiant stance in which an attempt is made to shock bystanders by opposing aspects of their belief and value systems which are not directly relevant to specific issues of the protest. Having issued this caveat, it seems necessary to mention the other side. Changes brought about in angle beliefs or practices, drawn from a complex ideological system, are not likely to last. The changed belief then becomes inconsistent with the remainder of the ideology and therefore subject to strong forces tending to bring it back into line. The successful employment of nonviolence must program its attack to hit the most vulnerable beliefs first and to gradually increase the range of attitudes against which pressure is brought to bear. Once again, it is clear that leaders of non-violent movements require knowledge of the ideological systems of their opponents.

Nonviolence and Ego-supportive Atitudes

Attitudes functioning as means of ego-support pose a different kind of problem to the nonviolent actor. As long as a target or bystander feels that his relevant reference groups support his opinion, he will feel little pressure to change. Indeed, the actions of the nonviolent protesters might even serve to increase the salience of the reference groups being opposed by the protest. As a result, susceptibility to unfreezing may decline as a consequence of the protest. In order to unfreeze a person's ego-supportive attitude, it is necessary to deprive him of the support of relevant reference groups or increase the salience of other reference groups which do oppose the goals of the protest.

Changing the relative salience of reference groups is probably the most powerful technique available to facilitate the acceptance of nonviolent actions and of the goals towards which this action is aimed. One way of accomplishing this end is to recruit the support of elite members of reference groups which are already in accord with the goals of the violent action. (See below.) For our purposes, elite refers to reference group members who are viewed as legitimate spokesmen for their groups and as legitimate enunciators of group values. Elites may be political, business, religious, or other leaders. Notice that the use of elites envisaged here does not alter the targets' or the bystanders' identification with their reference groups. It merely alters which of their many reference groups will be uppermost in their minds. The more salient the group, the more power its norms have to affect which attitudes an individual will bring to bear on the nonviolent action situation.

In order to bring about unfreezing, it may not be necessary that the salient reference group norms favor the acceptance of the goals of the protest. They need only favor the legitimacy of protest action. Such acceptance might prevent violent countersteps by targets and bystanders; it might also prevent them from summarily, dismissing the action as unworthy of attention. The use of reference group elites in this manner requires a knowledge of the reference groups that might become or be made salient and also of the identity of the reference group elites. At the very least, the demon strators should try to obtain visible police protection. It would clearly indicate the legal status of the protest.

The power of reference group elites can be used and often is used to thwart the objectives or nonviolent action. The thwarting can occur by virtue of simple inaction on me part of elites who know about the violent opposition to non-violent protests. Such inaction may be interpreted as tacit approval of the violent response. A study by Levin and Turgeon provides some relevant evidence. In this study, children were engaged in two sessions of doll play. In me second session, each child was allowed to play. With toys in a in the presence of his mother or an unknown stranger. In both conditions nothing was done by the adults to punish or discourage aggressive behaviour. It was found that children who played in the presence of their mothers exhibited more aggression than those who played in the presence of the stranger. The authors suggest that in this situation, the mothers, but not the strangers, were perceived as legitimate moral authorities. The role of the mothers was similar to the role of the inactive elites referred to above. The children probably expected that their mothers would disapprove of aggressive play. When this expected disapproval did not appear, it seemed as if the children assumed that they were being given a "green light" for further aggression. Strangers, on the other hand, did not have the power to suspend the norms against aggression; hence, their silence did not remove the children's normal inhibitions against aggressive behaviour.

It may also be difficult to change ego-supportive attitudes when there are no societal reference groups salient for the targets and bystanders. The bystanders, in particular, might be very marginal members of their communities, either because of age (adolescents are typically in this position), or because of their socio-economic status The community in which the nonviolent protest occurs may, itself, be poorly organized so that most members cannot look to stable reference groups for ego-support.

Under these circumstances, the immediate group of bystanders is likely to become a powerful, albeit temporary, reference group.

In such a situation there may be instigators whose hostile behaviour is likely to spread. People in a state of rootlessness or anomie are generally frustrated and therefore aggression prone. They are likely to welcome the opportunity for aggression that the instigator provides. In temporary groups of this sort, there is no tradition or other basis on which an appeal for restraint can be made. Therefore, the general disapproval of the nonviolent protest is quite likely to engender a violent response.

There is at least one possible exception to the poor prognosis for the success of nonviolent action undertaken in anomie communities. There are some individuals who can influence persons suffering from an anomie state. It may be improper to think of these influential persons as elites in some reference group because there is no special group or class formed about them. They appear to engender direct ties between themselves and those who are adrift in disorganized communities. Kate Smith is an example of such a person. Her great success in selling war bonds during World War II was probably based on toe trust and admiration she evoked from people who had little that bound them to their communities. It is likely that power such as hers would have a decided effect on changing the attitudes of her listeners toward greater acceptance of the methods and goals of nonviolent protests. Billy Graham and General Eisenhower might be others with this power.

Nonviolence and Ego-defensive Atitudes

The surprise created by nonviolent action is note likely to un freeze attitudes serving an ego-defensive function. The departures from established ways and the social change demands of the protesters are likely to be anxiety arousing for people holding relevant ego-defensive attitudes. The act of challenging authority, however nonviolent it may be, may stir up the defensive person's own ambivalence toward authorities and lead him to rely all the more heavily upon his defensive attitudes. The intense respond iterated by the destruction of draft cards and the even less frequent instances or flag desecration may be examples of this process. It probably impossible for the nonviolent protesters to do anything that would change the defensive person's orientation.

It is in connection with ego-defensive attitudes that one of the assumptions of the nonviolent protest movement must be questioned. This assumption is that the movement must the demonstrator, the less able the more nonviolent the demonstration as a personal attack on himself and the more inclined be will he to see it as a protest merely against certain practices. As a result be is presumed less likely to react defensively. Richard Cregg in *The Power of Nonviolence* speaks of the nonviolent resister's respect for the personality of his attacker which his refusal to counterattack illustrates. However, it should be recognized that the absence of violence does not necessarily imply the absence of threat. For the ego-defensive person, any change which interferes with the maintenance of his defensive system if threatening. Furthermore, the target whose established and valued ways are the focus of a demonstration is being threatened, be cause his values are an important part of his self. It might be that the unexpected or unorthodox nature of the nonviolent threat makes it all the more anxiety evoking The person threatened by the protest cannot rely upon traditional means for eliminating the threat. This loss of control over the threat-producing situation compounds the anxiety. While this anxiety might be the prelude to unfreezing, it is more likely that it will result in unrealistic stubbornness or in violent attack upon the protesters.

As in the simple case of the Allport and Postman study, described above, the threatened person who is moved to violence or who observes physical attacks upon nonoviolent actors may reverse things and come to perceive the protesters as the ones who first used violence. The tendency to reverse responsibility for violence is probably stronger in people who receive their information from the mass media. A news reporter might simply describe the violent events surrounding the protest, leading the reader or listener to decide for himself who started the fighting.

Given the general disapproval of the protest movement, it is likely that the responsibility will be placed on the demonstrators. Such a belief would be considerably more consistent with a reader's attitudes than would the opposite belief. Having reversed responsibility for the initiation of violence, the bystander interprets the physical assault upon the protesters as deserved punishment. This is probably particularly likely when the assault is made by law enforcement officers.

The actual or vicarious expression of aggression against the protesters in such circumstances is likely to be a rewarding or exhilarating experience. When this is the case, the next nonviolent protest might be met with even more violence by those whose appetites were whetted during a previous attack. People who are considered martyrs by the protesters might well be considered subhuman knaves by their opponents.

The danger of defensive distortion makes it particularly important that the demonstrators make their goals dear and manifest good will in their behaviour toward their targets. When the demonstrators help keep paths dear, cooperate with legitimate police requests, and perform other helpful acts, anxiety distortion in ego-defensive targets may be minimized.

The Effects of Coercing Targets

Most of the discussion thus far has been oriented toward the effects of nonviolent action upon bystanders, for some kinds of actions, no further considerations need be introduced because there are no specific targets or because the targets are so remote as to be unaffected in an immediate way by the nonviolent action. For example, picketing the White House, while that President is at his home 2,000 miles away, can probably be thought of as a demonstration designed primarily to influence bystanders. However, there are actions in which the target is dose by and in which some specific response on his part is one or the goals of the nonviolent action. Because the target must often do something, e.g., serve a Negro, register a Negro, call the police to remove the protesters or to protect them against a violent attack, be subjected to more and different pressures than is the bystander. Many of these are not attitude-change pressures. Rather, they are coercive pressures from the protesters and coercive or milder pressures from the nonprotesting segments of the community. The operation of such pressures falls outside the scope of this chapter. Nevertheless, it should be noted that the actions of the target may have an important effect upon the altitudes of the bystanders, particularly if the target is a political, business, or religious leader. Coercion of leaders by protesters may lead to unfreezing and perhaps change in the bystanders. Changes in the bystanders may prevent the target from slipping bade to his old practices once the nonviolent pressure is removed. Similarly, failure by the protesters to coerce the target is likely to lead to increased vigor in the community's opposition to the goals of the protest.

The attitudinal effects of coercion discussed in dissonance theory seem quite applicable here. The target's coerced compliance with the demands of the protesters might not change his attitudes toward the issues of the protest. But impact is different for the bystander who, without coercion, accepts the target's change and who begins to act in accordance with the change, e.g., eating at a desegregated lunch counter. According to dissonance theory, this kind of compliance should produce changes in the attitudes of the bystander which will bring them into congruence with his new actions. The attitude change accomplished in this manner may not generalize to other demands of the nonviolent actors, but it is probably a step in the right direction.

Legislation and Atitude Change

Legislation regulating discriminatory behaviour probably affects attitudes much in the same way as a bystander's attitudes are affected by the coerced compliance of the target. Most people who obey laws do so more or less voluntarily and not because of the threat of negative sanctions imposed upon those who violate the law. In the case of anti-discriminatory laws, it is likely that initially compliance is dissonant with the attitudes of the individual concerned. Such compliance can lead to attitude change in a direction congruent with the new law-abiding behaviour.

In order for this outcome to take place, the theory requires that the people involved do indeed make decisions in conformity with the law. If they are never faced with the opportunity for such decisions, the attitude-change forces stemming from dissonance would be quite weak. Some studies suggest that simply making a verbal commitment to conform will produce enough dissonance to lead to attitude change. For example, the signing of a pledge to sell one's home on an open occupancy basis, if and one decided to sell, might lead to a more favourable attitude toward open occupancy housing. This should be particularly true for persons who were quite ambivalent about open occupancy and signed the pledge only after moderate, but effective pressure.

Conclusions

The application of attitude-change theory to the study of the effects of nonviolence does not leave one with a feeling of optimism. As has been emphasized throughout, attitudes or ideologies resist change through the effects of a variety of equilibrium maintaining mechanisms. Nonviolent actions often do not seem to have characteristics which guarantee the undermining of the resistance to change. However, there are two reasons for hope by the proponents of nonviolence. The first is that the theories might help in avoiding tactics which increase resistance to change. The second and more important one is the recognition that under the proper conditions, coercion can ultimately lead to attitude change. For this hope to be realized, the nonviolent agents of change need to know about the sources of the attitudes they wish to affect. They need to know the content of the beliefs brought to the protests by targets and by bystanders. They need to know the reference groups supporting the attitude to be changed and also the reference groups or individuals who might soften the opposition to the goals and methods of the nonviolent protests. Neither of these two types of knowledge is easily acquired. Under these circumstances, it is probably best for the protesters to concentrate on coercing behaviour change in a way which uses as little force as is possible to ensure the desired changes and to focus on changing attitudes only when the information needed to apply attitude-change theories is available.

Chapter-3

Cultural Forces for Peace and Violence

Chapter-3

> **One way to understand a culture is to identify those values that are emphasized in child rearing.**
> **-Maureen B. Slonim (1991), p.6.**

Statements made in preceding sections of this book support the idea that culture has a powerful influence over people and; consequently the course of history. The purpose of this chapter is to consider some of the violence and peace-causing forces that come from cultures. A few components of culture have been discussed from the aspect of individuals and families (e.g., values, beliefs, child-rearing practices, and family relationships). These become components of culture when they are accepted as guiding principles throughout a group and have extensive power to sway personality development and societal systems.

Although other systems discussed in this Part could be considered segments of culture, here they are separated for convenience sake. Not all forces that influence personality development are here considered to be a part of culture.

Included in this chapter are: the meaning and significance of culture; why there are cultural chasms and walls; prejudice (e.g., ethnocentrism, racism, ideological bigotry, intolerance, and sexism - being discussed here as a basic example of prejudice); and other cultural promoters of violence and peace such as competition, cooperation, and communication systems (especially television).

Culture: Its Meaning and Significance

Culture Defined

Society and culture are not synonymous. Society is a group of people organized or related in some way. Most societies have one or more cultures within them. There are many definitions of culture as a vital concept in anthropolgy and other social sciences. Culture as being discussed here means; a unique way of life shared by members of a group of individuals - an aggregate of people, social relations, and commonalties. *Elements* of culture include the learned meanings, beliefs, values, customs, ideas, norms, social habits, patterns of behavior, competencies, and accumulated knowledge common to a particular group, internalized by them, transmuted, and transmitted to succeeding generations.

"Culture is society's blueprint for behavior," wrote Peter Farb (1978, p. 352). Kazuye Kumabe and colleagues (1985) clarified this statement when they wrote: Cultural norms specify what must be done, what ought to be done, what may be done, what must not be done, and prescribe solutions to basic life problems. In this respect, tradition provides stability (p.9).

Although there are sundry individual differences among the people in a culture, they stand rather solidly together on types of thinking and practices such as religion, child rearing practices, gender roles, and types of recreation.

National culture. Since there are so many strong differences among various groups within nations, it is only in a limited sense that nations can be spoken of as national cultures. Nations usually have components that are widespread among the people (e.g., democratic convictions, competitive economic practices, and personal freedoms in the U.S.; national religion and public welfare services in Norway; and family loyalty and social conformity in Japan). Cultures are characterized more by one or more common types of feelings, beliefs, and practices than by location of residence, community, or nation.

Sub-culture. People in a given nation do not have all elements in common, but there usually are groups within nations that have cultural likenesses. They are cultures within cultures (e.g., "gang cultures," "drug culture," "right or left-wing culture").

Practically all nation -states and regions have more than one ethnic and linguistic grouping, or sub-culture. Indonesia has 3,000 separate groupings according to Elise Bolding, 1988, p.58).

The Mexican American culture is one among many others in the U.S.

Cultural Verse Individual Priorities

The development of self-otherness requires finding a balance between being a completely self-centered individualist and being entirely group centered. Where do we draw the line between the rights and freedoms of the individual verses the needs and welfare of the group - family, community culture, state or world?

Merriam - Webster (1986) defines individualism as:

> a doctrine that the interests of individuals are or ought to be, ethically paramount; conduct guided by such a doctrine; the conception that all values, rights and duties originate in individuals; a theory maintaining; the political and economic independence of the individual and stressing individual initiative, action, and interests; conduct or practice guided by such a theory (p.615).

The extreme of this si selfishness or self-onlyness. On the other hand, collectivism refers to a doctrine in which the interests of the group should be ethically paramount and the individual is less significant.

Most cultures seem not to have done very well in reaching a balance between these two. There seems to be a tendency to either coerce people into servitude to the group or to sanction complete individualism. Neither of these alternatives meets human needs for individual freedom and for interdependent community. These two interdependent type human desires/needs are frustrated by most modern cultures. There is a very strong desire to grow independent of obstruction having the power to get and achieve what one wants. The need to be free from excess burdens is important to people. Standing almost in contradiction to this need is the personal and cultural needs to relate closely to others, to share, to trust one another, to cooperate, and to serve one another. There can be a healthy balance between these two great needs by modifying both. This is **freedom with interdependence and responsibility**. It is a component of self-otherness. It is also part of cultures' responsibilities not to require excessive individual sacrifice. This has often been done by cultures' demands of laborers, racial groups, women and family members. Reaching an appropriate balance between freedom and responsibility, equity and self-interest, and independence and interdependence should be a primary goal of all people. This may seem too much to ask, but it we are to live in peace and happiness, it must be done..

In the past, people in the U.S. were accustomed to living in sparsely populated individualistic societies. Perhaps we need to be reminded that sharing has been the more usual lot of humans. Until recently, most people in most societies lived in stable cultures that took for granted the subordination of the individual to the welfare of the group. The aggrandizement of the individual at the expense of others was considered a crime.

Founders of the U.S. Constitution took an important step forward in declaring freedom for the individual and protection of personal self-directing rights. However, there was not enough stress upon responsibility to accompany those rights. There was not enough provision for a balance between individual privileges and freedom on the one hand and, on the other, the responsibility of individuals to society, the importance of equity for all, and the urgency for protection from exploitation. Hence, exploitation of people and Earth are rampant in the name of individual rights. This is a crucial issue which has yet to be equitably resolved.

The development of self-otherness, requires individual independence to develop one's potentials, meet one's needs, and enhance one's life, as well as accountability to develop integrity, cooperation, responsibilities for sharing resources with others, and the joy that comes with service. The idea is that we, the people of the world, are one people. We all share the same resources and we shall fare better if we cooperate for the common good. Hence, cultures should give priority concern to the growth of the self-other people.

Cultural Blending and Cultural Conflict

Culture is learned, not inherited. In recent times there has been a great deal of cross-cultural learning, as well as cross-cultural conflicts.

Cultures blend with each other. Presently, most cultures are not as isolated, close-knit, and distinct as they were when population was sparse, groups were small, often widely separated, and communication between groups was difficult. In this present heavily populated world there are closer contacts, more extensive communication, travel, and common education. Most cultural practices have been brought into nearly everyone's view. There is widespread cultural interchange, and cultures learn from one another various cultural elements that were once confined to a particular geography area have become widespread throughout other regions and across national borders. Types of clothing, tastes in music, political and economic ideologies, and ethical practices key examples of such cultural exchanges. These ideologies and practices are what could be seen as cross-culture culture.

People in various parts of the world are united in many common beliefs and ways of living which have broken down certain barriers. In today's world, people need each other. Unless they tolerate and accept each other and cooperate, they can not survive and universal destruction is inevitable.

Cultural conflicts can arise from bigotry and intolerance. Cultural distinctions can add vitality to living but unless there is acceptance of differences, conflicts can develop. It is unfortunate that cultures are often used as bases for harming each other. People are usually more comfortable living among people of a similar culture and this need to harm anyone. However, many people have felt the need, not only to screen themselves from other cultures with which they disagree, but also to try to force their beliefs and values upon others. One of the results has been tendencies to categorize people into classes and groups according to such things as religion, economic status, political parties, and ideologies. Often these are personal hostility, bigotry prejudice, conflict, and violence. When these qualities are present, injustice, conflicts, and even wars, result.

Culture can provide basic dynamic forces in the formation of peace promoting secure personality qualities. On the other hand, terrible conflicts and wars continue on the basis of ethnic and religious differences. Hostility centered people tend to see differences as evil. These hostile ways of thinking have resulted from consistent teaching of intolerance, or from autocratic humiliating parenting practices. It is surely true that some aspects of some cultures are very harmful, but violence toward them does not encourage desired change.

If cultures, sub-cultures, and cross-cultural forces promote the well-being of people and other living things, they advance peace. To the extent that they encourage intolerance, prejudice, bigotry, authoritarianism, and harmful conflict, they foster violence. It would not be possible, or necessarily desirable, to bring homogeneity to all the diverse cultures of the world but they could be (and many are) tolerant, nonviolent, cooperative and peace-promoting. The United Nations Coordinator for the International Year of the Family, 1994, Henryk Sokalski (1992, March 12) reminded us that culture is:

> ...much more than the content of our social inheritance, it is an actively produced and experienced way of life. The living culture implicates all of its members as active participants in the creation of new ideas, modes of conduct and interpretations of the world. Culture is not a static form made up of formulae and immutable information. It is evolutionary and is progressively affected by the advance of human civilization, particularly, in the modern context, by technological innovation and progress...In today's shrinking world of effective communication technology, we are witnessing the birth of, and participating in, an emerging world culture...Time and space do not insulate cultures as they once did...The multisource cultural information available to individuals around the world offers us and families, both an opportunity and a challenge (p.3),

Part of the opportunity and challenge is for families and society to evaluate the effects of cultural practices and changes upon family relationships., children's personality development, and society in general. Since cultures do change, whether we like it or not, we should help to create constructive changes rather than being victims of harmful changes. We should endeavor to be uplifting, not degrading, in our cross-cultural influences.

Sokalski, his colleagues, and Year of the Family projects throughout the world have encoruaged constructive child-rearing practices, and peace promoting marriage and family relationships. through its research findings, conferences, consultations, human rights documents, convnetions, and educational projects, the United Nations has promoted constructuve changes and reduced cruel cultural practices. this si particularly true of the **Year of the Family** efforts and influences.

If religious/racial/tribal wars and destructive conflicts are to be eliminated, greater numbers of parents and significant others must help children develop self-other qualities with kindly feelings toward all people whether they are different or not. Other cultural forces must also promote peace, not violence.

It is also vital that intergroup discussions become more systematic, widespread, and persistent. This could help to bring about greater tolerance, understanding, cooperation, and intercultural peace.

It was mentioned earlier that one of humanity's goals should be to develop enough consensus on values to create a cooperative, compassionate equitable world with acceptance of harmless cultural differences and widespread concern for the well-being of all people and the Earth. Thus we seek equity and cooperation, whether we become a global culture or remain differing cultures.

Cultural Chasma and Walls?

Chasma and Walls between peoples are outward expressions of people's inner fears, hostilities, and unmet needs that have, in turn, resulted from harmful past experiences. These chasms and walls are of numerous types including: bigotry, authoritarianism, discrimination, exploitation, racism sexism, and other types of prejudice.

These are irreconcilable with peace. Permanent peace is impossible in a world permeated with or controlled by feelings of hostilities and fears in one or many of their various expressions. Emphasis here will be given to prejudice.

A variety of types of prejudice that people harbor within themselves have created for holding deep chasms and high walls between themselves. These barriers have prevented peoples of differing cultures from cooperating in peace. They deny human rights and cause harm of many kinds.

Prejudice

If you are debased, I am debased
If your identity is distorted, so is mine.
-Robert Lifton (1982)

What and Why?

Prejudice means pre-judgment. It is an attitude for or against something that is not founded in truth. It is a harmful preconceived judgment (i.e. an irrational attitude or mistaken idea, feeling, or belief about an individual, group, or their characteristics). It is debasing to people's identity and damaging to their human rights.

In this brief discussion of prejudice, two general causes and a number of types of prejudice will be mentioned. Then, because sexism is perhaps the oldest, most basic, and affects the most people, special consideration will be given to it is an example of cruel prejudice. The present situation of inequity between men and women will be briefly discussed, some secondary societal causes of sexism will be mentioned, and a number of reforms will be suggested.

Why prejudice?

Prejudice is one of the harmful expressions of self-other personalities that were discussed in Chapter Five and throughout this book.

Gorgon Allport (1958, p.282) described two types of prejudice.

One he called "adopting prejudice." In this type, the child learns and accepts without question, attitudes and stereotypes from his family and/or cultural environment. It may be simply false beliefs with no involvement of underlying hostility toward self and/or others. This type prejudice which is based upon false information may be learned from parental opinions, peers, cultural patterns, traditions, and/or social structures of various types. Some people are prejudiced simply because they have been given "misinformation." As Allport wrote, "Much prejudice is a matter of blind conformity with prevailing folkways" (p.12). since hostilities and fears are not a part of this type prejudice, thought-promoting factual education can eliminate such prejudice.

Another type prejudice Allport called: "developing prejudice." Such prejudice results for parenting practices such as neglect, ridicule, and unmet needs. This kind of child-rearing builds hostile psychic feelings, creates dominant/violent tendencies, and hampers healthy growth. The psychic attributes that result include:

feelings: self-disrespect, distrust, jealousies, resentments, greed, hostilities, personal hurts, and fears of the unknown or differences;

ways of thinking: illogical, unclear, rationalization, selfish, denial, false, submissive, rigid, and self-denying.

beliefs: myths, misunderstandings, ideologies, dogmatism, superstitions, and falsehoods; and

attitudes: inferiority, superiority, disrespect, demeaning and dehumanizing.

These psychic forces cause:

behavioral patterns: discrimination, unhealthy communication, isolation, physical abuse, cruelty; and

cultural patterns and societal structures: bigoted religions, patriarchal family patterns, unjust laws, inequitable governmental policies, exploitative economics, and discriminating education.

Hostile/fear-based prejudices can be expressed in many types of including sexism, racism, elitism (classism), ageism, militarism, imperialism, neocolonialism, authoritarianism, and materialism.

These are all manifestations of self-disrespect and hostility toward others Prejudiced people with psychologically damaged psyches do not fully respect themselves or others. They have great difficulty relating constructively and cooperatively with others and are not capable of coping effectively with personal and societal crises. They are ineffective in contributing equitably to economic, political, and educational systems. Their dominant/violent personalities often cause them to project their hostilities onto individuals or groups. This in turn builds the walls and digs the chasms of prejudice involving deep-seated hostilities in interpersonal relationships.

Prejudice of any kind can do great harm to people's rights and well-being. All prejudice is violence and it continues in many forms. Humanity has made tremendous progress in material and technological advancement; but, as Allport wrote, "by contrast, we appear to be living in the Stone Age so far as our handling of human relationships is concerned" (p.ix).

Many people do not yet understand that prejudice in people causes inequity and resentment in all human relationships. More people should realize that

- each person can be happier and more productive by cooperating than by competing and being greedy;
- male-female partnerships and sharing give more joy than dominant submissive patriarchal relationships;
- peace-promoting preventing with love, mutual respect, dignity teaching and cooperative rule-making are more effective in promoting self-otherness than authoritarianism, punishment, and rebuke.
- fairness, justice, and equality is better in the work place than is exploitation; and
- in international conflict, understanding, empathy, and cooperation are more effective than threats, military strength, and competition.

The following figure shows important similarities between the ways forces in social systems manifest prejudice in four examples: *sexism*—holding women in submission to men; *racism*—keeping minority groups in less privileged positions; *elitism*—suppressing many people into poverty slavery of semi-slavery to the rich; and *neocolonialism*—forcing weaker nations into economic servitude to stronger nations. Four societal systems used here as examples are: economic, ideological or religious, political and physical or military. In each case there are rewards if the group stays in obedience, and punishments if they do not (i.e., the old carrot-and-stick idea). Relationships are dominant/submissive.

It is encouraging to know that more and more people are agreeing that if there is to be peace in the world, acceptance of

Forees	Sexism	Racism	Elitism	Neo-colonialism
Econimic	Support ^Desertion ^Discrimination	Tokens ^Discrimination	American ^Poverty	*Jobs, Loans, ^Starvation ^Embargoes ^Unfair Trade
Religious or Ideological	*Promise of Heaven ^Hetred ^Disapproval	Promised Equality ^Infriority ^Injustice	*Accepance ^Ridicule	Heaven, ^Capitalism ^Hell, ^Communion
Political	*Tokens ^Neglect	*Tokens ^Annihilation	*Protection ^No-influence	Promises ^Annihilation ^Overpower
Military	^Abuse ^Beating ^Harassment ^Rape	*Protection ^Put-downs ^Police abuse	*Protection ^Harassment	*Protection from Communism ^Military occupation

Figure. The Dominant/Submissive Relationship
*Enticments and rewards fro compliance — "carrots".
Punishments and penalties for lack of subjection—"Sticks"

difference must take the place of prejudice. The obstructive walls of many kinds must be torn down. The chasms must be filled with feelings of empathy, constructive ways of thinking, beliefs based on truth, and attitudes of mutual respect, and love.

For such monumental tasks to be performed, prodigious efforts must be made by many men of good will as well as by liberated women. Transformations of people and all major world structures discussed in this book will have to be an ongoing part of the needed reforms.

Sexism: A Major Example of Prejudice

Sexism remains chief among the many prejudices—a powerful root of violence. However, I want to make it clear that I do not believe that most men are sexist in the way I am describing it. In fact, some men are as equitable, kind, fair-minded, and caring as any woman. Furthermore, some women have been brainwashed into accepting ideologies of sexual inferiority. Much progress toward gender equity has been made in recent years. I as a woman am grateful to men, as well as to women, for that advancement have hope for greater gender cooperation in the future.

Yet, the reality remains: one of the strongest cultural forces in practically every culture in the world is the persistent and continual drive to keep women; in subjection, in a subordinate position to men. Women have been made slaves in labor and in sex. They have had little control of their own lives, their bodies, or the fruits of their own labors. These sexist attitudes foster myths and discriminatory practices in an areas (economic, social, political, religious, educational, and legal). I like the way Betty Reandon (1985) describes sexism in, "Sexism and the War System":

> Sexism is a many headed, ubiquitous monster that has manifested itself in different ways in different historic periods and in different either. It is a belief system based on the assumption that the physical difference between males and females are so significant that they should determine virtually all social and economic roles of men and women. It holds that not just their reproductive functions are

> determined by sex, but that sex is the factor that rules their entire lives, all their functions in society and the economy, and their relation to the state and all public institutions and especially to each other. Sexism is manifest in all forms of behavior from subtle gestures and language to exploitation and oppression, and in all human institutions from the families to multinational corporations. It is as complex and pervasive a phenomenon as is the war system, Few human beings escape the social conditioning of both, and only a small minority have transcended them (p,16)

There will be no peace while the fires continue to burn under the forces of violence against women. The underlying human psychic hostilities that cause the worst forms of sexism also express themselves with fires of militarism, racism, materialism, fanatical religious conflicts and wars. Sexism is the most destructive expression of authoritarianism.

Riane Eisler (1987) clearly depicts the effects of sexism and holds out hope for the future.

> For millennia of recorded history, the human spirit has been imprisoned by the fetters of androcracy. Our minds have been stunted, and our hearts have been numbed. And yet our striving for truth, beauty, and justice has never been extinguished. As we break out of these fetters, as our minds, hearts, and hands are freed, so also will be our creative imagining (p.198).
>
> *(Eisler uses the word "androcracy" to refer to " a social system ruled through force or the threat of force by men.")

Is this possible? If so, humanity with all our differences, can reach out to each other in love and live in peace. We can then help each other with our inadequacies, struggle to eliminate our hostilities, and appreciate our strengths.

What Causes Sexism?

The discussions in this book give only a glimmer of the oppression which women have suffered through the ages and still continue to suffer. Why this terrible sexism—abuse, prejudice, discrimination, and degradation. From time to time, various possible causes have been suggested. Here is a brief glance at some of these theories.

1. *Psychic qualities.* At the most fundamental level, the causes of sexism are the same basic dominant/violent underlying psychic feelings and qualities that cause other types of prejudice (as noted above). Other causes are secondary causes.

2. *Males are biologically superior to females.* Reardon says: "The major attitudinal underpinning of sexism lies in the belief that men are biologically and intellectually superior to women" (p.16). If this is the case, some would reason, women should be kept in subjection. She is for his pleasure, his helper, his servant.

No! Anatomy is not destiny, as Freud thought. Although this is a controversial issue, and it is quite certain that all the facts are not in at this point, research which is available point very strongly to the conclusion that the choice to respond to anger and frustration in violent ways is conditioned by very early experiences, not by inheritance. Many of the related facts were presented in Chapter Three.

If there were biological tendencies toward the development of sexiest attitudes, that would be all the more reason for educating both sexes to develop equitable life-promoting qualities and value systems.

Certainly, real biological differences are significant. On the average males are physically stronger then females. Although males have more muscular power, females, biologically, have more physical stamina. They have greater resistance to disease and better life sustaining systems. More males than females die before birth and at earlier ages throughout life.

We should ask: "What real difference should these differences make? None should dictate work roles; qualify or disqualify one for making decisions in family or world affairs; justify inequities and rigidities; or vindicate authority over, or abuse of women. The fact that males are physically more muscular may indicate that they can, on average, do more strenuous tasks.

The fact that women give birth may help them to be more sensitive to life and the deeper feelings of people. But primarily both genders have been socialized to think and feel the way they do.

3. *"It's just that way and always will be."* So say some people, and dismiss the subject of causes of prejudice. Riane Eisler (1987) argues that it has not always been that way. She says that when, in the nineteenth century, evidence was unearthned concerning the existence, many centuries ago of peaceful caring, loving societies.

> ...it was concluded that they must have been "matriarchal." Then, when the evidence did not seem to support this conclusion. It again became customary to argue that human society always was - and always will be-dominated by men. But if we free ourselves from the prevailing mode of reality, it is evident that there is another logical alternative; that there can be societies in which difference is not necessarily equated with inferiority or superiority. (pp.xvi, xvii).

Eisler says that these early societies were "...based on the principle of linking rather than ranking [and] may be best described as the partnership model." She points out that since these early people knew that "...new life emerged from the body of a woman," It is reasonable that "..earliest depiction of divine power in human form should have been female rather than male." It is also logical that such a society would be governed by qualities of caring, compassion and nonviolence (qualities usually attributed to women). She says further "...that the original direction in the mainstream of our cultural evolution was toward partnership but that, following a period of chaos and almost total cultural disruption, there occured a fundamental social shift..." from a gylanic (partnership) to an androchic (male-dominated) type culture, probably in all parts of the world (p.xvii).

Whether or not there ever was a "gylanic" society we can not know for certain. But, this we know: the world as a whole is now certainly ruled by males. But, as she says, there have always been "peaceful and nonviolent men." and, soem women have not been so "peaceful and nonviolent." Therefore, we are referring to a way of thinking, behaving, and relating which is dominant, oppressive, hierarchic, and bigoted. Women sometimes have these qualities, but males have, in large measure been socialized and expected to be very authoritarian. Hence, what is needed is for people, both men and women, is to develop to a level of self-otherness in which they are caring, responsible, egalitarian, sharing, and self-directing.

If Eisler is correct in her conclusions that egalitarian societies have existed and were "truncated and completely turned around" by foreign invasions of dominant militaristic people, we still do not know exactly what caused the invading group to be that way, nor we can be entirely sure how the peaceful peoples maintained this spirit for so many thousands of years, if indeed they did. More research is needed. But, I am convinced that partnership and equity could be a reality in the future, if humanity chooses to make it so. If this is ever to occur, great changes will have to be made in social structures and most certainly in the way men and women think and relate to each other, especially in family relationships and parenting practices.

4. *The socialization process.* A very important cause of sexism is the warped commonly used socialization process. People's personal psychic qualities are what they are because of the kind of socialization they have received - relationship-experiences, what is learned, and the way one integrates these with native abilities.

Authoritarianism and social and personal hierarchies are backed by force, or the threat of force. Military strength has been the male security blanket. Eisler says:

> For millennia men have fought wars and the Blade has been a male symbol. But this does not mean that men are inevitably violent and warlike. Throughout recorded history there have been peaceful and nonviolent men. Moreover, obviously there were both men and women in the prehistoric societies where the power to give and nurture, which the Chalice symbolizes, was supreme. The underlying problem, is not men as a sex. The root of the problem lies in a social system in which the

> power of the Blade is idealized- in which both men and women are taught equate true masculinity with violence and dominance and to see men who do not conform to this ideal as "too soft" or eliminated (p.xviii).

From ages past males and females have been socialized very differently An early example of this conditioning can be seen in the type toys chosen for girls and boys. Baby dolls and cuddly animals are important in allowing the expression of loving empathic caring feelings and in helping both boys and girls develop gentleness, sensitivity, and cooperative skills - qualities are very much needed in this world by both men and women. Very early in life little boys are steered away from these toys, Girls are often discouraged from and boys are encouraged toward play that could develop large music strengths, courage, independence, confidence, creativity, and problem solving skills that every person needs. On the other hand boys are strongly pushed into competitive play and encouraged to develop strong, dominant, aggressive, chauvinistic qualities that tend to divided the sexes, and harm people.

> Nancy Carlsson-Paige and Diane Levin (1990) have well said: When play is rich, children have a chance to construct flexible and broad gender identities and to develop a wide range of human potentials...Toys linked to television programs trap children into imitating stereo typed behavior (pp. 98,99)

These writers suggest that people help children become aware of sex role stereotypes that are harmful; help boys and girls play together and expand their play behaviors; provide a variety of gender role models and encourage them to participate in tasks formerly performed by only one sex; and provide books that picture men and women in a variety of roles (pp. 100-105)

In these chapter on Nurturing it was nooted that from birth both parents relate differently to boys and girls. Especially significant is the ways in which boys are given less love and affection because parents think this makes men too soft and related too much to their mothers rather than their fathers.

From her research with people and a study of psychological

theories beginning with Freud (1905), Carol Gilligan (1982) has revealed and presented a new view of two ways of looking at moral problems and relating to self and others which usually correspond to male and female thinking.

Since for centuries male thinking and power has ruled everything outside the home and many things within it, it is understandable that not only social structures, but also research and theory are based on male assumptions and perceptions. The male life and developmental process has been considered the norm and women as deviants from that norm. This fact of seeing the world through men's eyes, has been far-reaching in its implications for both the lives of all people and the crises and problems which now threaten to destroy the world.

According to the studies reported by Gilligan, one of these omissions of truth is that since girls have not had to go through such severe separation from mother as boys are conditioned to do, they can maintain closer human relationships than can boys and have a former basis for empathy than do boys.

These researchers point out, for example, that in play girls are more friendly and cooperative, less bound by rules and competition than are boys. Girls are also more flexible and concerned with finding alternative ways to solve the inevitable children's conflicts, including stopping the game if a solution is not readily found. They then maintain friendship.

Misogyny (hatred of women) and gynophobia (fear of women) that plague many males are underlying psychic feelings that have been socialized into little boys, and are basic in the development of sexism. They are components of the dominant-violent syndrome of qualities in these men. They seem to be caused, in part, by the situation of infants and small children having to submit totally to the power of mother. A fear/love/hate emotional syndrome develops from this dependency relationship. The more punitive and harsh the power, the stronger the development of fear/hate aspects of the triad. The situation is aggravated when fathers and other men degrade everything which appears to be female and flaunt their humiliating attitudes and behaviors toward women. This hostility is inverted toward self in the case of girls, since they too are female - the hated sex. Hence, one reason for low self-esteem in many women.

Birgit Brock-Utne (1985) concluded from her studies that fathers have greater influence in "making boys into 'real' men than mothers had. They were even more instrumental than mothers in making girls into 'real' women (p.ix). Children learn rather early, especially in a patriarchal home, that males are in charge, that they must be respected, obeyed and imitated Girls, of course, are allowed only limited imitation of their fathers, and fathers can be very clear in impressing girls with these distinctions.

The authority structures that pervade the military are socialized to pervade the entire society. All are taught to obey authority and to fear violence. Men are conditioned to deal with their fear of violence by developing the capacity to use it competitively with "equals" and oppressively on "inferiors." Women are conditioned to deal with the fear of violence, not only by developing behaviors of accommodation and avoidance but also by learning to cope with it as a fundamental given of the human condition. Because they must cope with an avoid violence, women are permitted to express their fear to it. Demonstration of fear is seen as feminine in women but cowardly in men. The sexist conspiracy, however, secretly communicates to boys that, although macho men do know fear, they simply do not show it. Indeed, boys and then are encouraged to become more fierce, more aggressive when they feel that. Fear in men is channeled into aggression, in women into submission such behaviors are necessary to maintain patriarcnal authoritarianism (Based primarily on Reardon pp.38-39)

Furthermore, boys are encouraged to reject qualities of tenderness, nurturing, empathy, and expressions of feelings such as fears and affection. Since women are taught to be in touch with emotions-theirs and others' - they are often perceive men to be emotional and not responsible. Males are allowed and encouraged to be physically expressive, to show anger and even violence, to be adventurous and "foolhardy", whereas females are taught to sublimate their anger and to give expression to what seems to me to be natural tendencies of love, nurturing, kindness and sympathy.

Many kinds of deceptions, policies, and hostile techniques are employed to keep males in line. This puts an extra burden upon them. It should not be imagined that it is easy to be a male. They have many privileges, but they also are expected to carry many responsibilities. The most distressing thing is that what they are often expected to be is unhealthy and immature if comparison to what is good for human beings. They must try to prove they are superior to most men in win lose competition and superior women without objective proof that they are. If they can not do this, and of course, only a few can, they feel they are inadequate and hence, have low self-esteem. If they dislike themselves, they dislike and often feel hostile toward everyone else. These are unfair expectations and place burdens which one should not have to bear.

Furthermore, males are socialized to develop pragmatic minds that deal with quantifiable concepts and concrete relationships. They are expected to be precise, technical, logical, and to think scientifically and analytically. This analysis usually involves details or fragments, not wholes. It is assumed that they should always be in control, without a show of emotion. They are taught to stand on their own, to be separate from all others. They are to be courageous, dominant, powerful, and willing to fight physically for what they believe. Although analytical-type thinking and some other qualities taught to men are very important, taken as a whole, the qualities they are taught and the type thinking they are encouraged to use promotes materialism. National leaders with this type personality, feel they must be in control and show their strength and superiority before they attempt to negotiate. They may ignore the cogent need for worldwide cooperation and interdependence, for understanding on all levels, and for responsibility for nurturing and enhancing life.

Certain aspects of women's socialization help them to be

kind, loving, nurturing, respectful, compromising rather than confronting, and able to relate to their own and other's feelings. Since they must care for whole people, bring many details into perspective, and coordinate many facets of home and family welfare, they have learned to see situations in their entirety. The caring, nurturing, sacrificing role which women are conditioned to play, is better education for peace than the education males receive. This greater love for humanity which most women seem to have, has been of tremendous influence in creating and promoting peace. More often now women are learning to think independently make a more significant contribution to decision-making worldwide. Since they are beginning to learn how to be more assertive, they are beginning to get into managerial and decision-making positions without playing the male superiority role. It is unfortunate that sometimes they because, at least on the surface, as authoritarian as males. This may direct their efforts from peace to materialism. What a predicament!

Thus, various myth, harmful institutions, and violent practices are created when differences in the sexes are exaggerated; attempts are made to cramp people into prescribed roles; and dominance/submission qualities are encouraged.

The prejudicial practice of reducing some groups of people to inferior levels of being is an important factor in many types of exploitation. If a would be oppressor does not attribute full humanity to women, labourers, minority groups, third-world people, or the poor, it seems to give a justification for his/her oppression, or at best ignoring them and giving them little respect.

Julia Edwards (1988) implied that this is the reason both women and Afro-Americans have been practically omitted in history. Not only them but what they do seem of little importance to dominant white males. As insecurities, fears and hostilities mount, more excuses and justifications are fabricated to keep the feared "enemy" in subjection. This includes race, cultural group country, or class, as well as women.

Even when people are adults, if others around them continually simply word or deed that they are inferior, they tend to internalize those judgements and begin to feel inferior. Thus, the oppressed gives assent to the oppresson. It takes a great deal of reeducation, including attitudinal and emotional transformation to rectify this situation and for a person to gain self-esteem and feelings of equality.

5. *Cultural/social systems*. Much sexism arises from secondary causes in societal systems. Symptoms of sexist socialization practices mentioned above may be found in numerous social forces. Some of these forces are discussed in greater length in the following chapters of this book. A few examples are mentioned here.

Various religious teachings have been created and manipulated to give sanction and power to desired sexist practices. This is probably the most effective means of getting women's assent and cooperation. Women are persuaded that God will punish them if they disobey their men, but will highly reward them if they "keep their places."

The justice system is also on the side of the males who created them. Many civil laws are made to legalize practices which are harmful to women, or which disallow them opportunities and privileges. It has now (1995) been only the 75th year that women have had suffrage in the U.S.

Nearly all *television commercials and programs* portray and promote an image of women as sex objects and in other ways often degrade them.

As will be discussed later, most *economic* systems disallow women opportunities and keep many of them in poverty.

Political systems encourage the status quo and ignore potential contributions of women. Presently, they are gaining more opportunities to serve in public offices, but are far from having equal decision-making opportunities.

Women and their concerns and ideas seem completely invisible in the military part of the male system. Recently women have been entering the military in limited numbers but this brings up a myriad of questions.

These systems are not only a result of dominant/violent personality qualities, they also encourage dominant/violent qualities in the population. They are both primary and secondary causes of violence. Unless we work to minimize dominance and promote maturity toward self-otherness, our world stands in crisis.

Face Present Realities, Make Changes

I agree with Eisler that we must strive for "truth, beauty, and justice." We must also face the world the way it is -permeated with sexism. Women's rights and personal potentials are being denied, their thinking inhibited, their psychological growth stifled, and their spirits dulled.

It is, therefore, crucial that many reforms be made and constructive structures be created. Following are suggestions for changes in beliefs, attitudes, practices, and other forces that presently cause sexism.

Respect both women and men Perhaps the most important change needed is to give high respect and admiration equally to women and men. At present women are not respected for being as worthy, capable, and valuable as are men. This is the most insulting of myths. I am convinced that many women and most men, feel this disrespect because both have been conditioned to see females in this way. This degrades their humanity and distorts their identity.

Men are thus depriving themselves and society of women's wisdom and its potential human resources. The world needs, from all its people, creative thinking, cooperative participation, and a spirit of peace, enthusiasm, love, and joy. Women cannot make this type of contribution while being held in subjection or in invisibility. When people subscribe to out-worn destructive role models, harmful artificial behavior patterns, and personality qualities that disallow full development and expression to women, they are burdening men with a mission impossible and women are denied a fulfilling mission.

Although women are much freer than they were an hundred years ago, they yet have many *fewer* choices than do men. In some parts of the world women have little free choices even in choosing a marriage partner, having children, or divorcing. At the United Nations World Conference on Women held in Nairobi, Kenya (1985), a panel of Tanzanian women said that they would never be free until they could outlaw the "bride price." Several young men in Nairobi asked us what the women were doing at that big Conference. They said, "We own our women, we bought them with our possessions. We may do with them what we like." No apparent respect for them as separate human beings.

People can never be morally bought or sold. No such cruel system should be allowed anywhere. Women and men could and should be wonderful loving partners. They can cooperate in whatever endeavors are for their mutual well-being. They also can be helpful, or at lest not harmful, to the rest of humanity.

One of the most biased ideologies still being spread about is: "Wives be in subjection to your husbands." This, some religious doctrines declare means that men are to be the leaders and make the final decisions. The claim is that "families can not have tow heads," or "a car can not have two drivers." However, a couple is not one; there are two people and they should be two autonomous people. Few people would enter into any other partnership contract that required them to allow the other person to make the final decisions. As noted in Chapter Nine, couples can learn to make decisions cooperatively and live together lovingly with autonomy for both.

Women have long been encouraged and usually urged to make their life's work consist almost totally of having children, and taking care of them her husband, and their house. This may be best for some women, but certainly not for all. There is much to be considered. For example, being prepared to care for self and children if needed; the over-population problem and meeting life's gets for work and service. Please read Chapter Nine on couple relationships and especially the topic "should you have children?" at the end of the chapter.

In summary then, let us all endeavor to change attitudes which encouraged dominance, exploitation, and violence directed toward any individual or group, and let us destroy all prejudice and the undesirable "isms". Women have held the worked together with love. They can continue that influence for human good if they disallow themselves to be swept into a world of cut-throat competition. Instead they can teach men as well as their children to live by the power of love and equity. Dominance is now fostering destruction Equity can foster life, love, peace, and beauty.

Understand and encourage feminism. Feminism is the theory or belief that women are of equal intrinsic worth and value with men, that their thinking, values, and capacities are as important as men's. and that there should be no discrimination against them because of sex. It thus, means that they should have equal opportunities and equity in all matters. Feminists and women's liberation movement are still striving to being equity between men and women. They want to free women for discrimination of all types. They hope to reform societal structures that perpetuate myths that women are inferior. And they are eager to encourage practices of cooperation and partnerships between men and women.

Even now only a token number of women have been allowed in the male world's decision-making positions. Many men still insist that qualified women are not available. Qualified often means meeting masculine standards and tests for success and conforming to male ways of thinking. Just as important is the requirement to keep power in men's hands. Such attitudes are changing for the better. In some sectors, women are respected as are men. But still, men often fear women's thinking will change the status quo. But many men are now overcoming these feelings.

New men and women not only respect the equal intrinsic value of women and men, they also give equal recognition to the value of their work, paid as well as unpaid. Anthony Astrachan

(1986), in his book, *How Men Feel*, gives the following as his definition of "the new man":

> ...the new man is one who has abandoned or transcended most traditional male sex roles and the male attempt to monopolize power. He doesn't insist on being the sole or dominant earner of family income and he resists being a slave to his job even though he prizes competence and achievement. He believes that men are just as emotional as women and should learn to express their feelings, and he can talk about his own problems and weaknesses.
>
> At home, if he's married, he recognizes his wife's career as equal in importance to his own, and he trades off on transfers that mean promotion or on staying home from work with a sick child. Most important of all, he takes half the responsibility for house work and child care, in addition to doing half the work (pp.402,403).

Insure equal educational opportunities. The International Labor Organization (ILO) (1995) reports that in some countries 80% of the women are illiterate, and worldwide more than 65% (i.e., 600 mision), ILO urges that greater effort be made to insure the women receive equal opportunity for education and employment training.

Egalitarian equity education should be an important component part of all education for all people of the world. Some educational systems have made progress in their educational programs by such policies as:

- deleting some of the sexist language;
- reducing competition and increasing cooperation;
- eliminating awards and punishment, helping children enjoy learning for its own sake;
- showing the folly and destructiveness of greed and exemplifying the values and pleasures of sharing, and helpfulness;
- encouraging both girls and boys to develop their full potential range of non-sexist humanitarian personal qualities, skills, attitudes, and behaviour patterns;

- involving parents in the educational system and
- including in the curriculum the study of family relationships, child development, parenting education, and education for peace.

Girls and women need to develop their autonomy, self-esteem and confidence in expressing their opinions from their own perspective. They should develop their ability to refuse to be oppressed by male domination. They could also increase their ability to sure more effectively facts, logic and strength without losing their flexibility, relatedness, and willingness to care for others. They may also need to empathize more fully with men's probility.

On the other hand, boys and men need to learn how to be in touch with their own feelings enjoy close caring relationships, avoid competitiveness and use "win/win" practices, how to be nurturing. They should recognize the value and significance of women's contribution and try to see the need for closer examination of women's points of view and ways of perceiving rather than demanding that life be judged from male perspectives only. They need to develop flexibility in the use of roles and willingness to search for alternatives to dominance, hostility, and violence when differences arise. They should grow in sensitivity, kindness, and the use of principles of equal between men and women and among men.

Not only do I object to culturally assigned roles for men and women. I am also convinced that there should be no gender-designated qualities, feelings, and behaviors. Qualities, feelings and behaviors which are conducive to the promotion of equity and peace are human, not gender-based. If they are good for one sex they are good for the other. All people need to know themselves and accept their real feelings. They all need self-esteem, confidence, courage, concern for others, willingness to nurture and to be nurtured, and skill in independent creative thinking, decision-making and peaceful conflict-resolution. None of us need to be domineering, exploitative, manipulative, or violent.

Educators should recognize the traps that males are in and provide education that will help to escape and learn to be equitable. It is unfair to assume that women are the only ones oppressed. Males are abused when they are educated and prodded into being unnaturally objective, unrealistically dominant, unfeeling, greedy, aggressive and fool-hardy. Women, too often manipulate men, for example into marriage, security and money. Herb Golberg (1979) was right when he said that a woman can use.

> ...wiles, coyness, helplessness and other "feminine" manipulations to gain her end and to goad him into proving himself the big man, the succeeder, the dominant, fearless, powerful protector (p.145).

Girls and women need to learn to be aware of, and empathic with, the pressures they face. They should be encouraged not to imitate the domineering behaviors of many men. They sometimes fail to realize that equality and equity do not need to mean sameness. Mahatma Gandhi (1940), who argued that only women could save the world, also said: "She can run the race but she will not rise to the heights she is capable of by mimicking man" (p.35). Mimicking women is one of the last things most men want to do. The worst thing you can call a male is "sissy". This gives one indication of the difference in the way men and women see each other.

Another problem which seems to plague women is what Penelope Russianoff (1981) calls "desperate dependence." Why do women so often think they are "nothing without a man?" Russianoff has found that many of her patients are handicapped by a "whole dependency syndrome." She says that "although both men and women rely too much on the opposite sex for emotional sustenance, there are differences in the nature and degree of the dependency. Women's needs tend to seep into all areas of their lives" (p. xiv). This, she says is not true of men. This inability to be autonomous, self-directing, and self-actualizing can be a great handicap to living a productive fulfilling life. Women have been taught to believe Freud's theory that woman can not be complete without a man. This, of course, is not true. It should be remembered also that being autonomous does not prevent a person from living a companionable, loving, caring, interdependent life with someone of the other sex. In fact it makes possible a more vital enriching life for both.

Anthony Astrachan (1986) says his change has to do with power more than anything else. He says that women have been claiming greater power than they have ever had, "an equal share with men in political, economic, social, family, and sexual power, and the intellectual power to name and define. They not only demand this equal share, but in the process they also expose men's true powerlessness, the weakness that the majority of us disguise by identifying with the few, mostly male, who hold power" (p.400).

All humanity - males and females- need a great deal of education to reach heights needed to get "beyond war" as a way of resolving conflict, beyond sexism as a way of viewing and behaving toward women and men, and beyond I-win-you-lose competition. The human family can transcend the problems involved. Let us learn how.

Women and men can learn from each other and contribute to each other's development. We all need to recognize out interdependence, our need to contribute to each other's development, and the need to stop doing and thinking things which separate and antagonize each other. We can respect each other and accept our differences and stop imposing our expectations on each other.

Provide Family Life Education for Peace (FLEP) FLEP is most urgently needed if permanent progress is to be made toward the elimination of prejudice. As may be concluded from the discussion above, equity for women should begin in the family-with the couple who establishes the family and with their child practices. The spousal and family relationships should be examples of equity for both sexes, and the emotional/intellectual family climate should encourage healthy psychic growth rather than building dominant/violent psyches. Chapter Nine provides many suggestions for promoting couple partnership relations. Couples can learn how to give unconditional love and affirmation and how to contribute effectively to each others' growth. Peace with each other in the family promotes peace in the world.

Some psychic transformations within individuals and in child-rearing practices are necessary to stop the vicious cycle of self-hostility, insecurity, fear, violence, war, deprivation, inequality, and back around again. For example, people need to learn that punitive and authoritarian child-rearing practices, malformed human psyche, inequitable social structures, and militarization are all intricately interrelated with multiple directional causation. Authoritarian patterns can be continually conditioned into people at all ages but especially in childhood.

Establish economic equity for women. Economic inequity (as in noted in Chapter 14) is pervasive in all economic systems. Many women's state of economic living is most deplorable.

The May/June, 1995 issue of The Magazine of the International Labor Organization; World of Work, states that 70% of the world's poor are women and urges greater equality for women around the world. The editorial begins with this statement:

> Despite significant progress during the last two decades, equality of opportunity and treatment between women and men in the world of work remains elusive as we approach the 21st century. Society stands to be the loser for not fully harnessing all of its human resources towards its sustainable development (p.3).

Because one's economic situation also greatly determines one's opportunities in other areas of life, **women are economically disadvantaged in various ways**.

One reason women are less often elected to and advanced in political positions is that tremendous economic power is necessary: they seldom have it.

Industrial homework, which is becoming more prevalent, poses an insidious threat to women's already precarious economic position. Piecework results in lack of legal protection of any kind, hazardous technologies, substandard wages, child labor, and no labor organization. Sweatshops, now on the rise, offer jobs that are so poorly paid and often dangerous that they are filled mostly by immigrant women who have no other option.

In Scandinavian countries, women's economic situation is better with public professional child care, social services, flexible work schedules, total government health and medical programs, retirement insurance, and better work opportunities. However, worldwide women are not so fortunate.

All over the world, most women who work outside their homes double or triple burdens with care of children, home and sometimes agricultural. This is often the case even if husbands are also in the home. Years ago the ILO estimated that even though women are one half the world's population, they are only one-third of the paid work force perform two-thirds of the total hours of work, recieve only one-tenth of the income, and own only one-hundredth of the world's wealth. Percentages may not be accurate, but the principle remains the same. When women work outside their homes, men should share the responsibilities of homework and care of children.

In the U.S., women earn about 70% of the hourly pay rates of men. On worldwide average, they earn only slightly more than half what men do. Man hold more than three-fourths of all managerial and professional jobs while women considered about the same percentage on the clerical and essentially line work force

If women choose to stay at home with their children while they are young and then go back to work outside, they are greatly handicapped. Even when they are competent and fully qualified, they are discriminated against. Some women need part-time work; policies should facilitate such opportunities. It is vitally important that competent, professional, adequate, affordable child care be provided. Lack of childcare services is a chief handicap for women.

Because women's economic future is left primarily to the

workings of the business-dominated economy, more women, both employed and unemployed and their children, are entering the ranks of the poorest of the poor. Therefore, governments should guarantee; gender-balanced training policy a life-supporting minimum wage, equal access to credit; prohibition of abusive labor practices, hazardous work conditions, and harassment at work adequate health benefits and retirement insurance; and limitations on maximum income and wealth. This is controversial, but the gap between the rich and poor is becoming cruel and unfair and violence promoting.

When corporations move from "First World" countries to "Third World" countries, they pay no more for a day or even a week of work than it would cost them for an hour in their own countries. They have no trade union demands, no (or very few) health and safety standards to meet, no retirement payments or extra benefits, no environmental regulations, and when women's eyes fail or they become ill because of toxic chemicals and strenuous working conditions, no compensation is necessary and the women are readily replaceable.

"But," some will say, "this provides much needed employment, and the women prefer it to their former situation." That is sometimes true. Even so, their earnings provide only the barest subsistence-level living; they may have to live in conditions that are almost unbearable; unsanitary water; small and crowded rooms; and sharing beds with as many as three shifts of workers, one sleeping while another works.

Yet they are trapped. They have few alternatives, and feel they have no defensive or assertive power. Their own government officials have let them down by making bad agreements with the corporations either for self-profit or because they see no other option.

This type cruelty and exploitation, especially of garment workers, is rampant throughout the U.S. as well as elsewhere. Poor Asian women are being brought to this country by the thousands to work at almost slave labor in the garment industry. A most shocking extreme sweatshop case was exposed in El Monte,

California. Christina Nifong (August 16, 1995) reported:

> ...there they were, 72 Thai immigrants forced to work around the clock, hunched over sewing machines in an apartment complex ringed by razor wire. The Thais were paid 69 cents an hour and allegedly threatened with rape and murder if they stopped working before repaying the cost of being smuggled to America (pp.1,3).

The Christian Science Monitor quotes Julie Su, an attorney for the Asian American Legal Center: "The garment industry is one of the most abusive industries in the country" (p.3).

> The California Labor Department found that 50 percent of the 69 garment manufactures investigated did not pay minimum wage. More than 60 percent paid no overtime. And more than 90 percent were guilty of breaking health and safety codes (*Christian science Monitor*, August 16, 1995, p.3).

A concerned person might ask, "What kind of thinking, feelings, and self-onlyness would allow people to exploit people in these circumstances in order to make themselves wealthy?" Again, we note the need for a higher level of self-otherness within people so that they will refuse to be an agent or an accomplice to such cruelty.

Abolish physical violence. There is, and had been throughout recorded history, a high incidence of *direct physical violence* against females in most cultures. But heinous comes against women have been ignored or mentioned only in passing by most male historians. An example of this is the abominable witch hunts and burning at the stake of thousands of innocent women (many were mid-wives, nurses, and wise women) over a period of over a hundred years. According to Barbara Ehrenreich and Deirdre English (1973) these murders were not only approved, they "...were well organized, initiated financed, and executed by Church and State" (p.7).

Cruelty toward women is common everywhere. Brock-Ume reviewed number of studies and concluded that atrocities toward females.

> ...take on different forms in various societies, but there are some common characteristics. In a majority of cases the violence against women is committed by men she is well acquainted with, her husband father, brother, or father-in-law. Another common denominator is that male society is reluctant to report and research such "private," personal violence against women. The official apparatus has been unwilling to explore and condemn acts of violence, especially of a sexual nature (p.16).

In all countries of the world women are being violently abused. Even though some of the more atrocious types have been reduced in number they still include suttee (burning women with their dead husband) and dowry murders in India; genital mutilation in Africa and Middle-East sex slavery in Taiwan and some other Asian countries; and wife beating everywehere. Rape, a cruel violent crime, is widespread. The most inhuman of all cruelties, women are being sold as sex slaves to vile sex fiends. This sexual slavery has been increasing in recent years, especially in the East. In some places girls and young women are "literally imprisoned in the brothels where they are forced to see 30 to 40 clients a day." They are captured purchased or persuaded (they are often told that they are being employed for factory work or domestic service).

In Asia, strong preference for males above females is now being shame fully expressed. Because Asian countries, especially China, India, Korea, and Taiwan, are urged to cut population growth, sex-selection abortions have become commonplace (according to Sheila Tefft, August 2, 1995).

These female abortions added to already prevalent practices of female infanticide, abandonment, starvation, and neglect, cause an undesired imbalance of the sexes in those countries.

Cooperate internationally to remove cultural injustices. Prejudices against women are so widespread throughout the world and are embedded so tenaciously within cultures that international cooperation is vital for their removal. Sexist practices have persisted for thousands of years and are rooted within family traditions, educational teachings, religious beliefs, and innumerable cultural practices.

The four United Nations' world conferences on women, other less major conferences throughout the world, and various projects and programs have provided information concerning conditions women face everywhere and encourage greater opportunities for women. The documents which resulted from the conferences have also been helpful in raising the awareness of people in various parts of the world. The most important of these document is "**The Convention on the Elimination of All Forms of Discrimination Against Women.**" This Convention has been ratified by most of the countries of the world. This means that it is a binding part of the legal systems of countries where they are ratified. This has promoted progress toward bringing equality to women. It is being monitored by the UN Committee. However, many countries that have signed are not living up to the agreements. When Japan was faced with their lack of compliance with the Convention, officials responded that these were only goals toward which they could proceed. The United States has not yet ratified. Hence this is an important work for women here. (The text of this Convention is to yeton to long to reproduce here, but the principles are similar to those set forth here).

Dozens of Non-governmental Organizations (NGOs), most with worldwide membership, hold their own conferences adjacent to the governmental conferences. They are dynamic forces working for women's equality and/or for peace. These movements are sometimes collectively called the humantarian movement. I also call them *equity-peace movement*. These organizations often work together for common goals-the eliminations of all "...ism" and others forms of violence. I hope they will emphasize more fully that the basic causes are primarily within people, thus giving emphasis to FLEP.

Media: Cultural Strength and Weakness

Influences from the *media* (in print and electronic forms) are both peace-promting and violence causing within and outside cultures. Except for families, child care-givers, and the formal educational systems, nothing has more to do with the promotion of dominant/violent thinking than do the media. The media have the potential for being especially powerful in promoting equity and peace. Their great power rests in the ability to motivate people (especially children) in various ways including shaping beliefs and public opinion, changing ways of thinking and behaving, and determining direction for decision making. For better or worse, the media advises and often persuades us on the purchase of every conceivable commercial item and it keep us somewhat up to date on what goes on in the world; they bring us the voices of politicians, and take us to the ends of the earth, broading our perspective of the world, and provide both constructive and desire forces.

The National Association for the Education of Young Children (NAEYC) reports that there has been a very marked increase in TV portrayal of violence in every aspect of life in the past few years, especially and the Federal Communication Commission's decision to deregulate children's commercial television in 1982. For example, air time for war cartons jumped from 1.5 hours per week in 1982 to 43 hours per week in 1986 (Carlsson-Paige & Levin 1987). Children's programs featured 18.6 violent acts per hour a decade ago and now have abut 26.4 violent acts each hour acts per hour a decade ago and now have about 26.4 violent acts each hour.

Those in control of the media argue that they only give people what they want, that the media merely portrays what is manifested in other institutions, and a few even say that violence on television or in movies is cathartic. It certainly is what a lot of people want, but the media also creates wants, both in types of programming and in kinds of products they induce people to buy. Indeed, the trends toward violence on television and in the movies echoes the militaristic tendencies in government, in terroristic religion, and in society as a whole; but it also accelerates the trend. "However," as the NAEYC report concludes, "media violence is not just a reflection of a violent society, it is also a contributor." There is certainly evidence to indicate that violence on TV promotes violence in society.

Leonard Berkowitz (1993) quotes a relevant statement made by the National Commission on the Causes and Prevention of Violence:

> Each year advertisers spend [billions of dollars] in the belief that television can influence human behavior. The television industry enthusiastically agrees with them, but nonetheless contends that its programs of violence do not have any such influence. The preponderance of the available research evidence strongly suggests, however, that violence in television programs can and does have adverse effects upon audiences (Commission Statement, Sept. 23. 1969 quoted by Berkowitz p.199).

Berkowitz reviewed relevant research in the field and stated a number of conclusions. These included the following:

> The mass media can have both short-lived and long-lasting influences on their audiences...media reports or depictions of violence can activate aggression-related ideas and action tendencies in the audience members. These aggressive ideas and inclinations will be activated, however, only to the extent that the media-presented material has a relevant meaning for the recipient...Repeated exposure to violent scenes on television may also help to foster aggressive modes of conduct among children...There is a significant change that children who watch a good deal of violent TV programming will grow up to be unusually aggressive adults (pp.233-235).

Berkowitz suggests that "Parents, educators, and the mass media can and should take steps to mitigate the harmful consequences of heavy does of violence on TV and movie scenes" (p.235).

There are many problems and issues regarding the media that need to be considered. They include the following:

1. Children become desensitized to people's suffering and to violent behaviors.

2. Children may become more emotionally distressed, fear

and anxiety may heighten, and anger and irritability increase.

3. Brutality may be normalized in people's minds and they will more easily accept and sure it personally and approve of its use in foreign and domestic policy. Children conclude that the way to resolve conflicts and problems is through violence (TV violent characters have become favourite models); violent is fun (about the only kind of fun for some people not seems); life has little intrinsic value; in war men are heroes; people are either "good guys or bad guys"; women are sex-objects to be dominated, exploited and controlled by men; heroes are macho figures and women are portrayed as weak, ineffective, emotional, or unreasonable; and families are middle or upper class or should be ashamed if they are not. Caring, cooperative self-other attitudes are much less often portrayed.

4. Violent behaviour may be mimicked and criminal behavior results. Many adults also mimic those whom they see around them or on television.

An example of the power of movies to influence behavior was demonstrated in "The Deer Hunter." The movie depicts a lengthy terrifying scene in captured American soldiers in Vietnam were forced to play Russian routed with handguns and are killed. The *Christian Science Monitor reported* effect of that movie" Quinn Redeker, one of the four screenwriters of film, said in an interview that by four years after its release, when the midland played in theaters across the U.S. and on cable TV, 27 young men taken their own lives playing Russian roulette after seeing the film (p.11).

5. Children's intellectual and emotional development and be retarded Imaginative play may be reduced, creativity stifled, language retarded and objective thinking and self-direction replaced by ready-made ideas. Concerning "The Empire's Old Clothes", Ariel Dorfman (1983) wrote:

> Industrially produced fiction has become one of the primary shapers of our emotions and our intellect in the twentieth century. Although these stories are supposed merely to entertain us, they constantly give us a secret education. We

> are not only taught certain styles of violence, the latest fashions, and sex roles by TV, movies, magazines, and comic strips, we are also taught how to succeed, how to love, how to buy, how to conquer, how to forget the past and suppress the future. We are taught, more than anything else, how not to rebel (p.ix).

6. Humanitarian values may be distorted in people's minds. They may adopt values which glorify physical force, aggressive behaviors, consumptive life styles, and sensationalism. Much of real-life relationships and values may not be given adequate consideration. The power to change the general tenor of life and the tendencies toward certain attitudes may very well be dangerous. This is particularly true for children, young people and for adults who have not thought through their value systems. Some scholars of the subject fear the possibility of mind control and the manipulation of individual choice.

7. Rather than searching out facts and analyzing statements and depictions, people may become docile spectators who may be manipulated by distortions of the truth and may accept superficial nonfactual answers and avoid deeper analyses of complex controversial issues. "The media can be used to manipulate us into giving up individual choice in favor of collective conditioning" (p.139), says Aaron Stern (1979). Being aware of this tremendous power of the media, candidates for office spend most of their time raising money to put their messages on television.

8. Instead of participating in many other healthy activities, children may spend much too much time with television. Studies indicate that most parents give little thought or attention to what their children watch on television or on videos. For example, one study of the use of VCR's by sixth and 10th graders in Flint, MI, and other cities, by Bradley S. Greenberg of Michigan State University, showed

> ...that only 6 percent of the American parents in the study ever nixed a child's use of VCR. Flint parents were more likely to impose restrictions on how late their kids watched

videos than on what they watched (as reported by Kierman, 1990, p.66).

Dorfman found violence and other harmful materials in other forms of media. He examined various comic-books, fictitious characters such as Babar the Elephant, Donald Duck, the Lone Ranger, and also the *Readers Digest*. He showed how these misinterpret reality, promote violence, give over-simplified disarming answers to social dilemmas.

Dorfman seems most disturbed by the fact that some of this fiction keeps us thinking of ourselves (Americans) as innocent, child-like characters who would not harm anyone while at the same time we condone without serious objection harmful actions of our government. He says our ways of thinking about ourselves and the world have become so comfortable, so much of us that, like "The Empire's Old Clothes" we dislike throwing away our mis informed ideas. It is time. I think, that we consider throwing away of our old clothes and getting new ones.

9. It is very important that values and issues discussed on radio and television. This is done on Public television and radio. They, provide discussions that are helpful in clarifying issues values as well as provide good sources of education.

Education that comes through the media is far being value-free from in reporting the news, values determine which events are chosen to and how they are reported. Indeed the media cannot be completely free; values are necessary part of what is portrayed, but the question is whose values should be portrayed? This is a very complex question. It is problem which should be cooperatively discussed and evaluated.

Television Should be Controlled

It is easy to understand why some other countries are very unhappy about the United States television being imposed upon their cultures. They are that their people are demoralized by the violence and conflicting values. He brings up the issue of: Just who should control the satellites? It is not that one society should dominate another. What Aaron (1979) has to say about this is very relevant:

> By controlling the satellites, one society can inflict its ideology upon another; one country can undermine the basic beliefs of another...who is to say that one nation has the right to impose its values on another? Who controls the air-space that surrounds the earth? Who monitors the light and sound waves? Who studies the messages they carry? Who designates appropriate territories for transmission and reception? Who designates the right of some of us control what belongs to all of us? Who ensures that what belongs to all of us is not used only by few us, and only then to harm the rest of us? (p.144)

This tremendous power of the media should not be allowed to continue unrestricted, molding the minds of people everywhere including ourselves and our children all in the name of free speech? Should freedom of speech and press be interpreted to mean print anything, say anything, or portray anything? I think not. **Free speech should not be free to hurt people**. Isn't it about time we think for ourselves and together about what is good for people, especially children, and act as responsible citizens? Censorship is dangerous for freedom. However, uncontrolled license to hurt others with violent portrayals is like freedom to kill while disallowing police protection. In the case of freedom in the media, as in other types, freedom without responsibility instigates violence.

As we become willing to put forth more thought, dialogue, time, exploration, and resources, we shall find many ways to nudge legislators to provide guidelines and legislation for television programming and set up standards for industrial advertising; and we can give assistance to **parents** in their efforts to monitor, evaluate, and interpret television visualize a time when television will have changes its violent/exploitative nature. Instead we would like to be educational; show examples of compassion, justice, equity, positive social values, and entertainment without competition; provide programs that enlarge aesthetic appreciation and knowledge of other peoples and places; show ways to save the biosphere; furnish in-depth reporting of **news** of various types; portray discussions of important issues; and allow a wide range of opinion to be voiced by all cultures, races, ideological groups, and women as well as men. In short, provide more of what could be termed peace education and equity in the media. Education through the media has almost unlimited potential.

An example of prejudice coming through the media was played out in news reports of the United Nations Women's Conference held in Beijing (1995, September 2). Important speeches and discussions were being presented at the Forum that would have been of much interest to thousands of people in the U.S. However, about the only thing reported here was the sideline arguments. This is the way it was at the three former (1975, 1980, 1985) Women's World Conferences that I attended. (I can understand the anger of women at this kind of reporting. But, we must remember that women have assisted men in socializing boys to feel that theirs should be the only voices listened to and followed.)

What kinds of control, if any, should we and our public laws and policies have over the media?

It is unfortunate that present 91995) trends in the U.S. are toward releasing governmental controls instead of tightening them. Hence, the media remains a large part of the violence problem. Self-other people can change that. They have the responsibility to contribute whatever abilities they have in various forms of the media so that equity/peace oriented media will take the place of dominance and violence.

Competition and Rewards

Competition and rewards, as well as punishment, are interrelated deepseated cultural values. They are nearly universally accepted as being constructive motivating forces cocive to human growth and well-being. Hence, their values are seldom questioned.

The basic premise is that if people do what they should (meaning; do what parents, teachers, and other leaders direct them to do), they will be rewarded. If they do not they will be punished, and they must compete and win over others to be appreciated.

Alfie Kohn has written two books contradict these premises and show them to be "intrinsically objectionable and counter-productive." in other parts of this book, I also have indicated my disagreement with them. Space does not allow extensive consideration here. I urge you, the readers, to give study and discussion to these issues. I highly recommend Alfie Kohn's books: No Contest: The Case Against Competition. *Why we lose in our race to win*, 1986; and *Punished by Rewards,*: The *Trouble* with Gold Stars, *Incentive* Plans, A's, Praise, and Other Bribes, 1993.

Competition

> Life for us [Americans] has become an endless succession of contests. From the moment the alarm clock rings until sleen overtake us again, from the time we are toddlers until the day we die we are busy struggling to out do others. This is our posture at work and at school, on the playing filed and back at home. It is the common denominator of American life (Alfie Kohn, 1986, p.1)

The issue of *competition* was extensively explored by Kohn (1986). He sees the U.S. as the country must obsessed with competition. People complete in practically everything and most people seem to assume that it is a good way to live. But Kohn sees it as destructive.

Paul Wachtel (1989) **argued** that: "Right or wrong, we have assumed that efficiency is maximized by encouraging each to out do his compatriots" (p.68). and that competition is almost our official state religion" (p.284). He also wrote. "we are not used to thinking of competition as something that reflects a particular decision to set up the rules in a chosen way (p.282). but it does. It is not needed for the well-being of people. It is not a constructive way to work or play or teach children. But because we have been taught to compete, most people accept it as we do the air we breathe without analysis, and as thought it were human nature. Wachtel predicts that we shall not be able to solve our mutual problems through competitive approaches and that it is only through cooperation that we ideal effectively with the issues we face.

Competition is probably most damaging when carried into the family. Kohn says of this: "Even within the family there is rivalry-a muted but often desperate struggle that treats approval as a scarce commodity and turns love into a kind of trophy" (p.2). What a tragedy that our most vital needs-for love and affection-become a desperate competitive struggle! Kohn writes that his concern regarding competition goes far beyond the business world. He asserts that. "Competition is a deeply ingrained, profoundly enduring, part of our lives. And it is time to look more closely at what it does to us" (p.2). This he does in his book.

Kohn defines two types of competition-*structural and intentional*. "Whereas structural competition has to do with the win/lose framework, which is external, intentional competition is internal; it concerns the desire on the part of an individual to be number one" (p.4).

Structural competition is a part of culture or social systems and does not necessarily mean that the participants hold psychic feelings of hostility or harmfulness toward their competitors. The activities are set up by others and are thrust upon those involved, but it requires that one person or group lose as the other wins.

Internal competitiveness means "a proclivity for beating others", (i.e. making others fail), and/or fearing that others will make us fail or lose. People who continually measure themselves by others' progress, or on their opinions, are emotionally insecure with low self-esteem-self-onlyness. They have experienced psychic mistreatment, including embarrassing competitive failures. Because they look at others with envy, fear, or host city, their human relationships are marred. Both types are harmful.

There are many misunderstandings regarding competition.

Kohn discusses and refutes the four following myths concerning competition:

> "competition is an unavoidable fact of life, part of "human nature."

> "competition motivates us to do our best we would cease being productive if we did not compete."

> "that contests provide the best, if not the only, way to have a good time. All the joys of play are said to hinge on competitive games."

> "competition builds character."

Space does not permit full discussion of these, but evidence indicates that competition is taught, urged upon people, is not natural; is discouraging and inhibiting to most people; harms friendships and is fun for only a few, if any; and definitely causes psychic qualities. Competitive spirits are not compatible with feelings of caring, cooperation, and equity that are necessary for loving relationships in marriage, among siblings, and between friends. Competition is not viable in a peaceful world.

There is no good reason for cultures to create competitive situations and there are many damaging effects from competition created by parents, schools, and society. There are better alternatives. Admittedly in the present atmosphere, other options are often hard to find. We may work *cooperatively* with others toward common goals or we may work *independently* toward individual goals (this does not mean competing with one's self). Research shows that either of these succeeds better than competition. Promotes psychological health, and encourages enjoyable relationships.

Kohn urges that people find constructive alternatives to competition. For example: games and recreation that employ cooperation and mutual consideration; education that encourages growth toward each individual's potentials (not in relation to others progress); deliberations and discussions that result in consensus on values, behaviours, and cultural structures; and international; interaction that fosters "mutual security" and peace.

Girls are often taught an unhealthy submission, but in the same process are usually taught to be cooperative, kind, caring, and helpful. This situation has sometimes led to confusion. They have often been accused of fearing success when in reality they back away from competition and other practices that harm themselves and others. But they do very well on constructive efforts. These days women have often been pushing themselves and other women to become more competitive; whereas what everyone needs is to be guided by their own growth potential and a need to help others succeed rather than competing to put others down. Peace-promoting qualities are fundamental for all people Let us discourage women from trying to imitate men, but instead learn to succeed equitably in whatever endeavors they decide is best for them.

Competitive Sports It has long been understood that sports are very instrumental in inducing competitive attitudes. Although sports of various types may sometimes provide models which are helpful, they can also promote unrealistic ambitions that detract from education and some boys are made to feel inferior of they do not succeed in sports. Competitive sports can teach children to see each other as rivals and they endorse hierarchical power values.

There has often been the assumption by some that violent feelings could be calmed by aggressive sports, watching full fights, violent shows on TV (Aristotle proposed dramatic plays as a "purging" of emotions) or in other ways vicriously experiencing violence. It has also been found (Perry & Perry. 1976) that winning or losing a competition either reinforced or increases aggressive responding, especially in children. Aggression can thus be self-perpetuating.

Rewards

It sounds reasonable that people be rewarded if they do what they should. Following are some reasons that awards are harmful.

- When awards follow directed behaviour, the result is that

one person is controlling another. There is thus, a degree of loss of self-control.

Harm is done to one's need to feel competent, worthwhile, and capable of directing one's own life.

•Being controlled can result in a form of punishment. For example, if one does not follow the prescribed behavior and does not receive the desired award, that person feels punished.

•Rewards such as prizes, awards, and bribes often "rupture relationships". It sets one person against another. Where as, as Kohn (1993) wrote:

...cooperation does not just make tasks more pleasant; in many cases, it is virtually a prerequisite for quality. More and more teachers and managers are coming to recognize that excellence is most likely to result from well-functioning teams in which resources are shared, skills and knowledge are exchanged, and each participant is encouraged and helped to do his or her best (p.54).

Rewards are especially harmful when the number available are very limited because: anxiety is created some see no chance of winning and hence, are "demotivated" from the tasks that need to be done.

•Rewards ignore the real reasons that something needs to be done. They also may hide the real reasons the behavior is not being done without the reward. It is easy to conclude that without the award, the task is not worth doing.

•Rewards discourage creative thinking, innovative approaches, and challenging undertaking. They have "long-term negative effects on intrinsic motivation...Extrinsic motivators are most dangerous when offered for something we want children to want to do" (pp..85, 87).

•Incidental learning seldom results from rewards because the person does just what is required to get the reward and nothing more.

•Rewards are more likely to kill interest in tasks than to stimulate eagerness, especially if the person does not continue to be the winner.

Kohn summarizes: "Do rewards motivate people? Absolutely. They motivate people to get rewards." He says that parents, teachers and managers are discouraging interest in the very things they are bribing them to do. They "...smother people's enthusiasm for activities they might otherwise enjoy" (p.74). he documents the above reasons with considerable research.

In Conclusion

Humanity's most promising frontier-its greatest challenge-is its own maturation. The need to grow is a powerful force. Children's need and desire to grow will continue throughout life it is not hampered by damaging experiences. But growth is stifled by humiliation, demands for nonthinking obedience, discouraging contests and there damaging practices. If growth is stagnated by cultural practices, bigotry, and nonthinking beliefs, people become very slow and resistant to change. This is true of personal, cultural, and structural changes. As I glance out my window and up at the magnificent enormous live oak tree, I respect the time and the power which has gone into raising b the .billions of molecules of moisture and nutrients up the trunk and branches to build that beautifully tree. It reminds me of the greater number of eons of time and the untold change which have gone into the evolvement of our world, its peoples, and their social structures. Earth has provided abundantly for humanity. Primitive peoples within many cultures grew mature enough to meet the contingencies of the times and to live, multiply, and continue to grow.

However, people have never been able to develop to their highest potential personally or socially. They have built social systems, customs, and personal relationships-patterns which have served them less then perfectly. Their cultures and social systems were rigidly constructed; and like the tree, they need modifications and renewal. Occasionally a tree-trimmer arrives here and cuts away the dead wood in order to encourage **new growth**, enhance its beauty, and serve the purpose for which it was planted. The new growth than needs nourishment to grow properly. Our cultures have old dried-out parts (myths, superstitions, prejudices, inequities, exploitations and dominant/violent practices) that need to eliminated. There are new growths that need to bc nourished (e.g., with higher levels of love, cooperation, creative efforts, and additional learning).

Not only are there opportunities for refurbishing our cultures, it is also inevitable that we shall self-destruct if we do not succeed in doing so.

Chapter-4

Scientific Realism, Human Emancipation, and Nonviolent Political Action

Heikki Patomäki

Chapter-4

INTRODUCTION: EPISTEMOLOGY, ONTOLOGY, AND POLITICS

"ISN'T THE MOST general of political problems the problem of truth?" asks Michel Foucoult.[1] Foucoult is not alone in seeing a very close connection between politics-or its failures-and epistemology. Hard standards, criteria, and measures have lost much of their credibility to a great extent because intellectuals today would like to freeze and dismantle the guillotine as well as other machines of violence stockpiled in North-East, North-West, and South.[2] As Hannah Arendt puts it: "At least we can learn from them (Rousseau and Robespierre) that absolute goodness is hardly any less dangerous than obsolute evil,"[3] and the same applies to absolute truth and its negation, total lie or absolutely untrue (or arbitrary) proposition/theory, at least as well. Thus it seems that the Robespierrean dilemma of hard standards should be avoided somehow. This practical-moral line of thought points towards relativism, towards understanding that "we" may be wrong-whoever the "we" are.

The relevance of practical-moral problems related to any kind of social criticism should be quite obvious also from the point of view of peace research, because it seems that peace research has typically endeavoured to be critical towards some present conditions of social life. Johan Galtung, for instance, characterizes, his project as "empirical", but it also critical and constructivist, with a heavy emphasis on the lattr.[4] Because of its leftist critical nature, structuralist peace research has often been associated with the advocacy of people's wars, especially in the periphery of the world: "The goal of peace research is a revolutionary peace, and the means to its attainment is power politics, including, if necessary and appropriate, the use of force."[5] The aim of people's wars has typically been, as Mao Zedong expressed it, defined by a historical movement from capitalism to socialism.

> Once man has eliminated capitalism, he will attain the era of perpetual peace, and there will be no more need for war.[6]

This view is based on a certain theory of history and social world, as well as on the judgements concerning the truth of that theory. However, the same Robespierrean dilemma is not a problem of Marxism and radical structuralist peace research only (note however, that for example Galtung's position is in fact much more sophisticated and, as it is, pacifistic than the picture drawn above). The Kantian idealist strand of peace research, or rather Kantian idealism, too, ahs face it. For instance, Wilson's USA took part in the intervention in the Soviet Union in 1918; for, Wilson saw, in accordance with Kantian theory of world politics, anti-democratic Bolsheviks both as a threat to peace and security in general, and as an obstacle in the defeat of Germany in the "war to end all wars" in particular. Hence, in idealist thought, too, there can be "wars to end [all] wars." Moreover, in this manner the United Nations has been used as an imperialist/anti-communist force, although only to an extent.[7]

Does the solution to this somewhat Nietzschean problem of clash of truths, or rather "truth/power-regimes," require total relativism? In this regard, Roy, Bhaskar's emancipatory scientific realism is both significant and interesting; for, he makes a clear distinction between relativist epistemology, judgemental rationality, and realist ontology. Bhaskar also presents an elaborated schema of explanatory critique and connected emanicipatory political action, which provides conceptual tools for a detailed argumentation and analysis. In the following paragraphs, Bhaskar's theory of truth as well as his normative theory will be analysed and appraised, his theory of explanation, social criticism, and emanicipatory political action will be scrutinized, and finally a suggestion concerning a very strong connection between scientific criticism and nonviolent political action will be put forward.

My basic aim is to show—with the help of notions and arguments presented in particular by Putnam and Harre—that

Bhaskar is not explicit enough on his view concerning the refutation of the metaphysical correspondence theory of truth, and that after this shortcoming is corrected, a very strong "prima facie" case for exclusively nonviolent emancipatory political action follows immediately. Note, however, that problems of explanatory criticism do not exhaust moral and political problems. Hence a few words on the relations between explanatory criticism and other types of practical moral or practical-political arguments will be put forward at the end of this paper. It is not easy to give a short summary of a complex theory which is, moreover, developed to a great extent by way of criticising other philosophical theories. Nevertheless Bhaskar himself crystallizes his ideas by stating that transcendental scientific realism entails the necessity of ontological realism, the actuality of epistemic relativity, and the possibility of judgemental rationality. The meanings of these notions can be clarified as follows. First, ontological realism includes two claims, namely that there are objects which, in most cases, exist and act independently of their identification by any scientist or any observer in general, and that this world is differentiated, structured, and stratified he real word is differentiated because it does not consist merely of some kind of "grey", shapeless and deformed "mass". It is structured because these differentiated elements can form different kinds of structures. It is stratified because there are ontological levels in the real world. One of the these levels can be called "social", and it is at this level where science itself operates.

According to the thesis of epistemic relativity, all beliefs are socially produced, so that all knowledge is transient, and neither truth-values nor criteria of rationality exist outside historical time. However, this thesis should be distinguished from the (incorrect) thesis of judgemental relativism which asserts that all beliefs (or statements) are equally valid, in the sense that there can be no (rational) grounds for preferring one to another. This distinction is necessary because even any kind of action presupposes some criteria:

[...] it is cleat that if one is to act at all there must be grounds for preferring one belief (about some domain) to another; and that such activity is typically codifiable in the form of systems of rules, implicity or explicity followed.

Thus anything does not go. To take one example (from Putnam): if anyone really believed that, and if they were foolish enough to pick a conceptual system that told them they could fly and act upon it by jumping out of the window, they would, if they were lucky enough to survive, see the weakness of the view at once. Moreover, Bhaskar claims that judgemetnal rationality depends upon the (at least implicit) recognition of the ontological realism and epistemic relativity. It seems that the first part of this point is a Habermasian reconstructive one, although Bhaskar is not very clear on it. If I am right, judgemental rationality depends upon the ontological realism because it is not possible to assert something (to make a historical speech-act) without at least implicity claiming to be saying or writing something of the world, i.e. giving something to understand. In the same manner, it can be argued, action in general presupposes the reality of the world. Furthermore, judgemental rationality depends also upon the epistemic relativity; for, if there were absolutely true or self-evident statements, claims or propositions, there would be very little room for historical human judgements. Finally, since choices between theories and models are, in fact, a matter of historical human judgements, these choices depend also upon ethical responsibility of the commitive agents concerned, as will be seen.

Duality of Truth?

What is "truth" in this theory, then? It seems that it relegates the notion of correspondence between epistemic statements and ontic objects merely to the status of a metaphor for the goal of an adequating practice, in which "cognitive matter is fashioned into a matching representation of a non-cognitive object." In other words, it seems that it is not possible to know the world except under particular more or less historically transient descriptions, as Bhaskar himself argues. However, Bhaskar continues his analysis of "truth" as follows:

> [...] truth effectively functions bivocally- to designate, on the one hand, claims, judgements and values [...] which are, or could be, made or avowed within social activity; and, on the other, conditions, states of affairs and [...] composite referents (truth-conditions or more simply truths) which exist quite independently of us. (Thus, although truths are not things, laws, natural kinds, etc., it would be misleading to deny that the latter, were, in some sense, truths). Truth thus has a genuine ontological and not just an ontogenetic (e.g. heuristic or regulative) use [...]; but its ontological use depends upon the possibility of ontogeny (and hence human practice) in a way which the concept of a natural law, for instance, does not.

Bhaskar is of the opinion that his theory of truth is able to sustain a duality of epistemic and ontic aspect of the truth, instead of the reduction of these aspects to the "duplicity" implicit in the (more conventional) correspondence theories of truth. This advantage notwithstanding, there are still problems in his account of truth. Self -proclaimed pragmatist Richard Rorty, for example, would strongly object to Bhaskar's views. For the pragmatist, Rorty argues, the notion of "truth" as something "objective" is just a confusion between:

(i) most of the world is as it is whatever we think about it, and

(ii) there is something out there in addition to the pragmatically known true statements, or in addition to the world called "the truth about the world."

The pragmatist assents to (I) but cannot make sense of (ii). When the realist tries to explain (ii) with;

(iii) the truth above the world consists in a relation of "correspondence" between certain sentences (many of which have yet to be formulated) and the world itself,

the pragmatist can only fall back on saying that many centuries of attempts to explain what correspondence is have failed. What is Bahskar's position on these theses? There is no disagreement between Rorty and Bhaskar as far as (i) is concerned, but there certainly is a disagreement in respect of (ii); for, this is one of the basic claims of Bhaskar's transcendental realism. Let me, however, leave this point aside for a while, the concentrate, instead, on (iii). This is, in effect, the "metaphysically realist notion of truth," as Putnam labels it—truths as "correspondence to the facts" or something of that kind. Putnam denies the validity of this view by arguing that we do not have notions of the "existence" of the things or of the "truth" of the statements that are independent of our conceptual constructions, procedures, and practices. This is a view he shares with Rorty who claims that "all awareness is a linguistic affair." However, Bhaskar, too, admits that it is not possible to know the world except under particular more or less historically transient descriptions. Where does the difference then lie?

Evidently, Bhaskar not arguing for a metaphysical realist notion of truth, i.e., he does not accept (iii): "the supposition of the possibility of a (logocentric) correspondence, if interpreted as a logical thesis, is meaningless or at the very best unverifiable." Nevertheless, Bhaskar speaks of "a matching representation of a non-cognitive object" and he argues that there is an ontological aspect of truth—namely independently existing truth-conditions—as well. First, let me scrutinize what Bhaskar means by "a matching representation." In order to understand this, we must be able to understand why Bhaskar accepts, contra Rorty, the claim (ii) Bhaskar's argument is based to a great extent on the presuppositions of natural scientists' historical practice of experimentation:

> In an experiment scientists produce a pattern of events. There is nothing in itself special about this. For as causal agents, we are co-responsible for events all the time. And scientists could, in fact, produce a vast array of events, most of them of no conceivable significance. What is so special about the patterns they deliberately produce under meticuously controlled conditions in the laboratory is that it enables them to identify the mode of operation of natural structures, mechanisms, or processes which they do not produce. What distinguishes the phenomena the scientist

actually produces out of the totally of the phenomena he could produce is that when his experiment is successful, it is an index of what he does not produce. A real distinction between the obejcts of experimental investigation, such as causal laws, and patterns of events s thus a condition of the intelligibility of scientific activity.

More generally, philosophy as a fallible mode of investigation of the necessary presuppositions of historical practices can tells us that it is a condition of the possibility of scientific activities that the real world is startified, differentiated, and structured, independently of our knowledge concerning its specific content. Hence the claim (ii) that there is something out there in addition to the world called "the truth about the world," is not only meaningful and possible but also necessary for scientific practices (note that Rorty does not reject scientific practices or their fallible results). And because we are able to speak of and imagine- in abstract- the world beyond our present conceptual construction, procedures, beliefs, and opinions, we can also speak metaphorically and regulatively about the manner in which "cognitive matter is fashioned into a matching representation of a non-cognitive object," and we can also make historical judgements on this (mis-) match..

What is then the "ontological aspect of the truth"? What does it add to Bhaskar's scientific realism? Are there really, and in what sense, independently existing truth-conditions? According to Rom Harré, a statement using the word "true" is typically used merely (i) to refer to a statement or theory, and (ii) to pass a judgement on it. There are contexts where what matters is whether a statement metaphorically "corresponds" to the objects of the knowledge, but there are others where our assessment depends more upon whether the statement under review coheres with other statements. In both cases, inter-subjective evidence and/or reasons for a (rational) judgement is required. The judgement concerning "truth" may refer to an existential or casual hypothesis, to a theoretical or logical thesis, as well as to particular interpretations. Moreover, one additional characteristic of truth can be distinguished. Moreover, one additional characteristic of truth can be distinguished. (iii) Truth is in a sense independent of all justifications of here and now, but not at all independent of all justifications. To claim that a statement is true is hence to claim that it could be justified according to ideal standards (which, in fact, might not be the case), but also that it, indeed, is justified (here and now).

What is the role of Bhaskar's "ontological aspect of truth" in all this? It must be said that I think that is is wrong to say that the truth-conditions are genuinely ontological; rather truth-conditions, too, are historical and theory-dependent, although the real world, with which they are in many ways in touch is (mostly) not. Furthermore, I can see only two possible roles for the "ontological aspect of the truth," and both of them are negative. First, the duality theory of truth merely adds to the complexity of Bhaskar' scientific realism without improving its explanatory or illuminatory power, or any of its characteristics for that matter. Hence, because a carefully balanced simplicity is *ceteris paribus*, one scientific "desideratum" among others, the ontological interpretation of the truth-conditions should be abandoned. Secondly, as Bhaskar himself writes about the metaphysical correspondence theory of truth his duality theory of truth, too, is politically reactionary, in that it reinforces the authority of dominant or any other accepted interpretations (or "ways of reading") by ontologisizing human judgemetns. This is unfortunate, too. For these reasons, Harrés modest and normative theory of truth—"truth" as it is contigently used in the scientific practices—seems to be better grounded than any ontological theory:

> If we read the realist manifesto, "scientific statements should be taken as true or false by virtue of the way the world is." As a moral principle, it would run something like this: "As scientists, that is members of a certain community, we should apportion our willingness or reluctance to accept a claim as worthy to be included in the corpus of scientific knowledge to the extent that we sincerely think it somehow reflects the way the world is." Put this way, the manifesto has conduct-guiding force. It encourages the good and the worthy

to manifest their virtue in trying to find out how the world is, seeking [ontological] truth is a hopeless epistemic project, but trying to live a life of virtue is a possible moral ambition.

Thus attempts to define truth (and possibly those of scientific realism, too) either in terms of a principle of bivalence or bivocality are a mistake, which confuses normative thesis about truthfulness, honesty, and openness with a connected epistomological thesis about how to achieve the highest standards of representational quality for scientific cognition, or with the ontological thesis that (the startified, differentiated, and structured) world is mostly independent of any particular description of it. Read in the normative manner, Karl Popper's fallibilism, for instance, would hence say something like this: "However much personal investment one has in a theory, one should not ignore contrary evidence" or "one should seek harder for evidence and reasons that would count against theory than for that which would support it," and so on. A simple, pragmatic and, in a sense, "post-modern" truth relegates thus, after all, the notion of correspondence between epistemic statements and ontic objects merely to the status of a metaphor—although a well-grounded one—for the goal of an adequating practice, in which "cognitive matter is fasioned into a matching representation of a non-cognitive object."

Social Scientific Explanation and Social Ontology

Scientific realism requires that some of the substantive terms in a discourse denote or purport to denote beings of various metaphysical categories such as substance, quality, and relation, that exist independently of that discourse. This picture will need to be qualified in fundamental ways for the social sciences. Because for scientific realism it is the nature of the objects that determines their cognitive possibilities. The qualifications of the above picture in the case of social sciences should be approached as the ontological question to the properties that societies and social beings possess. As i see it, this is primarily a theoretical and conceptual question, not an empirical one, although, as always, there is and should be some dialectical interaction between these modes of dialogical research. However, this is not a place to discuss basic social theoretical problems, and hence I shall only give a short summary of the basic ideas of the theory of structuration and the transformational model of social activity (TMSA). This summary is necessary for the general argument of this paper, because otherwise the schema for social criticism and emancipatory political action would be incomprehensible.

There are tow aspects in the ontology of the theory of structuration and the TMSA. First, the recognise the hermeneutical, i.e., meaningful nature of society, and the knowledgeable—in respect of discursive and practical consciousness—character of social conduct. In other words, the substances, qualities, and relations of oscial world are not independent of human discourses (scientific discourses included) and related meaningful practices. On the other hand, social structures, which are generated and (re) produced by human action and social rules and resources, make possible, or enable, as well as constrain historical modes and forms of social action. In the worlds of Bhaskar:

> Society is both the ever-present condition (material cause) and the continually reproduced outcome of human agency. And praxis is both work, that is conscious production, and (normally unconsious) reproduction of the condition of the production, that is society. One could refer to the former as the duality of the structure, and the latter as the duality of the practice.

This kind of social ontology makes the relationship between a scientist and his object of knowledge quite complicated; for, they both (subject and object) are, and can be, internally and externally related to each other. On the other hand, precisely this relationship connects social scientific explanation to social criticism in a necessary manner.

However, before proceeding to that connection, let me say a few words on the social scientific explanation in general. It can be argued that there are five types of interconnected elements in society which together from the causally sufficient (but unnecessary) ontological condition for producing a socially generated effect: rules (constitutive and regulative), actors, action, which is relectively monitored, resources (differentiated according to the modes of action), and relationally positioned practices. Basically the task of social scientific explanation is hence to form a plausible, empirically confirmed but fallible and corrigible teleiomorphic-sometimes perhaps paramorphic, too-iconic model of these historical elements and their relations. A necessary condition for this model—construction is permeneutical meaning—analysis, which is needed in grasping the element and relations of a social complex. The analysis of unintentional causal consequences of social action is as well as necessary condition for a good social scientific explanation, because unintentional consequences play such a central role in social life. There may be other necessary or useful methods as well: carefully done and hermeneutically reflexive statistical analysis, and/or structuralist combinatorial possibility-analysis, may be needed, or may be of help, too.

One crucial metatheoretical question of social scientific explanation is: "is it possible to generalize beyond the concrete context of social action?" Equivalently significant question is: "to what extent does a good explanation allow the possibility of prediction and control"? A preliminary answer to the former question can be stated as follows: the forming of an iconic model involves always abstractions and idealisations of the world according to our theoretical presuppositions and prejudices, i.e., modelling involves and "analytical accentuation of certain elements of reality." Thus a telemorphic iconic model is by definition more general than the concrete context which is its source, and it is necessarily based on prejudices and pre-understandings of the scientist, and these pre-understandings are typically connected to still more general views and opinions. However, it may be that there are many historical episodes, practices and /or systems, which can be reasonably and plausibly identified with telemorphical (or paramorphic) iconic model A, for example, and hence causal theories and other hypotheses concerning A may suffice to explain them all. Another way to generalize is to form higher-order models Man with larger range but with lesser accuracy than the concrete models Aa-I, Ba-I, Ca-I, etc., which can be in some relevant respects identified with each other, and which are consequently the source of the hermeneutically deeper (higher level) model M_n. From these considerations we cannot, however, infer anything concerning the possibility of prediction and control, as will be shortly seen.

EXPLANATORY SOCIAL CRITIQUE

The future of any society cannot be predicted, except in very general terms or for narrow time intervals. The reason for this is, according to Galtung, that we can reflect on predictions about our town future and at least to some extent base our actions on our reflections; we have the capacity to make predictions self-fulfilling, or self-denying, depending on how we evaluate the predicted state of affairs. The reflexive nature of predictions is related to the more general phenomenon of (qualitative) openness of all social systems. Bhaskar uses this notion in developing a theory of necessary connections between social scientific explanation (which does not imply prediction), critique, and emancipatory social change. Critique is claimed to be possible because a social scientific explanation is able to say that the beliefs of actors are false or superficial. It is almost self-evident that this idea requires careful analysis.

It can be argued that the reasonable assumption of relative privilege for an agent's account of his reasons depends upon the notion of the causal efficacy of his beliefs -for, otherwise, there would be no reason to prefer his to an outsider's account. However, this establishes an ontic distance between the agent's belief and any particular expression or statement of it, grounded in the existential intransitivity of the belief at the moment (or for the duration) of its causal efficacy. This entails the corrigibility of any description of agent's (real) beliefs; and includes the idea that even the description of our own sensations, beliefs, needs, and passions is heavily affected by a host of conceptual choices. Now, a social scientific explanation may be able to demonstrate why some false beliefs are also necessary for the occurrence of an episode, or for the reproduction of some positioned practice or system. This is one aspect of the partially irrational "prophasis" of historical episodes: the rationalisation of action does not necessarily correspond to the real causes of the action, or to its consequences. Both these aspects are captured by the stratification model of human action and agency, as presented in Table I.

Table I.

Stratification of Human Agency and Action

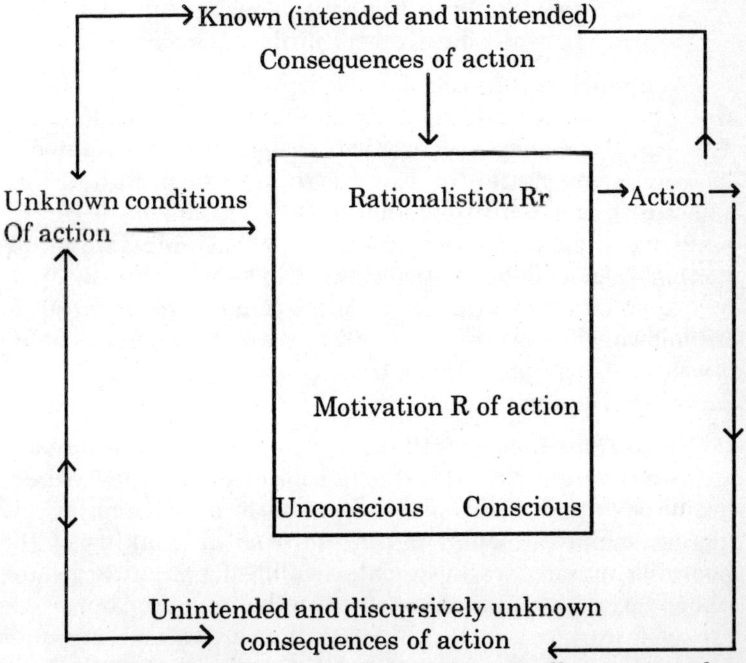

According to this model, action is causally connected to unknown conditions of action, which are also partially responsible for the unintended consequences o action; unintended consequences and unknown conditions may become known conditions of action, actors are able to learn more about their environment as well as about themselves; motivation has in turn two sources, unconscious and conscious; motivation is affected, through rationalization, by the consequences of action, whether unintended or intended; and rationalization of action indicates that human action is reflectively monitored.

It was asserted above that the rationalisation of action does not necessarily correspond to the real causes of the action. Now, according to Bhaskar, this idea is directly connected to the emancipatory political change:

> ...the object that renders illusory (or superficial) beliefs necessary comes [...], at least in the absence of any overriding considerations, to be criticized in being explained; so that the point now becomes, ceteris paribus, to change it.

My opinion is that Bhaskar, though being right in general, somewhat exaggerates the aims and force of the explanatory criticism. The main reasons for this exaggeration are related to his vacillating notion of social structure (especially "deep structure"), and to his somewhat unclear version of the correspondence theory of truth. Bhaskar is not able to analyse thoroughly enough the relation between facts and values, because he has not explicated his notion of truth in sufficient detail. In the following I shall attempt to substantiate these critical points as well as to explicate in detail the necessary connection between explanation and criticism.

Bhaskar distinguishes three ways in which an "interference" between the subject's interest in the object and its knowledge of it could operate. It could operate consciously (as in lying); it could operate semi-consciously (as in the wishful thinking of the incurable optimist or the special pleading of a pressure group); or it could operate unconsciously (whether or not it can become accessible to consciousness). Further, there are two subcategories in the third possibility: either the conclusions of such an unconscious mode of "interference" are rationalisations of motivation, or they constitute mystifications (ideologies) of social structure. Clearly the suggested third way of "interference" is the most controversial one, because lying is analytically a simple case, and because "plausibility" of a theory or thesis can understandably stem also from the wishful thinking (but how unconscious might wishful thinking be, especially if it develops gradually within a relationally positioned practice)?

Now, according to Bhaskar, one is only justified in characterizing a set of ideas P as "ideological" if both (i) P is false, that is, one possesses a superior explanation for the phenomena in question; and (ii) P is more or less contingently (conjuncturally) necessary, that is, one possesses an explanation of the falsity of beliefs in question. it should be noted that the necessity may only be the necessity for some false idea, rather than any particular one; and that where different theories are required for the satisfaction of (i) and (ii), they must be at least consistent with each other. (i) is the critical, (ii) the explanatory condition. (i) suffices to criticism in general, but (ii) is required if the criticism is to be explanatory and directed to emancipatory social change. Now, one can write these criteria and their normative conclusion as follows.

(Arg.1)

(a) T > P
(b) T exp R (P)
―――――――――――
(c) ~ V (A -> P)
―――――――――――
(d) V ( )

Where	">"	=	"has more explanatory and illuminatory power than... and covers the range of...
	"exp"	=	"co-explains"
	"->"	=	"causes"
	T	=	an existing theory
	"R"	=	"reproduction of..."
	"V"	=	"positive evaluation of..."
	"A"	=	an object (a social structure)
	"O"	=	strategic action di rected at removing/ changing A

This argument, which I do not accept in this unqualified form, entails the imperative; change it," if change is possible, in the absence of overriding considerations, and without any conditions on means of change. Now, let me ask: is this argument substantially valid? Might it be objected that this argument is valid only because one is committed to the prior value that truth is (morally) good, as was argued above? According to Bhaskar, this certainly is so, but

> ...that truth is a good (ceteris paribus) is not only a condition of moral discourse, it is a condition of discourse.

Thus Bhaskar claims that the (Arg. 1) is "naturalist", not moral, in character. This claim is further substantiated with his peculiar correspondence theory of truth:

> The notion of false consciousness employed here simply involves in the first instance that of disjuncture, mismatch or lack of correspondence (representative adequacy) between belief and object.

As can be seen, the "most general of political problems, namely the problem of truth," is again under discussion. Above I concluded that Bhaskar's attempt to define truth (and possibly scientific realism, too) in terms of a principle of bivalence is a mistake, confusing a normative thesis about truthfulness, honesty, and openness with an epistemological thesis about how to achieve the highest standards of representational quality for scientific cognition. In this sense, truth cannot be "naturalist." However, on another occasion, I also interpreted Bhaskar as saying that judgemental rationality depends upon the ontological realism because it is not possible to assert something (tø make a historical speech-act) without at least implicity claiming to be saying or writing something of the (real) world, without giving something to understand. In other words, I suggested that Apels's and Habermas's universal pragmatics and Bhaskar's scientific realism might be very closely connected. This suggestion is again confirmed by Bhaskar's claim that "truth is a condition of discourse at all." To clarify the matter in question, let me quote Bhaskar:

> Might it not be objected, however, that the fact/value distinction only breaks down in this way, because one is committed to the prior valuation that truth is a good, so that

one is not deriving a value judgement from entirely factual (natural) premises? But that truth is a good ("ceteris paribus") is not only a condition of moral discourse, it is a condition of any discourse at all. Commitment to truth and consistency applies to factual as much as to value discourse; and so cannot be seized upon as a concealed (value) premise to rescue the autonomy of values from factual discourse, without destroying the distinction between the two, the distinction that it is the point of the objections to uphold.

Now, Haberman and Apel, too, have argued that the truth of an assertion is one of the circumstances "what we must always already presuppose in regard to ourselves and others as normative conditions of the possibility of understanding; and in this sense, what we necessarily always have, we already have accepted." However, as can be seen, Apel and Habermas consider this to be a normative condition of all speech-acts, and, in effect, their view dispels the distinction between facts and values, although it does not destroy the distinction between them. After rejecting the bivalence and bivocality theories of truth, I cannot see any other option left. This is the only possible conclusion for Bhaskar as well, it seems. The only question that remains is: is the truth merely a moral value of (realist) scientific practices, as Harre claims; or is it one of the universal conditions of understanding, as Habermas claims; or is it a transcendental condition in a Kantian sense, as Apel asserts? Apel's assertion stems from the project of searching for Ultimate Foundations, and to him we could answer, as post-structuralist Ashley does, that we should eschew grand designs, transcendental grounds, or universal projects of humankind because of the seemingly arbitrary pluralism of these projects and because of the potential Neitzschean clash of these projects (wills); But is it still the case, as Habermas argues, that a necessary condition for a successful speech-act is that the speaker (or writer) must have the intention of communicating a true proposition or a propositional content, the existential presuppositions of which must be satisfied (i.e., that when we are communicating, we have always already presupposed the normative condition of truth)?

My suggestion for the (cautiously) affirmative answer to this very difficult question goes as follows. First, a possible argument against Haberma's claim would be a counter-example, which reveals that truth is not a universal normative condition. It might be possible, for instance, to imagine a culture, where people do not make any difference between "lying" and speaking the truth, although it is almost impossible to imagine how they could understand each other or coordinate their actions (or, for that matter, how they could have a language in the first place). Moreover, in concrete communicative situations actors can always challenge each on "ad hominem" grounds, if there are reasons to believe that a person does not believe in what he or she is claiming about the world. Nevertheless, there still might be objections against Habermas's argument, and thus his thesis is, in principle, fallible. Secondly, and more significantly, there might be other normative considerations which could override truth on many occasions. Winch offers us an example:

> [...] question concerning the importance in human life of knowing the world as it really is. I am thinking of the moral question which so exercised Ibsen in such plays as the "Wild Duck" and "Ghosts": How far is it important to a man's life that he should live it in clear awareness of the facts of his situation and of his relations to those around him? In "Ghosts" this question is presented by considering a man whose life is being ruined by his ignorance of the truth about his heredity. The Wild Duck" starts from the opposite direction: here is a man who is living a perfectly contended life which is, however, based on a complete misunderstanding of the attitude to him of those he knows; should he be disillusioned and have his happiness, disrupted in the interests of truth?

Habermas has been accused of privileging the illocutionary act involved in asserting (normative) claims, rather than the substantive content of the judgements which are fixed firmly in those illocutionary acts. Moreover, he has also been accused of privileging consensus, instead of conflict. As a consequence of these almost "a priori" preferences, Habermas contends that, because speech is essential to human life, the normative conditions which are presupposed by speech—like freedom and justice in an unconstrained, and basically consensual dialogue—possess universal justification. Peter Winch challenges this in his conservative way, and I think that his general point is apt, although it might be possible to question the validity of his concrete counter-example. Further, truth cannot be defined by a consensus in an ideal speech situation, as Habermas has done, because we as historical beings have no access to ideal speech situation. Note, however, that Habermas has recently weakened his position in this respect. Rather truth of a proposition or a theory is a historical validity claim, which is based on a historical human judgement, which is often concerned with the metaphorical correspondence between proposition/theory, and state of affairs in the real world. This judgment, in turn is founded on (always historical and contested) reasons and criteria.

For these reasons, despite the fact that truth is a universal normative condition of communication and an important *prima facie* value, this condition (value) and /or some (two) other formally similar conditions (values) are not, and cannot be, sufficient premises for a deduction of a utopia, which is society as an "ideal speech situation." This criticism of the Frankfurt School notwithstanding, my conclusion is that truth really is more than merely a moral value of (realist) scientific practices. Truth is a universal as well as strong *prima facie* value, which is based on the always already supposed normative condition of any discourse where problematic validity claims are thematized. On the other hand, it should also be understood that the explicit and continuous problematization of truth claims can be associated with the (rise of the) Western scientific culture, and especially with "Galilean style of thought."

Qualifying (Arg.1)

It can now be concluded that there is no objectivist, or naturalist, position from where to put forward any concrete critical (Arg. 1). Moreover, the trade-off situations between different normative scientific criteria, which are crucial to any theory choice, should be remembered as well. In realist sciences, the explanatory and illuminatory power of a theory are the most important criteria, as is indicated in (Arg.1$^{\neq}$). However, there are always other criteria as well, like the standing of sources of evidence in point of authoritativeness, the probative strength of confirming evidence, and the tendency of principles of systematization like simplicity, regularity, uniformity, and normalcy, which form part of the plausibility of a thesis or a theory. Hence science is a value-based social enterprise, relying on practical judgements which are in principle structurally similar to pay-actor's judgements. Science has thus no a *priori* privileged position (outside of society) for making normative judgements, although it is inevitably committed to making such critical judgements.

In respect of the (Arg. 1), I am still faced with the following problems; (i) is it possible to decide rationally, psossibly relative to some sub-audience X_e of "universal" audience X_u, at some definite moment t, that (Arg.I) is valid; (ii) should "we" give to "the accused" a chance to answer to the accusation; (iii) what conditions, if any, there are for the sub-audience X_e; (iv) if I, or rather "we", have decided at t + I (i ≥0), possibly after a dialogue with "the accused," that (Arg. 1) can be applied, is ∅ then unconditioned, e.g. does it include the possible use of violence? Or should "we" specify ∅ somehow?

As stated, scientific activities include always judgements which are themselves subject to debatable-normative criteria. Thus the answer to (i) must be positive. Consequently, in a conflicting and contradictory world, it seems that from the epistemological and normative point of view the answer to (iii) is the crucial one as far as the possibility of (Arg. 1) is concerned. Transcedental realism admits the speculative possibility that even one person, who is opposed to all other human beings, may be, in principle, and may in the long run turn out ot have been might in matters of truth; but an epistemology, which relies on intersubjective judgements and criteria denies the rationality of any monological judgements: rationality is always dialogical in nature. But does this imply that there must be a consensus between all actual human beings before we can make real judgements? Or can we make some sub-audience X_e, say a group of Islamic priests, a Communist party, the "community" of Western diplomats, or an Occidental academic intelligentsia, to whose critical examination we should submit outs judgements, and whose decision should be decisive? In my opinion, both questions should be answered simply in the negative.

To begin, rationality on its minimal sense is internally related to reasons. Further, rationality is connected to openness to criticism from whatever source: if openness is not guaranteed, there would be no basis to claim that the probative strength of all possible relevant evidence is considered. If a person is "deaf to argument," he may either ignore contrary reasons or reply them with dogmatic assertions, and hence openness is the basic normative criterion of realist sciences, as Harre points out. This notice is further confirmed by the observation that there is an actual non-consensus in most matters; we have different possible, and contradictory, sources of knowledge. But the possibility of criticism, as well as the presumption that the world is mostly undependent of any particular description of it, implies that everyone cannot be right. Thus we are neither able to name any decisive sub-audience X_e, nor do we need any kind of universal consensus before making rational judgements. It should perhaps be added that a rational judgement is also not a matter of voting.

For these reasons, it can now be concluded that rational judgements imply both the actual existence of good reasons and openness to further critical debates. A rational judgement cannot, and consequences of a rational judgement should not, ceteris paribus, contradict these notions. However, although a judgement is made according to "the well-grounded rules of the art," it is quite likely (because of the holistic basis of plausibility, because of the need for pragmatic simplicity or economy of work since we are finite human beings, as well as because of many non-scientific reasons of stubbornness), that only a relatively small—unspecified—sub-audience can agree with the judgement in a reasonable period of time, and even they possibly only fairly. Nevertheless it can be claimed that as far as the person thinks; she or he has publicly presented good reasons for dialogically made honest judgements, a far as he or she is open to criticism—

which can always break through established holistic contexts—and far as he or she does not know any relevant counter - arguments made against judgements, he or she is justified in making them.

Consequently we can, in principle, make judgements concerning the validity of any concrete form of (Arg.1). However, Bhaskar claims that once we have fulfilled the explanatory condition, too, we must conclude V (∅) = positive evaluation of an unspecified strategic action directed at removing/changing the social object which has co-caused the false belief(s). This inference is valid, ceteris paribus, if and only if the relation between A and P is internal (i.e., conceptually necessary), not causal (i.e., contingent), as it, however, often or typically is. In the latter case, the false belief(s) can be removed and changed, at least in principle, for example by the way of rational dialectical persuasion (Ω), instead of some form of strategic action. Moreover, there are good reasons for v (Ω), isntead of V (∅), as well: Ω is in perfect accordance with the rational method of making scientific judgements, while ∅ is, at least thus far, unconditioned, and hence may be contradictory to W. Consequently we should re-write (Arg.1*) as follows:

(Arg. 1*)

(a) T > P

(b) T exp R (P)

(c) ~V (P)

(d) ~V (A->P)

(e) V(Ω), CT

where CT stands for "ceteris paribus"

The *ceteris paribus*—clausal—indicates that there may be other than scientific-rational considerations, too. Moreover, concrete rationality, including a specific normative scientific criterion, is always embodied in a historical context, and is subject to other normative considerations. The most important of these is the following, suggested by Hannah Arendt:

To be sure, every deed has its motives as it has its goal and principle; but the act itself, though it proclaims its goal and makes manifest its principle, does not reveal the innermost motivation of the agent. His motives remain dark, they do not shine but are hidden not only from others but, most of the time, from himself, from his self-inspection, as well. Hence, the search for motives, the demand that everybody display in public his innermost motivation, since it actually demands the impossible, transforms all actors into hypocrites; the moment the display of motives begins, hypocrisy begins to poison all human relations.

From these practical moral considerations, Arendt concludes that in politics, more than anywhere else, we have no possibility of distinguishing between being and appearence; and, indeed, that being and appearence are one and the same. However, even though there clearly is an important problem here, this conclusion is not a necessary one. Actually, it is partially false and contradictory; for, Arendt herself first makes a distinction between being and appearance, accepting the existential hypothesis implied by this distinction, and then she concludes, after practical moral considerations, that "being and appearance are one and the same". The question rather is: do we have practical political possibilities to distinguish between being and appearance?; is it possible to put froward critical (Arg. 1*) without destroying the trust which is necessary for all communication?

Suppose that it is practically possible to put forward (Arg. 1*). Consider then the case that Ω have no success, and that there are good reasons for the belief that this is simply because the accused is "deaf to argument," i.e. irrational, or because there are no practical political possibilities for rational disputation (note that these states of affairs cannot be decided *a priori*). Should we conclude V(∅) ? In my opinion we should, on the condition that ∅ is restricted and specified in a way which captures also the problem of trust presented above. Now, remember that I have claimed that rational judgements cannot, and consequences of rational judgements should not, ceteris paribus, contradict the notions of good reasons and openness to further critical debates. Hence we should continue the (Arg. $1^{\neq}$) as follows:

(Arg. $1^{\neq}$) (f) $(\Omega$ & $P)$ or $(\Omega \sim$ PP wrt. Y)

(g) V(∅) & [∅ ⊥ ∅ PPwrt. (Y & Y`)]

Key: PPwrt. = "is politically possible with respect to"

Y = the relevant political situation

Y = changed Y co-caused by ∅ and its consequences

∅ = rational dialectical persuasion that the proponent of the (Arg. $1^{\neq}$) has been wrong

I have claimed that it is possible to decide rationally, at some definite moment, that (Arg. $1^{\neq}$) is true; that we should always give to "the accused" a chance to answer to the accusation; and that there are no substantial conditions for the sub-audience X_e, except the normative, procedural, and historical criteria of rationality. The final question to be answered is concerned with the possible use of violence. Does (g) of (Arg. $1^{\neq}$) allow the use of violent means to achieve the desired end described by ∅. The answer is, in my view : no, it does not.

However, I am not going to argue for a simple-minded pacifism. The point is not that there may not be, on certain occasions, good moral reasons for using violence (e.g., self-defence, "just war"). The point is merely that emancipatory explanatory critique does not allow the possibility of use of violence. Perhaps, surprisingly, the reason for this almost categorical denial point towards the need for a theory of nonviolent political action, which is compatible with the structurationist ontology, like the one preliminarily developed by Sharp:

> [...] political power can be viewed as fragile, always dependent for its strength and existence upon a replenishment of its sources by the cooperation of a multitude of institutions and people-cooperation which may or may not continue.

According to Galtung, Sharp's work is by far the most comprehensive and analytically useful study produced in the field of nonviolent political action.58 There are, however, problems with Sharp's theory, namely its narrow view of political power (as governmental power) and its still somewhat unelaborated form. Nevertheless, it is a good beginning, and we have to start from somewhere.

CONCLUSION

If peace research is to be critical, it should be able to present its normative basis. This paper can be read as an attempt to form such a basis, although not in a modern foundationalist manner. First, I have argued that truth is a normative notion which is internally connected to honesty, openness, good reasons, and justification. Although the real world is differentiated, structured, and stratified, any "correspondence" to the real world can be only metaphorical in character. Further, the normative notion of truth gives, in turn, force to explanatory social criticism, which is founded on a theory that can explain (also) the necessity of (some) false beliefs, if they are connected to the reproduction of social structures (of domination, in particular). However, the dialogical nature of rationality, and the position of truth as one value among many, conditions modes and forms that emancipatory political action can assume. In particular, emancipatory political action should restrict itself to the forms of nonviolent political action.

Relations between explanatory criticism and more general normative discourse are manifold. For one thing, truth is only one value among others, despite the fact that it is a strong and universal prima facie value. On the other hand, however, it can be argued that truth—in a sense of description and explanation, or a "true theory"—is a prerequisite for many/most normative judgements. For, how would it be possible to judge what is right and wrong if it is not known what the world is like? And if true understanding of the world is a prerequisite for normative judgements, then these judgments often involve explanatory criticism also.

Finally, it should be emphasised that criticism and connected emancipatory political action are not enough in themselves. "Peace research," or "international relations" for that matter, should be also constructive (as, for instance, Galtung, too, notes). In other words, they should be able to open new political possibilities to create new concrete and realistic political alternatives. Following Rorty, this could be called "the edifying aspect of social sciences." Political possibilities could be opened, for example, by studying modes and strategies of nonviolent political action, by revealing—in a somewhat post-structuralist manner—the repressed political possibilities already immanent in history, or by inventing new possible practices and institutions which could be subjected to the scrutiny of historical experimentation.

Notes and References

1. Michel Foucoult, "Questions of Method: An Interview with Michel Foucoult," in Baynes et. al. (ed.) *Philosophy*: *End* or *Transformation*? (Boston: The MIT Press, 1987), p.111.
2. See Reiner Schurmann, "Deconstruction is not Enough: on Glanni Vattimo's Call for "weak Thinking," *Graduate Faculty Philosophy Journal*, Vcl. 10, No.1. Spring 1984, pp.175-76.
3. Hannah Arendt, On *Revolution* (Bungay, Suffolk: Penguin Books, 1973, 1965), p.82.
4. Johan Galtung, *The Ture Worlds* (New York: The Free Press, 1980), p.28.
5. A.J.R. Groom, "Paradigms in Conflict: The Strategist, The Conflict Researcher and the Peace Researcher," *Review of International Studies*, Vol. 14, 1988, p.112.
6. Quoted in H. Alker, T. Biersteker, and I. Inoguchi, "From Imperial Power Balancing to People's Wars: Searching for Order in the Twentieth Century," In J.Der Derian, and M. Shapiro, eds, *International/Intertextual Relations*: *Postmodern Readings of World Politics* (Lexington Books, 1989), p.152.
7. *Ibid*., especially pp. 146-50.

Chapter-5

Political Systems: Crises in Governance

Chapter-5

**The well-being of society depends
On the well-being of its citizenry.**

-Neil J. Smelser (1989, p.1)

Governments are powerful forces in people's lives. They can ensure tremendous opportunities, security, and guarantees of human rights and freedoms. They can also do much to promote peace among nations.

In contrast, governments can, and throughout history some save, caused many kinds of suffering. They have deprived many people of their basic needs. They have brought anguish to their citizenry and horrors of war to neighboring states. Hence, it would be easy to agree with Thomas Paine who said that whereas society springs from men's virtues, government springs from their vices, and is therefore a necessary evil (referred to by Carl Becker, 1949, p.5).

Yes, government is necessary, but it does not have to be evil. Whether it is a force for peace, violence, or both, is determined by the psychic qualities of people - those who created the government and/or those who maintain it ("We the People"). Governmental policies can, therefore, be secondary causes of violence and peace, in people and in other societal systems.

Because a goal of this volume is to encourage study of some important sources of violence and peace, government must also be examined. This chapter will briefly consider some of government's important functions and responsibilities for:

•general defense, well-being, and peace;
•the security of human rights and freedoms;
•fall systems of justice, penal, and legal policies; and
•interaction and cooperation with other countries is fostering peace and well-being for all people.

Chapter 6 gives consideration to the responsibility of

government for promoting economic equity. Hence, this is not a chief topic here.

This chapter will also make suggestions for a continuous process of evaluating and reforming government and for upgrading our valued, unfinished democracy. It encourages thinking, discussion, and action pertaining to the nature and responsibilities of government and our roles in it.

Governmental Functions and Responsibilities

Why government? Paraphrasing Abraham Lincoln's answer to that question, Mario Cuomo (1995) wrote: "...government is the coming together of people to do for themselves collectively what they could not do individually." Cuomo says that, "Lincoln's definition...helps on questions where Americans haven't always agreed about the need for government action of any kind." Cuomo includes among such issues: the use of common resources such as the airwaves; the protection from "...harms that cross state lines like air and water pollution"; national parks; protection from crime; checking for safety of medicines, drugs, and foods; old-age insurance; regulation and monitoring of banks; and unemployment following layoffs. On the other hand, government should not interfere in people's private affairs if they do not harm other people.

If Thomas Jefferson were here today and could witness the conflicts over welfare, capital gains tax cuts, minimum wages, and the like, I think he would again write the following words.

The care of human life and happiness, and not their destruction, is the first and only legitimate object of good government (1809).

"Care if human life and happiness..." requires that government perform various *functions* and accept many *responsibilities*. It means also that if government is to be by and for the people", those people must cooperatively carry out these functions and responsibilities in a way that is equitable and for the well-being of all people. If equity is honestly followed as a guiding principle, government will be effective in promoting human well-being when governments are not equitable, they should be reformed.

Guidelines and rules for people's behaviors (i.e., governance) have been a par human affairs since primitive groups and families were formed. As populations have grown, groups transformed, and needs and conditions have changed, so have behavior guidelines and governing policies become increasingly complex.

People have differed, sometimes violently, concerning type and amount of government needed. At present, some people advocate abolishing all government except its role as protector form outside invaders and inside criminals. A movement in support of a "government-hands -off policy" seems to be gaining popularity. Some even foster cutting all public assistance funds for children the unfortunate, aged, and handicapped. They support the idea that charity can sustain these groups. Even worse a few leaders have advocated moves such as removing children from their unwed mothers and putting them in orphanages.

In addition, some of these people think government should subsidize their business efforts and grant them special privileges. Still others take government for granted and ignore it. Many seem quick to condemn government but take no responsibility for participating in or changing it.

Since crises such as economic inequality, pervasive violence, educational urgencies and environmental degradation are looming large, we should look carefully at the role of government in helping to cope with these crises. This means that we need to examine our own responsibilities in these processes Government needs us - "we the people" - to monitor, and when needed, to change and provide a more equitable, humanitarian, democratic government. There us much for citizens to do.

Chapter Eight briefly discussed some ways in which society, including governments, can share functions and responsibilities with individuals and families. The requires insuring families, especially children, against some of the contingencies of life that can devastate individuals and families if they are not cooperatively safe-guarded. Such guarantees include public education, healthcare, retirement insurance, and protection from some types of catastrophe. If government (i.e., with all of us sharing equitably) will provide these basics, we can obstruct violence and advance peace. Citizens should require government to perform these functions.

The following is a brief discussion of some governmental functions and responsibilities.

Provide for Defense, General Well-Being, and Peace

The Preamble of the United States Constitution commits government to certain responsibilities. It is written:

> We the people of the United States, in order to form a more perfect Union, establish justice, insure domestic tranquillity, provide for the common defense, promote the general welfare, and secure the blessings of liberty to ourselves and our posterity, do ordain and establish this Constitution for the Untied States of America.

Governments, past and present, have had as a chief priority the defense of their populations from outside invaders. It is unfortunate that this has sometimes been necessary. Too many governments (including our own) have used their power to also invade and/or dominate other countries. It is not a purpose of this book to debate the validity of these undertakings. However, if more people become self-other oriented this will not happen, and freedom, justice, and equity can be a possession for everyone throughout the world without interference by aggressors

Functions of governments include not only insuring numerous freedoms, but also protection from various types of danger, security of persons and possessions; security against military power, and the fostering of peace on Earth.

Secure Human Rights and Freedoms

Freedoms one of our most prized opportunities and conditions. There are **freedoms to do** something, and there are **freedoms from** something (e.g., freedom to grow and learn and freedom from mind control). There are freedoms are human rights that are inalienable and vital to the well-being of everyone. The following are included among these.

Freedom of mind, speech and press. Freedom of mind is the foundation of democratic government. Freedom to speak and publish thoughts is very closely allied. For centuries people have struggled for the rights to think freely, seek truth, believe their own thinking, express those ideas, and be masters of their own lives. Some early creative thinkers were forced to recant their own words (e.g., Galileo); others lost their lives in struggle (e.g., Giordano Baurno and Socrates).

Freedom from the compulsion of church and state were rights that our founding fathers were determined to have written into the Declaration of Independence and the United State Constitution. They were convinced that, as Carl Becker (1949) wrote:

> Democratic government rests on the assumption that the people are capable of governing themselves better than any one or any few can do it for them; but this in turn rests on the further assumption that if the people are free to think, speak, and publish their sentiments on any subject, the consequences will be good. Well, sometimes they are and sometimes not. If we have faith in democracy, we get over this inconvenient fact by saying that by an large and in the long run the consequences will be good (p.27).

This means that self-other people must work to prevent harm, or the "long run" may be a *long dictatorial run.* Democracy can succeed only if people are well enough informed on public affairs to base their decisions upon facts; they do not allow themselves to be swayed by special interests who have clouded facts and indoctrinated with misinformation; and are self-other oriented having integrity, responsibility, and the willingness to subordinate purely selfish desires to the general well-being. These are prerequisites to freedom.

Freedom to learn and teach. When helping to form our government, James Madison said, "A popular government, without popular information, or the means of acquiring it, is but a prologue to a farce or a tragedy...a people who means to be their own governors must arm themselves with the power which knowledge gives."

Without much question, leaders of government have concluded that a functions of government is to provide for public schools, teaching, and opportunities for learning. Democracy will surely fail if this responsibility is turned to profit-making private enterprise of other special interest groups. People should be free to build their own private schools but not at the public's expense. It is also vitally important that children and youth gain a wide range of facts from many areas of learning with interactions among them. They need to learn much more just about technology. What should and what should not be taught in public schools an issue which needs to be discussed and continuously decided by the people. Chapter 16 discusses various educational issues.

The right to work and to receive a living wage. In a democracy in which people are interdependent and cooperative, every effort is made to provide work for everyone who is able and of a legal age to do so. A living wage should be assured for such labor. The official minimum wage should be high enough to provide for an adequate family living. Governments and corporations should guarantee this. When it is not done, workers are unable to provide for their most basic needs. They also tend to believe that they are inferior, which they are not.

It seems that most everyone agrees that welfare should be reformed. Arguments have been loudest from those who contend that welfare should be denied to single mothers. In a television panel debate on welfare (March 3, 1995), not one person said that many young women on welfare do not work because they can not provide childcare, health care, and support for their children and themselves on the present minimum wage level. Yet earlier on the same station a group of young mothers were interviewed. They stated that they wanted to work and some has tried to do so but could not because of the low wage. This is an example of belittling a group of people who are in a distressed condition, regardless of who is at fault. Our legislators need more compassion and knowledge of the real conditions.

Government and the people should accept responsibility for providing education of young women and men that includes; learning employment skills; development of self-esteem and self-otherness; autonomy and adult responsibilities for their behaviors; and family life education that could do much to prevent early pregnancy.

Promote Fuller Democracy

The following are a few of the many ways our government could make participatory democracy more complete.

1. It could encourage a fuller representation from citizens in the voting process by providing authentic voter-information, general education, and by changing election procedures.

2. It could reform the outworn party system; make destructive campaign practices illegal; and prohibit special economic interests from financing candidates campaigns and bribing legislator to pass laws that cater to their greed. A **prime example** of this bribing is the lobbying by tobacco companies. They have **provided** campaign funds and luxuries for congressmen in exchange for their **votes** to continue government subsidies for their industries. Many companies use this practice. In the care of tobacco, they are also killing millions of people through addiction to nicotine. There is presently no pending **legislation** to drop these subsidies, even though Congress is now working to reduce **aid** to dependent children. These types of buy-outs and other kinds of fraud are serous blocks to participatory democracy. We are much in need of reforms.

3. The power of the wealthy elite over government and the people could be reduced by **bringing** greater equality. This could include a higher minimum **wage** and a ceiling on individual income and wealth. No person should be **allowed** to earn of possess the immense portions of Earth's resources which are now being permitted. This means regulating speculative finance; the harmful effects of stock markets; the national and

international power of **corporations**; more equity in the tax system; more control and reforms in the welfare system, providing positive programs for raising the well-being of the poor; and reducing the national debt.

4. A national single-payer nonprofit health system should be provided Reduce unnecessary federal programs, but not by shifting functions to states that would cause inequalities across the country.

Restrain Unjust Freedoms, Require Responsibility

Liberty consists in the power to do
Whatever does not injure others.

—The French Declaration of the
Rights of Man

This truth continues: freedom must not be unlimited. Governmental restraints should prevent people from using freedom to exploit or harm other people and Earth's resources. There are nor enduring rights, freedoms, or democracy apart from responsibility to live equitably. With the present state of **many** people's self-onlyness, controls must be placed upon freedom and **opportunities** to do harm, it democracy is to survive.

For **example, restraints** must be placed on freedom of speech and the press if what is **said and** printed is injuries. Through the democratic process, people must determine what is harmful and what is not. Much thought must be given to this process to promote the **greatest possible** freedom with the **least amount of** restriction. Such judgements are difficult but necessary especially to protect the ignorant and gullible from self-only people's manipulation, violence and misrepresentations as the lies flood the air-waves before elections.

Ross Stagner (1967) quotes an aphorism often used by Robert L. Lynd: "Each for himself, and God for all of us, ' said the elephant as he danced among the chickens." Stagner concludes, "Autonomy an self-determination are fine for the elephant. But his unrestrained freedom presents a major threat to the chickens." Someone else said, "You have no right to hit me in the nose. Your freedom ends where my nose begins." Does this mean giving up some of our freedom? Yes, in a sense. But that is a price we pay for being allowed to share this Earth with other life, and provide a way of living which is **EQUITABLY GOOD FOR ALL.**

It is unfortunate that the highest status and greatest praise is often granted to those who take **advantage** of freedom and excel over others, even when accomplished without equity. There is still this tremendous admiration for the *winning man who can excel* over others in various kinds of encounters as well as in war. The **attitude** still prevails that to be a worthy male, a man must be superior to **most** other men, and of course, superior to all women. The emphasis has **shifted somewhat** from status through physical prowess (although that still exists) to military power, political influence and material wealth. The idea **remains** the same: **complete**, win, dominate others, and gain glory for self. A result is patriarchy in the family, control in the community, exploitation in the work place, manipulation in the economy, power in politics, and destruction of Earth's resources. On the international level, there should be restraints upon corporations' freedom to exploit poorer countries and upon nations to prevent their abuse against each other. Too often there is demonizing, coercion, warnings, and threats of military strength. You know the approach: "Negotiate only from a position of power." There are all forms of violence. Success could come more often if opponents' views were heard, their intrinsic worth respected, and constructive conflict resolution and cooperation were employed. Self - other type governmental policies could lead the way.

In this country, the power ethic is often combined with a promulgation of the "American Dream" in which it is assumed that everyone can be rich, happy, powerful, and *admired* for their acquisition of material possessions. Hence, many people *are engulfed* in a struggle which consumes and isolates them and often denies *them deeper* human relationships and higher values. This "rat-race", as it is *often called*, has pitted people against each other; it has been a factor in the *demotion* of self-respect, since only a few can win over many others; it has not been fulfilling even for those who win; and it has been a cause of *other types* violence. Running concurrently with this syndrome of ideas has been the view that empathy, cooperation, kindness, and sensitivity are signs of weakness. This self-only condition is illustrated in the following story:

Two men were backpacking in the wilderness when they saw a large vicious-looking bear bounding toward them. One man threw off his backpack and started to run. The other man, trying to think of a way our of the situation, said, "You can't outrun that bear." To which the other replied, "I don't have to outrun the bear. I just have to outrun you."

Some people see others as things to be used and exploited. Alfie Kohn (1986), Eric *Fromm* (1976), Robert Bellah (1985), and others have warned us that competition, consumerism, and individualism are getting out of hand and unless we modify them, we may lose our precious freedoms.

The drive for freedom has gone to an unhealthy extreme in the United States. *One person's* freedom, without limits, can become dictatorial power resulting in other people's deprivation or servitude. On the other hand, excessive controls on freedom can mean totalitarian government. There must be a fine balance these two extremes. In this country we have the alternatives to find that balance and act in the best interest of everyone or lose democracy. Since power s ultimately in the hands of the people, the responsibility rests with us. Business entrepreneurs need freedom to use capital and hire workers. However, if that freedom allows, and their greed urges them, they can gain excessive profits while the workers receive below-living wages. Such entrepreneurs freedom ahs gone too far without responsibility. There should, therefore, be controls by legal means.

When people are self-other oriented, their psychic qualities of empathic thinking, equitable attitudes, constructive values, compassionate beliefs, and peace -promoting behaviors lead them to balance freedom with responsibility. If power is not based upon such qualities, tyranny will be the consequence. Since many **people** are not yet at this stage of self-other maturity. Some carefully chosen **constraints** and regulations are necessary. Such controls are not burdensome to **those people** who are willing to live within the context of what is best for **everyone**.

How much **governmental** control should there be? Since present views range all the way **from** complete laissez-faireism to totalitarianism, much creative thought, **research**, analysis, impartial deliberation, and honest cooperation should **be invested** in this question. There is a way between these two which promotes **peace** and encourages freedom with responsibility.

English Laws and Maintain Justice

A necessary function of government is to make and enforce laws needed to provide for order in society. It is the responsibility of citizens in a democratic society to monitor these processes and to keep them serving the needs of the *peoples*. If this responsibility is not *carried* out, special interest groups conspire to pass laws which are for their advantage and not for the good of all people. If law enforcement agencies are operating from the philosophy that violence must be used to control violence, then a cycle of escalating violence results. Certainly there are extreme cases where violent control is necessary. Usually there are better ways. The most fundamental one is to solve the social and psychological disturbances in society that promote violence. Victims of injustice and inequity can easily, and often do, become villains.

When laws are broken: Who is responsible? What should be done? In the U.S. the policy has been that courts of justice should determine innocence or guilt, decree appropriate consequences, and order enforcement of the verdict if guilt is determined. It has been assumed that care should be taken to place responsibility on the guilty party when justice is being determined.

Notwithstanding prior conditions, it has been assumed that

when people are guilty, they should be punished. This may result in injustice. For example, judging children in adult courts and administering adult-type punishment may expose children to adult criminals who teach those young people how to become more hardened criminals. The cycle is perpetuated. What these young people really need is reeducation, respect, help from caring people, and if possible, parenting education for their parents.

There should be consideration for prior conditions, not to escape a guilty verdict, but to *determine* what should be done to and for the guilty person. Emphasis should be placed on *root causes* in order to decide how the person could be helped to reform and *return* to society as a respected citizen. There is a recognition of the truth that a *victim has become a* villain, and therefore, the victim/villain should not be *punished* but reeducated or held away from society. Responsibility is placed on the guilty party, but the root causes should be recognized. These causes may encompass parents, spouses, community, conditions, gangs, *schools*, racism, or even poverty. Efforts should be made to correct underlying causes.

Innocence is sometimes plead on the principle that "the means justifies the end." Thus, the crime is justified if it helped to advance goals of a political movement or a cause to which one is dedicated. At this point in time the courts seem less willing to grant this plea. But danger lurks in possibilities for tyranny in the future. If people disagree with established law, they should work through the legislative process of reform rather than taking the law in their own hands.

Criminals are sometimes not found guilty because of spurious technicalities such as: there was not a search warrant when the evidence was collected; or the arrested people were not "read their rights." This is an abuse and misuse of constitutional law.

These and various other arguments are flawed because:

1. If a person committed a crime, he/she is guilty. Matters of root causes, pre-conditions, special causes, age of the person, or special technicalities are different questions which must be considered but they do not change the matter of guilt. Releasing

the convict does not resolve the root causes, conditions, are reform the guilty party. It may cause more violence on this generation and perhaps the next. The question remains: what should be done with, or for, the victim /villain?

2. Since punishment seldom. If ever, solves a problem, much more emphasis should be given to positive approaches than to punishment.

3. The concern of what should be done with the guilty, involves questions such as : Was there an intent to harm? Is the character flawed and the person a threat to society? What programs of action should be required, should the person be in therapy, receive some other help, or be incarcerated?

4. If there are other root causes or extenuating conditions, should not society be responsible to make reforms in whatever ways possible? For example, in cases of dysfunctional families, remedial and educational programs for parents and family may be a possible solution, as well as preventive measures for others. Sentencing for the criminal may or may not be combined with changes in conditions involved. What factors should given consideration?

5. The way the evidence was collected does not change the facts of guilt or innocence. Perhaps the people who collected the evidence should be held accountable, but if the evidence is proven to be true, it should be used as evidence.

6. The consequences for both the guilty person and the public should be given great consideration. The follow up action is vital for all concerned. People who have deep respect for all life, are opposed to capital punishment. Other means can be used to deal with the criminal. For example, if a person commits an intentional murder that is not in self-defense, that person could be confined in prison for life to protect society.

All prisoners, regardless of the crime, should be required to work for their room, board, and services received. They should be helped to change behaviors, understand their personal psychic qualities, and reform, or to make a life for themselves inside the walls if they can not be released. They can learn to find satisfactions an ways to contribute to society. The prison environment and living conditions should not be based upon the person's wealth and outside influences but upon other factors that best meet the needs of all concerned.

Change laws and practices concerning justice to foster equity and improve societal conditions. Efforts to improve laws and enforce them are to be applauded; but when police become unnecessarily violent, cruel and unfair, they are fostering retaliatory violence rather than discouraging, controlling or repressing violence. Many more improvements are needed including reducing: fraud, dishonesty, bribery, delays in law enforcement, and inequities in the judiciary system.

However, *violence* can only be substantially reduced by promoting greater equity in all aspects of society and giving greater attention to meeting human needs.

Evidence substantially supports the thesis that major types of civil violence and disturbances "...flow from the well-springs of unsolved social problems." This was the conclusion of Monica Blumenthal and colleagues (1972). From their studies three Presidential Commissions were appointed to study civil unrest and violence. They wrote regarding the Commissions findings:

> The Commission on Civil Disorders Report describes pervasive racial discrimination and segregation, in employment, education and housing...it depicts urban centers as ghettos where segregation and poverty converge to **destroy** the opportunity of the young. The Commission report cities the **frustrated hopes** and unfulfilled expectations of Black Americans, their **political powerlessness**, and an ambient climate of approval and **encouragement of** violence as the bases of the ghetto disturbances. (pp.5,6).

Participate in International Cooperation and Action

(This sub-section was written by R. Carroll Cannon)

We all share this tormented earth, and harm done inany part of it will exact a heavy toll from all of us.

-President Robert Magabe of Zimbabwe

President Magabe spoke these words in a meeting of "The Nonaligned Nations" in which they were urging the United Nations to declare a decade for peace and international law; and to promote law as a means of solving international problems including third-world poverty and global pollution.

In the 20th century there has been an acceleration in the development of international laws and agreements designed to foster the security and well-being of all human beings. In the latter part of the century this process is being applied in maintaining the health of the planet and all forms of life it sustains. The development enables local, regional, national and international governments to increase the human capacity to achieve the process of sustained development while preserving life. Hence, we are witnessing continued development of global cooperation in the establishment of international laws and agreements in economics, environment, security and conservation.

The United Nations Charter was ratified in 1945 by the United States Congress, signed by the President, and thus we are bound by this international agreement, as law.

Note The Preamble of the United Nations Charter:

•We the peoples of the United Nations determined to save succeeding generations from the scourge of war, which twice in our lifetime has brought untold sorrow to mankind, and

•To reaffirm faith in fundamental human rights, in the dignity and worth of the human person, in the equal rights of men and women and of nations large and small, and

•To establish conditions under which justice and respect for the obligations arising from treaties and *other sources* of international law can be maintained, and to promote *social* progress and better standards of life in larger freedoms, and

For these ends

•To practice *tolerance and* live together *in peace* with one another as good neighbors and

•To unite our strength to maintain international peace and

security, and

- To ensure, by the acceptance of principles and institution of methods that armed force shall not be used, save in the common interest, and
- To employ international machinery for the promotion of the economic and social advancement of all people.

Additional fundamental human rights and guiding principles were more fully detailed in the body of the Charter, in the United Nations Universal Declaration of Human Rights, in alter conventions and in Charter amendments.

Nation States have elected to use the structure and processes of the General Assembly of the United Nations (UN) to respond to the growing challenge for security and peace. The 185 nation states belonging to the UN participate in the Assembly. In 1947 the nation states acting through the General Assembly established the International Law Commission that now meets annually in Geneva

By 1985 there were sixteen international agencies in working agreements with the UN. Some o the concerns of the agencies are: atomic energy, food and agriculture, educational and scientific cooperation, world health, and children.

The International Court of Justice (ICJ) was established to succeed the Permanent Court of Justice of the *League* of *Nations*. Nation states may take their disagreements to ICJ for settlement. By 1985 the Court had given 43 judgements on contentious cases and handed down 18 advisory opinions.

Recent incidents of *massive* crime, for example in former Yugoslavia, have stimulated serious discussion on the international level for creating an International Criminal *Court*. Prospects of success are increasing.

The UN has served *and is serving* as a vital vehicle whereby Member States cooperate in drawing international agreements and establishing international law.

No doubt the highest goals ever set for achievement in the welfare of human beings took place in December 10, 1948 when the General Assembly adopted the Universal Declaration of *Human* Rights by a roll call of 48 in favor to none against, with 8 abstentions.

The Assembly declared the Declaration as "a common standard of achievement for all peoples and all nations." In 1996 the Assembly adopted two major Conventions negotiated by the Commission on Human Rights. One dealt with civil and Political rights and the other will economic, social and cultural rights. These have been ratified by the majority of the members of the United Nations.

More than 20 *Conventions* and 17 Declarations have been negotiated for the purpose of achieving security for all peoples.

It is clear that tremendous progress has been made in the development of international agreement and law. A major weakness has been, and continues to be, the failure of nation states to develop and implement educational programs designed to promote among citizens and understanding of the UN its documents, programs, activities, laws, and contributions to human well being throughout the world.

Certainly, the above mentioned the documents were not first to set forth some of these high ideals. I have learned from an article by J. Dennis Blover in the *Christian Science Monitor* of September 17, 1987, that some of the U.S. Constitution was copied from the Six -Nation Iroquois Confederation Agreement which began with these words: "We the people, to form a union, to establish peace, equity and order..." Glover called this the "Oldest United Nations in the world." They were a thousand years at peace with each other. Two important principles of this document were that , "Leaders were to be the servants of the people, not rulers." And "Women had the right to participate in government equally with men." Equity was a key word.

International laws are needed to prevent injustices, protect smaller countries, and foster the common good- the foundation essential for individual good! Internationally agreed-upon laws could prevent such actions as a country sending armed forces and/or arms and support to overthrow another government. Such actions are unjust, **cruel**, criminal, and should not be allowed to continue. Therefore, **we should strengthen, support, and improve the Untied Nations**.

Former President John F. Kennedy had the right idea when he wrote:

> We seek to strengthen the United Nations, to help solve its financial problems, to make it a more effective instrument for peace, to develop it into a genuine world security system...capable of resolving disputes on the basis of law, of insuring the security of the large and the small and of creating conditions under which arms *can finally* be abolished...This will require a new effort to achieve world law.

Work Toward a More Perfect Government

Ordinarily it can be said that: it dictatorial governments, people are used as servants of the dictators; in a republic -type state, elected officials often serve best those who are most influential in getting them elecated; in a true democracy, government is by and for all people's well-being. If we believe that democracy of is the best government and want to make it that way, we must work to make sure that we as citizens are informed and have -self other qualities.

We, in the Untied States, have been fortunate in being able to make changes on our government. Respect for the dignity and worth of the person and the provision for numerous freedoms have made it possible for us to move about in many self-motivated constructive ways. The democracy as set up in the Constitution by our founding fathers was a great step forward,. I contend, however, that this democracy is yet unfinished and that people should work to participate more fully or be in danger of losing those precious freedoms. Citizens can have tremendous power and constructive influence if we are responsible and prepared. We must be vigilant in maintaining and/or reforming our democracy to meet the needs of all people and prevent laws and governmental policies that are inequitable and harmful to the common good.

The U.S. Declaration of Independence proclaimed:

> We hold these truths to be self-evident; that all men are created equal; that they are endowed by their Creator with certain unalienable rights; that among these are, life liberty and the pursuit of happiness; that so secure these rights, governments are instituted among men, deriving their just powers from the consent of the governed; that whenever any form of government becomes destructive of these ends, it is the right of the people to later or abolish it, and to institute new government, laying its foundation on such principles.

It is then, our responsibility to monitor our government and reform or change when necessary to guarantee that it is serving the needs of all the people, not the desires of a few.

We, in the U.S., are told almost from birth that our founding father dreamed of a government by and for the people which would provide for justice tranquillity, common defense, general welfare, protection, equality and the blessings of liberty. We were told that they then framed these dreams into a constitution. Overwhelming evidence indicates that "the people" they had in mind were the wealthy privileged class, not the people as a whole. Protection was primarily of property and position; equality was for the few, while slaves, women, Native Americans, indentured servants, and non-landowners were not included at all; and democracy for all people was openly rejected by most of the framers of the Constitution. Jerry Fresia (1988) cities documents and considerable evidence which substantiates these claims.

On the other hand, many of our forefathers and foremothers of the less privileged classes struggled for democracy and against the ratification of the Constitution because of its lack of provision for full democracy and for the opportunities it allowed for the wealthy to exploit the poor. Even if the Constitution was a step backward from the Articles of Confederation, as Fresia seemed to think, it left open areas within which people could, and still can, work for fuller democracy. The United States has more potential for constructive change than many other countries.

We have the freedom to speak out and to act in accordance with our conscience. We have the resources; and we have people who can be constructive. We can make changes in unjust economic and social practices which have resulted from the unfinished democracy, as well as making those changes needed in the Constitution itself.

There are avenues through which democracy has grown and can grow. Amendments have been added to secure human rights, to emancipate slaves, and to give women a vote. Other needed changes can be made, if the people want them and will put forth the needed effort. Full democracy is a tremendously worthy dream. It has been espoused by philosophers, sages, and peace *activists*. Courageous people have brought us rather along the road. For *example*, Mahatma Gandhi, who visualized a nonviolent approach to solving *conflicts* and *achieving* independence for India, and Martin Luther King who had a *dream* for *equity* and brought Afro-Americans closer to this reality. Many *less* prominent people have implemented democracy in their own worlds. Such endeavors as the United Nations Charter, the Universal Declaration of *Human Rights*, the Convention on the Elimination of All Forms of *Discrimination Against* Women, the *day-to-day* work of the various UN Organizations, women's *organizations*, and environmental groups have all helped to facilitate *important* steps toward greater democracy.

In the 1994 elections in the United States, barely one-third of the citizens voted. In *today's* changing uncertain world there are heavy work obligations pressures from many directions - economic, social, political, family and opportunities of many types. Hence, it is easy to see how difficult it is for everyone to become informed and accept citizenship responsibilities. Many people work very hard long hours at very *low* wages. They have neither the time nor the energy to study issues involved in governance. Many times they do not have enough education to pursue the needed study. We need reforms to provide more widespread better education and higher wages. It is our role with freedom and responsibility to make these changes,. In a democracy, this is our task. *We* can enlarge our participation even though our voting is by representation. *If* we expect government to serve us, we must serve it. Government can be by and for the people or it will be by and for the few. The few are these with power, influence, and /or wealth. if we expect government to secure the rights of everyone, everyone must take responsibility. For example, we could make it possible to vote for "none o the above" when we do not approve of any of the candidates, and then require that they get over fifty percent of the votes of those voting. We could also change the present reality that "only the rich need try to run for public office." We can urge our representatives and we can promote initiatives. These kinds of obligations must be accepted if we can have the continued *right to freedom*. This fact is truer than it was when Carl Becker (1949) told us, in 1944, that if we preserve our freedoms we must give

> ...more serious attention to public affairs than we have hitherto been willing or found it necessary to give to them... it is necessary for us to insist somewhat less stubbornly upon our individual freedoms, and to recognize somewhat less grudgingly our communal responsibilities (p.21).

Efforts to promote the well-being through government is seen in the following example:" John Vasconcellos (1989), California Legislator, wrote "In its essence, after all, politics properly understood is nothing more than the making of *policy* for all of us together, the sum of our individual beings" (p.xv). He was concerned about billions being spent on prisons and on programs for containment of crime and *violence, alcoholism,* drug abuse teenage pregnancy, child abuse, and welfare dependency; educational needs not being met; and almost no attention being given to prevention or cure of problems, only condemnation and punishment.

He believed that low self-esteem was a central factor is most social problems. It seemed, therefore, *both* morally and fiscally responsible to create a formalized governmental *effort* to explore whether in fact self-esteem might be a "*social* vaccine." He believed that the quality of self-esteem was capable of strengthening people and *making* them less vulnerable to problem behavior. *Hence*, he set about to propose, and got passed,

Assembly Bill 3659 which directed the establishment of "California Task Force to Promote Self-Esteem and Personal and Social Responsibility" and directed it (a) to compile research concerning the role of self-esteem as a possible factor in the above major social concerns, (b) to compile current knowledge about how healthy self-esteem is developed, how it is damaged or lost and how it can be revitalized, and (c) to identify and model self-esteem programs, including institutions to which people can turn when they need help for themselves or their families. These kinds of efforts to discover ways to solve underlying human problems should be pursued more extensively by government officials and by the public.

We must control our government or our government will control us. Injustices will be done if people do not cooperatively act for the good of everyone and keep their governments under their control. According to Amnesty International more governments than not engage in human rights violations. In July of 1990 the London-based Amnesty issued a 300-page report summarizing human rights violations in 1989 in 138 countries. Lucia Mouat (1990) reports, "It is a story of real-life violence that makes the action-packed summer movies look mild by comparison" (p.7).

John Healey, Amnesty International, U.S. director, told Mouat that much of the human rights abuses perpetrated by governments are against political protesters, ethnic, or racial groups - "the powerful against the powerless." He gave examples: China's *human* rights behavior against protesters; attacks of Indians in Guatemala *and* Brazil; Turkey and Iraq against the Kurds; unarmed Palestinian civilians short dead by Israeli forces in the Occupied Territories and U.S. death penalty policy more often imposed upon Afro-Americans than on Caucasians (paraphrased from p.7).

Ross Stagner (1967) pointed out (p.58) that most countries have a history of violence. Justifiable or not, in our short history, 30 years have been spent in war. We have been involved in at least nine major wars, one of the most bloody of all wars (Civil War) was with each other. The United states is not unique in regard to its violent past, many countries have similar histories we should, with humility, evaluate our own institutions and think of the reforms might be appropriate for improving our situation.

Being called a democracy does not guarantee the welfare of the people Citizens participation in government is more important than being considered a democracy. Under present conditions, there is always a danger in any country that special power groups can influence the masses enough to deprive them of their freedom. There are presently many efforts in that direction perhaps in all countries. Therefore it is very important that people be in control. If we lose our modest control, it could be most difficult to regain.

To strengthen our democracy, secure our freedoms, and willingly accept our responsibilities, we must work on the Persia family levels. As Carl L. Becker (1949) said: **The preservation of our freedom depends less upon the precise nature of our constitaons and laws than it does upon the character of the people.**

If we agree with this statement, we should urge governmental policies that endorse and promote FLEP (Family Life Education for Peace). This is urgent because FLEP can promote competence in creating loving families and parenting that foster peace - promoting characters, we can start our efforts for better democracy by encouraging families to begin democracy in the family and in the schools.

Since child-rearing is primarily relegated to women, it is seen as being relatively unimportant compared with those things which men usually do that are seen as the major affairs of the world. Personality changes in people are often seen as impossible and/ or impractical; dictators and power-hungry people would even find these changes undesirable; and both changes in people and in child rearing practices are seen as unrealistic approaches to peace. Conversely they are the most realistic and most important of all approaches to fostering peace. Thus, government policies should reflect these need. Government officials and policies should recognize that peace can never be possible unless people *move* out of their greedy approaches and raise their children to become *loving*, caring adults.

Secondary roots of political fraud are in the economic system, the roots of inequitable economies are in self-only or misled people. Deep-seated greed develops along with other psychic qualities as result of harmful experiences and unmet needs in the early years of life (discussed earlier). Such greed is deep within the human psyche—part of an insecure person's syndrome of qualities such as fear, hostility, dominant/submissive urges, and violent tendencies. A less deep-seated greed can also be caused or encouraged by inadequate government.

This cycle was brought to my mind when I was on a ship in a Norway ford. An English woman remarked that she would be afraid to live in the United States. When I asked why, she replied, "Because you have no stable healthcare system, pension plan, equitable taxing *and income* systems, and other security guarantees."

Freedom and participatory democracy can not develop in a society where greedy exploitative people are in control. Also international or even local cooperation can not thrive in the presence of hierarchies, triarch prejudices, cultural superstitions and harmful mores.

I am optimistic enough to believe that humanity is very slowly moving in the direction for self-otherness and peace. One problem is that the movement toward dominance and violence is so very strong that we may not move fast enough toward self-otherness to save our world from environmental devastation and /or corrupt degeneration. We are, I think, coming very close to the point of no return. Changes in ourselves and in our child-rearing practices is not the only primary work to be done, but I fear that without them all is lost.

We can demand that governments provide opportunities, conditions, laws, and policies that promote the well-being of all people and the resolution for crises, through participation and advocacy.

There are many ways of advocating for peace. Esther

Peterson, an 88 year "young" active advocate has, not only served in government by working for three presidents and Eleanor Roosevelt, but as a citizen in many capacities as well.

Vicki Kemper (1995) shares many of the beliefs which Peterson has activated that serve as guidelines for taking responsible action:

- "...one person can make a difference and, even more important, that people working together can do anything."
- Individuals need to take responsibility for the decisions they make.
- Activists should have "a great feeling of empathy" for what others are going through and put themselves in their situation.
- All people should know that they are important and be taught that they should stand up for themselves.
- People should understand that poverty of one group feeds the wealth of another group and likewise, that excessive wealth of one group causes poverty for another group.
- An effort should be made to get people to work together; to "...tear down fences between people"; avoid "..antagonistic us–against–them' attitude..."; "...find a common denomiantor"–and agree upon compromise that is to the benefit of everyone.

Many people have been activated by Peterson's "deep-seated love for life" and a core conviction that if you believe in the work you are doing. "you can do so many things!" Her attitudes and actions provide a model for working together as individuals and groups to change political systems and create a less violent more peaceful world.

(Excerpts from Kemper's article in *Common Cause Magazine*, Spring 1995).

Chapter-6

The Economy: Crisis of Inequality

Chapter-6

The economy of a democracy is grounded on the political proposition that people have collcctive responsibility for one another.
-Marcus G. Raskin (1986)

Economic Systems

The theoretical purpose of an economy is to make possible an opportunity for people to provide for their material needs. An economy is the structure or system of forces of production, distribution, and consumption of goods and services (including information systems) in a country or area. It is a way for people to organize property, capital, labor, intellectual abilities, and the necessary technology to meet their needs. We are all a part of an economy because we all produce, distribute and/or consume both goods and services.

Economies, and theories about them, differ in a number of ways including: who controls them; the extent of equality and equity intrinsic to the system: the quality and quantity of life-sustaining systems such as health and old-age securities; the **extent** of harmful competitiveness deemed necessary; the type of status **awarded for** various behaviours and material acquisitions; the care taken to protect **and revitalize** the environment; the ways in which they respect or fail to **respect** human rights and meet physical needs; and the kinds of cooperative or imperialistic economic relations among countries.

Crisis with Hope

The present worldwide economic crisis is very complex. While this crisis could be considered to be many crises, this chapter approaches it as multiple elements of one crisis. Harmful policies conditions, laws, various inequities, and predatory practices are perhaps chief among the many components of this economic crisis.

Several of these harmful elements and some possible reforms are examined in this chapter. Among foundational catalysts basic to coping with this crisis and making needed economic changes are the following five vital qualities: **equity, cooperation, governmental responsibility, democratic controls, and self-otherness**.

Economic equity is a necessity for people to live in peace anywhere. It is given special emphasis later in this chapter.

As stressed throughout this book, *self-otherness* is most crucial to making constructive change in any area and building peace. **Self-other qualities in people is a necessity for an economy to be equitable**. As explained in Chapter Five, self-otherness means developing the self (e.g., growing self-esteem, knowledge, skills, autonomy, and freedom) and simultaneously becoming responsible and caring toward individuals, family, and society. It includes personal qualities such as: ability to love, honesty, empathy, caring and a willingness to contribute to the common good. If people do not have such qualities they may exploit others for their own gain.

Amending economic practices is an enormous endeavor which one person can not do alone. Therefore, **cooperation** is a vital part of the process of resolving the economic crisis. If present generations succeed in making needed changes, it will be done by cooperative, capable, willing, self-other people.

In Chapter Five, suggestions are made to enhance, strengthen, and extend our **democracy**. Fundamentally, people should have control of an economic system, Whatever developments or reforms are made they should be empowered through the democratic process. Government must be responsible to "promote the general welfare."

Interdependence is a reality and should be recognized and respected to make cooperation and democracy possible. All people have a number of basic needs. Some of these needs are necessary for physical survival and many others are important for general well-being. Most homo sapiens throughout time have had to struggle to meet these basic needs. They have succeeded because they have cooperated and contributed to the meeting of each other's needs. Millions of people from present and past generations have added to the world's knowledge, skills, and resources. All of us who live today have received much. We should give of our own efforts to the well-being of this and future generations. Just as every snowflake in a show scene can be thanked for its beauty and every flake in an availanche can be blamed for the disaster; so it is with us-most of our acts are small but they are significant. People of the world are so interrelated and interdependent that whatever affects one, more or less, affects all. Therefore, it is vital that we all harmonize our own needs for independence with our responsibilities and services to other (i.e., self-otherness) to effectively cooperate and attain full democracy. I am convinced that the greatest satisfaction cam come as a by-product of working for the good of all not just for our own greedy desires.

Individuals, families, society, and nations could live in relative peacc if these forces were guiding principles and they would:

- provide opportunities for their people have honest work with equitable adequate compensation to acquire their basic needs;
- cooperatively support high quality education, basic health care, primary security for retirement, competent loving child care, and any other needs that are usually most difficult for individuals to finance alone;
- maintain population. environmental balance with sustainable resources;
- enforce maximum levels of income and limits on possession of wealth; and
- together provide their communities with recreation, the fine arts, and education.

A few countries seem very close to this equitable condition (e.g., the Scandinavian countries). On the other hand many countries (including the U.S.) are in economic crisis. Economic inequality and inequity causes such things as poverty, starvation, homelessness, discrimination, and worker exploitation that are widespread.

In spite of problems, challenges, and gloomy features, they may be reason to hope that a better economic future is developing. More people seem to be recognizing the need for great equity in economic affairs. Some of the things that can be done to continue a movement toward equity will now be discussed.

Advance Economic Equity, Prevent Injustice

It is recognized by many thoughtful people throughout the world that economic systems should be transformed. It is basic to promoting equity and peace and resolving degrading human practices. To this, we the people should make a thorough reassessment of the economy. Alvin Toffler (1984) comfortably, there are no perfect economies for models. I shall not attempt to propose one.

However, I think most of us are aware of harmful economic policies and attitudes that have produced numerous destructive conditions. Moment by moment these destructive conditions are causing pain, suffering, and death. We also know changes that could be made to better meet human needs. Therefore, it is urgent that people in all parts of the world and in all walks of life participate, if possible without politics, in studying and discussing long range and short term economic reforms. As with other issues being examined in this book, we should not be dogmatic. But each of us, seeing conditions from different perspectives, can put our ideas together and discuss them interrelated ways. A quantum leap forward in the field of economic thought and action will be required to meet people's urgent needs and resolve the world's economic crisis.

Economic equity is a fundamental vital guiding principle. It can guide people in making reforms. If humanity is ever to live together in reasonable peace, we must live in greater equity than we are now doing. When examining every aspect of the economy, we should ask: "Is this policy, condition, or approach equitable - is it fair to everyone concerned?"

It is not complete equality (or sameness) that we need, can have or most of us want. Differences in people's conditions, solutions to problems and personalities are necessary and desirable and so are their needs. This does not mean that we should ignore pervasive inequalities that produce indirect and direct violence in the world. In a large complex society, even under the best circumstances, it is unrealistic to expect that there will be perfect equity, and certainly not complete equality of income and wealth Absolute equality would be impossible to determine,

However, in many countries of the world a large part of the population does not have the opportunity to provide for their crucial economic needs while small segments live in excessive luxury. Where this tremendous economic disparity exists it is not jut inequitable, it is nothing less than cruel unjustifiable heartless indirect violence. This cruelty also engenders potentials for direct violent retribution from those who have been unfairly exploited. As I have written several times in this book: the victims often become villains. There is then much suffering, unhappiness, and despair. Mahatma Gandhi said, "Poverty is the worst form of violence" (as quoted by Jeanne Larson and Madge Micheels - Cyrus (1986), p.127).

Prohibit "Trickle-Down Economies"

> **Some economic systems provide socialism**
> **For the rich and capitalism for the poor.**
>
> —Anonymous

The theory that the wealth going to the rich benefits everyone has been applauded, not only by the wealthy, but also by a large segment of the lower income population. This is what President Reagan called "supply-side" economics. Prior to that time it was labeled, "trickle-down economics". When George Bush was running in the primary elections against Reagan, he called it "Voodoo economics". This policy has made, and is making, the rich richer and the poor poorer. "Trickle-down economics" extends the gap between the rich and poorer peoples. Wealth given to the rich does not "trickle down." *Mink Coats Don't Trickle Down*, asserted Randy Albelda, Elaine McCrate, Edwin Melendez,

June Lapidus, and The Center for Popular Economics (1988).

Through the great power of their wealth and influcnce, people who own the large corporations control the media, bribe legislators and determine whom and how people can run for political office. With their financial power over the media, these same corporations propaganda has won much of the public over to their theories. They have expanded to dominate sub-entities of the U.S. economic system. This is highly inequitable and violence promoting.

Economic theories and structures have been constructed to create and maintain the inequity, and the wealthy have spent part of their wealth on processes that convince large masses of people that the system is just. For example tax breaks for the rich are called "growth incentives"; unfair international trade practices are spoken of as "protecting our interests"; taxes on th lower classes are called "revenue enhancement." Such deceptions are violence against the unwary and the poorest of the poor who do not have the strength, time, or courage to protest.

The economy was already in rather rough seas when Ronal Reagan came to power in 1980. He persuaded the American public that nothing was needed except to accentuate the glories of the "supply-side" economic system; to keep government controls out of the unrestrained, unregulated economy; place emphasis upon the build-up of the military-industrial complex; and to meant tremendous government subsidies, the prevalence of rations and fraudulent activities, government-guaranteed loans to these corporate enterprises, tremendous increases in government debt, little or no taxes for the rich, prosperous rewards for the speculators, cuts in social programs, a growing poverty-stricken lower class, enlarged numbers of homeless, a wider gap between the rich and the poor in both income and wealth, and degradation to every corner of the environment. "Profit, the bottom line, became the top value" and many people are now suffering the consequences.

Certain aspects of the program looked great. A nation, as well as an individual cal look good and live luxuriously for a time on credit, greed, graft, and fraud, but a day of reckoning usually arrives and someone has to pay. The result is that the middle class and the poor pay for the tremendous national debt, for the "Savings & Loan mess." For malpractices such as the "Housing and Urban Development debauchery." and for the effects of collusion between political corruption and financial greed. These policies have created what Sidney Lens (1975) called "corporate socialism" (p.19).

An editor of *The Nation* (1990, May 7) spoke of the Reagan years as having a "rotten core...beneath the triumphal façade of freedom, prosperity and power." We have not yet been informed of the exact damages of this example of an *out-of control economy*. It was a though the Government had an unlimited line of credit that would never have to be repid. This is certainly an example of a debacle that originated in some people's self-only oriented psyches. This editor of *The Nation said further*:

> The Reagan Administration made the "magic of the marketplace" the national religion, and deregulation was its daily ritual. Every hindrance to corporate freedom came under fire: environmental controls, labor organizations, health and safety guidelines, welfare benefits, trade restrictions and, not least of all, financial oversight. Banks, including the "thrifts," were not only let loose to engage in any activity they fancied, the practice of strict examination and auditing that had begun during the Great Depression was all but abandoned. The unsupervised banks thus became a prime source for the credit that fueled the "Reagan boom" of the 1980s. Much of the growth was speculative and confined to reat estate deals of dubious merit and exotic financial transactions, such as mergers and leveraged buy-outs, which created more debt, which the banks then refinanced, and infinitum. The snake grew by feeding on its tail (pp. 619,620).

Although these are perhaps the largest of this type of greedy manipulation of the economy, they are not only type. It is obvious that more regulations on many segments of business are greatly needed. Michael Parenti (1986) says,

The capitalist class, that tiny portion of the population that lives securely and affluently principally off the labor of others, has a commanding say in how and for whom the wealth of the nation is produced. The imperatives of the private market determine the kinds of jobs that are (or are not) available: the wages we earn; the prices, rents, and mortgages we pay; the quality of the goods and services we get; and even the quality of the air we breathe, the food we eat, and the water we drink (p.1).

It certainly is true that, for the most part, corporations have one purpose only and that is to make all the profits possible - "the bottom line," Parenti asserted that to the extent that "Private profitability rather than social need is the determining condition of capital investment" to that extent it is a hazard to human welfare (p.2).

According to *The Washington Spectator* (1995), Volume 21, No.10, page 3, there is a growing concentration of wealth in America among a privileged few—the top 1 percent holding 40 percent if it, while the bottom 20 percent earn barely 6 percent of all after-tax income.

In that same issue the editor quoted from the front page of the *New York Times* (1995, April 17). That the high -income top 20 percent of American (U.S.) households own more than 80% of the nations wealth and receives 55 percent of all after-tax incomes, shares larger than in any other democratic nations (p.4).

If this type power is violence toward people as a whole, and if people also hold the real power, then why do they not choose to exercise that power, especially in this country where they could do it nonviolently? Part of that answer is short—they are misinformed and unaware. Another part of the answer is that many poor people also aspire to wealth and position and see possibilities within the systems as it is. A more complex part of the answer is that the tyranny of that ruling power group is not often seen as tyranny because of their subtlety, and their ability to, as Parenti wrote "...so insinuate themselves into the imagery of our consciousness and the fabric of our lives as not to be perceived as tyranny" (p.7). In addition some people are greedy and self-only oriented.

The middle class has continued to slip downward into the poorer classes. It has became more difficult for a blue-collar worker to make an adequate income. After the Democrats were elected in 1992, they could not or did not make immediate reforms and were swept out of control in Congress in 1994 and the Republicans came in with what they called "A Contract with America." They began implementing what some are calling "The New Harshness." In this Contract they are trying to cut nearly all programs that were established to help children, disabled, aged, sick, and abused women. They denied reforms in the health/medical system that could have provided care for everyone, as is done on other industrialized countries.

At the same time there is no lack of funds to subsidize the tobacco companies because those industries provide congressmen with funds for reelection even though they may cause the death of many people.

The minimum wage is not raised to a living wage nor is the present low wage even enforced. They seem to be trying to push the country back to the level of deprivation of 150 years ago. Hence, one of the greatest potentials for indirect violence is government, corporate, and media collusion.

In 1963 President John F. Kennedy said, "Those who make peaceful change impossible, make violent revolution inevitable." However, aware citizens can use their nonviolent power to reform both government and the economy and bring more equity. If people do not succeed in reversing present economic tides, bloody revolution may result.

Provide Employment

People live long assumed that, except for the young, the old, and the disabled, people must work to live. But today, throughout the world, there is a crisis of unemployment. Millions are faced with a lack of opportunity to work for living wages. Richard Barnet (1993) recognized this when he concluded that:

The global job crisis is so profound and its interrelated causes are so little understood that the best of the currently fashionable strategies for creating jobs just nibble at the problem; others are likely to make it worse (as stated in the Institute for Policy Studies (IPS) *Quarterly Report*, Winter 1994, p.1).

Practices that make the situation worse include: "incentive packages" to wealthy corporations (e.g., giving taxpayers' money to corporations to create jobs which may never come through as such); corporate practices that more factories from industrialized countries to countries where they get labourers al almost slave wages; and flooding the market with goods "far in excess of what people want or the planet can afford" (Barnet, p.6).

Barnet's suggestions include: shortening the work-week, thus creating more jobs; hiring workers in jobs for which government is responsible; confronting the international dimensions of the problem with global cooperation and coordination; and providing small capital loans for poor people to start businesses such as the *Grameen Bank* provides in Bangladesh. *The United Nations Development Fund for Women* (UNIFEM), and the private *Trickle Up Program* are also of this type. Barnet also wrote:

> There is a colossal amount of work waiting to be done by human beings - building decent places t live exploring the universe, making cities less dangerous, teaching one another, raising our children, visiting comforting, healing, feeding one another, dancing, making music, telling stories, inventing things, and governing ourselves. But much of the essential activity people have always undertaken to raise and educate their families, to enjoy themselves, to give pleasure to others, and advance the general welfare is not packaged as jobs...We have yet to summon the courage and imagination to face the human assault on human beings that we call the "job problem" (p.6).

In the long run, the unemployment component part of the economic crisis can not be resolved without a sharp curb in the swift growth of population. The Planet can not sustain an unlimited number of people.

Greater equality among wages, salaries, and profits is necessary to reduce unemployment. Equity, and perhaps survival, demands limitations on the amount of Earth's resources one person is allowed to possess. Controls could provide for more employment and higher wages. The present system requires unemployment to keep wages low and wage-competition high. Therefore, there must be controls to accomplish any reforms in the economy. Some of these controls are discussed in the following chapter.

Employers argue that they can not afford to run their businesses if they pay more than the present minimum wage ($4.25 an hour). If they can not, this may mean that their businesses are not viable in the economy (i.e., their products or services are not needed by the public), or they are taking more income for themselves than is justifiable by the share of the work they have contributed to the businesses. I agree with those who think that employers and employees should share equally the profits from their enterprise. The entrepreneur also deserves a reasonable interest on his/her investment; but no one deserves the inordinate amounts often received. The argument that some jobs are so menial and unskilled that they deserve very little pay is almost as inhumane as slavery itself. Much of such :menial" work is most difficult and deserves full rewards and much more respect than it now receives.

"The Poor [should not] Pay More"

The poor pay more than the rich, not only in the ways David Caplovitz (1967) discusses in how now classic book, *The Poor Pay More*, but also in many other ways. They not only pay more for what they get, they also get less income and have fewer advantages. On the whole, poor people are exploited both as workers and as consumers.

In the years following Caplovitz's writing, many consumer protection efforts have been made and various legislative measures have been passed, but because of powerful business and industrial forces aligned against the public, real progress has been spotty and not very effective in bringing about real equity.

It is also important to remember that many forces give special privileges to the rich and handicaps to the poor. Some examples are:

1. Higher interest rates are charged on small loans that low-income people get than on large loans taken out by business, industry and the rich.

2. The discrepancy in the amount of interest paid to small savers as compared to loans made by large investors, gives low incentives for poor people to try to save.

3. The policy of food and clothing stores charging more in low-income sections of the cities and shifting low-quality merchandise to these areas is a continued practice. Some efforts have been made to stop practices, but without complete success.

4. Because most low-income families live with numerous handicaps and lack educational , social, and occupational opportunities, they and their children have greater difficulty gaining the self-respect, knowledge, and skills needed for success.

5. Inequities of various kinds engendered by the powerful over the weak- the rich over the poor- cause feelings of pain, misery, inadequacy, jealousy, hostility, and can cause violence and war. When this results, exploiters become even more harsh, unfeeling, and uncaring toward the exploited and are more willing to defend their position, power, and wealth with any means available.

6. The poor are hit hardest by taxes and the "schemes, shams, scams, and strategies" of the exploiters.

7. In the United States, the poorest people can not afford health insurance; the middle-income groups can have it only with great difficulty; hence, only the wealthy have adequate health and medical care. Children are, of course, harmed most.

8. The very poor lack the cash to buy what they may badly

need; so they buy on credit. This causes them to pay more than if they were able to save and pay cash.

Caplovitz explains that the advent of installment credit brought a sharp rise in fraudulent and deceptive practices. He adds that,

> ...Nothing is saved for emergencies, and the hazardous result is a total commitment of future income. If that income stops through sickness, injury, or unemployment (worse still if medical bills are added to debts, the family sinks into the despair of economic disaster (p.xvii).

They often lose the items by repossession because a minor crisis can prevent them from making the payments. Exploitative schemes, bait advertising, and vicious rackets have increased and worsened since Caplovitz's study was done in the early 1960s.

Although Presidents Kennedy and Johnson set up consumer advisory bodies; and various other efforts have been made to protect consumers and bring about more equity. little of significance has changed. Caplovitz's description is still relevant" "...our interests as consumers have been submerged before the onslaught of the powerful lobbies of the business and financial communities" (p.xix).

Of the industrialized countries the gap between the rich and poor is greatest in the U.S., also the poor are the poorest. The poor are black and white, young and old. educated and uneducated, city dwellers and country folk: they are waitresses, day laborers, unemployed workers whose plants have moved to poorer countries where near slave labor is available. There are deserted middle-aged housewives, mentally deficient, mentally il, and disabled; they live in broken down ratty apartments, country shacks and on the streets: some are newly poor, pushed below the poverty line by an inequitable economy and many are becoming permanently poor as they are pushed into a straightjacket of limited opportunities. unwelcome dependency, and uncaring public policy.

In the least-industrialized countries millions are dying of hunger or are on the verge of starvation while their natural resources and often their labor are being exploited by transnational corporations from the U.S. The U.S. government and international law should disallow such exploitation.

Therefore, our plea is that we put the removal of poverty high on our national and international agendas. We recognize with regret the great injustices perpetrated upon other peoples by the U.S. and many other countries, going back to cruel slavery, colonization, inhuman treatment of native American people, to present-day unfair trade practices. We can join hand with all peoples of the earth in efforts to create world and national economies that are equitable for all.

Even though reforms are needed in all present economic systems in the world, most modern countries are far more equitable than they were during slavery or during the old feudal systems where there was no democracy, and little respect for human rights. We should be glad that most of such economies are gone. This may be evidence of human growth toward higher levels of maturity (i.e., perhaps human empathy, compassion, and awareness have grown).

Perhaps some day equity will guide all economic systems. Governments, laws, and practices can guarantee much greater equity among people in sharing the world's wealth and income. As responsible citizens, we can be aware and active in transforming abusive injustices into equitable economic practices.

In the U.S. we are fortunate that people have enough power (if they choose to use it) to allow then to prevent a totalitarian economic or military control over them. But there is nothing but the people to prevent the economically powerful from gaining total control. Neither is there anything but people to move the world toward equity. We should also be aware of the fact that there is still enough freedom for us to find avenues for making our ideas known, even though the media are primarily controlled by the richest corporate powers (I am grateful for Public Broadcasting). It is a responsibility of citizens to use this freedom before we lost it. It is not too late to make the economy equitable, democratic, non-abusive, and peace promoting.

It seems that perhaps more people are becoming aware of, and willing to exert more effort for, equity in the economy. As people become more self-other oriented and see the situation of people in the world, they are more willing to live more simply, even frugally, and help others live.

Government's Responsibilities for the Economy

Governmental policies and programs related to the economy are needed to protect. support and monitor human rights. Because our culture tends to encourage greed in income and possessions, some regulations are necessary. I am not a socialist and I do believe in individual initiative and personal marketing; but I support governments responsibilities to enforce justice and equity, and to provide certain nonprofit government programs. Some human needs that individuals can not meet alone, can best be provided cooperatively through government. Examples include: health and medical care; education; protection of the environment from contamination and from over-use of resources; and because the Earth's resources are finite, there should be limitations on the amount of resources, profit, or income one person can possess and the minimum wage that can be paid.

Laws that promote equitable ethical economic practices are essential. Most people are law-abiding. They would be kind and caring if there were no laws. Moreover, no law will adequately protect people from economic exploitation because extremely greedy people will find a way around such laws. However, laws deter some offenders; good laws are practical guidelines; supportive laws are helpful in promoting individual growth toward self-otherness; and just laws can regulate practices that are discriminatory, inequitable, and cruel.

Rights of Children, Women, and Families

Some of the questions that need to be considered by society as a whole include: What is the role of the economic sytem in the process of meeting family needs? How does the economy strengthen of weaken families? Should society accept more responsibility for the care, health and welfare of children for the sake of society as a whole and for future generations? What effect do roles assigned to women and men in relation to the economy have upon their well-being and on society? How does prejudice (e.g. racial, gender, and age) influence the economic well-being of people?

The impact of economic forces on children, women, and families is very significant in the area of human rights and in encouraging peace or causing violence. Children are most vulnerable to harmful forces in the economy. Since children are economic liabilities, not assets, poor families with children have the greatest economic difficulties. Women and children are particularly hard-hit by present conditions. This is especially true for minorities.

Children's are the world's only hope for the future, they are earth's most precious entities. Although their parents have the major responsibility for children's care, children are not possessed by them. Sometimes parents are not able to care for them, and certainly they are not all-powerful in controlling the many situation which affect their lives. Children also have their own rights and needs and society is responsible that these needs be ment and that their rights be honored.

From the economy, hunger, malnutrition, inadequate medical care, decrepit or non-existent housing, insufficient clothing and community dangers such as drugs, crime, and abuse do the most direct physical harm to children. Less obvious but often more damaging to the psychological development of children are the indirect effects of economic inequality, exploitation, deprivation, poor education. prejudice, discrimination, and the hidden effects of poverty. When parents are distressed with economic problems, feel discriminated against, overworked, or made to feel insignificant, helpless and unable to meet the needs of the family, it becomes most difficult to provide a loving, growth-promoting climate in the family.

According to a study done by Mah Jo Bane and David Ellwood (1989), "Twenty percent of all American children live below the official U.S. government poverty level." They suggest several solutions including: "...a federal tax credit for poor families, expanded medical coverage, and more government support for day care..." and raising the minimum wage. These are important, and there is much more. People can continually prompt legislators to place the well-being of children and families on top priority. There are many ways that they can do this instead of just cutting off support to them.

Prior to the 20th Century, respect for children's rights and public concern for their care, was almost non-existent. The seldom -told story of the efforts of diligent individuals and groups to establish international regulations for the protection of children, is a vital chapter in the history of the League of Nations, the International Labor Office (ILO), United Nations (UN) Relief and Rehabilitation Administration, UN Fund for Children (UNICEF), and the UN General Assembly. **The Convention on the Rights of the Child** was finally adopted by the General Assembly on November 20, 1989, and was opened for signatures and ratification on January 26, 1990. With enough ratification it came into force on September 2, 1990. One bright note is that it was approved by President Clinton in February, 1995. It has not been ratified by the U.S. Senate. As of that date 176 countries had either signed the Convention or had become States Parties to it by ratification.

This has been a long, tedious and at times, discouraging struggle. This Convention provides guiding value that can be inalienable rights when ratified by countries - it becomes law for those countries. Albert Thomas, first Director of the International Labor Office, would be pleased. He had emphatically stated: "This the exploitation of childhood which constitutes the evil the most hideous, the most unbearable to the human heart..." He insisted that "serious work in social legislation begins always with the protection of children" (P.4). Therefore, shortly after its beginning in 1919 the ILO adopted a Convention prohibiting work in industry by children under 14 years of age. Other Conventions followed.

The abolition of child labor is now ILO's top priority. Peter Sutcliffe (1995) announced that "it The ILO has launched a vigorous new offensive based on the absolutes of its human rights principles." He concludes by pronouncing this as an emergency: "Children have only one childhood. They can not wait. The best that mankind has to give must be given now" (p.5). Disturbing examples of damaging child labor reported by the ILO, in that same magazine, include:

- Many girls work as domestic servants in rich families (e.g, in Colombia they are 40% of working children).
- Thousands of children literally work as forced labor in brick kilns, rock quarries or mines.
- In Italy, tens of **thousands of children** work in the leather and shoe industries.
- In Portugal, girls have been cited working in clothing sweatshops.
- A Russian study shows that the social and economic changes there are leading to an increase in child labor.
- In Ankara, Turkey, 10,000 children are working in the streets.
- In Rio and other large cities of Brazil, at least seven million children live in the streets, abandoned to their own fates.
- Child prostitution and pornography are major **problems** throughout the world.
- The ILO's programs are helping to change these conditions and bring greater well-being to children. ILO is not opposed to all types of work for children. Certainly, some help around the house, or even a few odd jobs that do not hinder education, health or safety, can increase autonomy, encourage economic responsibility, and promote development of skills.

I agree with Maraian Wright Edelman (1995) when she wrote: "The results of the last national election (1994) were disastrous for America's children" (in a letter of CDF Supporters). These legislators have proposed cutting funds for disadvantaged children and giving tax breaks to the rich. Are they unaware or do not care that 15 million American children lived in deep poverty in 1994 and that 9 million lack health insurance?

Women make up nearly all of the increase in the poverty roles since 1970. Their number has increased so rapidly that experts are speaking of the "feminization of poverty." Barbars Ehrenreich (1983) reported that,

> In 1980 tow out of three adults who fit into the federal definition of poverty were women, and more than half the families defined as poor were maintained single women. In the mid-sixties and until the mid-seventies, the number of poor adult males actually declined, while the number of poor women heading households swelled (p.172).

Women who are the sole supporters of their children often suffer serious physical, emotional, and social pressures from economic deprivation. People who have never experienced this may find it difficult to empathize with these women. Ehrenreich wrote:

> For more and more women poverty begins with divorce. Over one out of three marriages now and in divorce and this usually means financial crisis for the woman and financial gain for the man (p.10).

Problems faced by these women are tremendous. For examples little or no child support is received from the absent fathers. Young women are often taught that they should stay at home and count on their husbands for financial support. When divorce comes, they may lack up-to-date money making skills because they have been taking care of children. home, and husband (sometimes supporting him while he gets his professional education). There fore, they are unable to get an income adequate for their needs. They are forced to move into cramped quarters and may have to go on welfare. which is humiliating and entirely inadequate. This present Congress (1995) is trying to force women with small children to work, even at minimum wage which is too low to provide a living income and with no adequate child care or health insurance. Is it ignorance one self-only qualities that fosters such cruel policies? I hope it is the former; that is easier to change.

Although divorce has been a blessing for some women who

would rather live in poverty than to continue with their abusive relationships, some reforms need to be made in regard to divorce proceedings, especially in provisions for father's child support. In some cases women have had to flee from abusive men to save the lives of children and themselves. They may then have no means of support.

As was explained in Chapter Twelve, there are positive alternatives to the battle of the sexes. On a personal level women and men need to decide carefully together how they can best arrange their lives together for mutual satisfaction in equity for both of them and their children. The economic system should make flexible work schedules available for parents. Laws should be strong enough to protect the equity for each party and couples should agree to share responsibilities for the care and well-being of their children. It is most difficult for both women and men to harmonize work and family responsibilities.

There should be leave from employment, without penalty, for women to give birth and leave for women and/or men to care for infants or young children. Educational opportunities and/or vocational training may be needed when women return to the labor force. Occupational choices should be such that fathers and mothers can share the duties of raising children.

Carl Becker (1949) wrote:

> ...what we need most is a heightened sense of individual and collective responsibility-less insistence on negative rights and the unrestrained pursuit of individual self-interest, ad more united and resolute determination to concern ourselves with the public good and to make the sacrifices that are necessary for it. This is to say that the preservation of our freedom depends less upon the precise nature of our constitutions and laws than it does upon the character of the people (p.122).

The roots of violence or peace in societal systems are secondary roots to the self-only and self-other qualities within the people who control those systems.

Corporations and various other systems within the economy

are not non-human self-operating structures. They are managed, controlled and operated by people, and the values, attitudes and behaviours of those people determine the activities of the systems. David Obst (1971) wrote:

> So long as we continue to think of corporate irresponsibility in the old way, as a matter solely of economic institutions, not of individuals who are products of a system and a society, we can expect the corporation to continue to devour the substance and spirit of America in the name of profit (p.VIII).

From families and the economic system, children often learn the insatiable desire for consumer goods, the love of power, greedy manipulation, and exploitation. High honor and status go to those who accumulate the most wealth through competition and even exploitation of others and by propagating the misconception that incessant consumption of consumer goods leads to happiness. Many people become greedy and abusive in economic affairs with their lives centered on accumulation rather than on community building and human well-being. Families have difficulty teaching them otherwise. Families rights for equity, education, and protection are frequently not respected.

Rights and Responsibilities of "Free Enterprise"

When examining various freedoms in Chapter Five. I did not mention the "**right of free private enterprise**." It was also not mentioned in the Bill of Rights. This was probably because by the time this document was passed, free enterprise was well-established and taken for granted since it was linked to the philosophy of "liberty and justice." A wide gap already existed between big land-owners and poor farm workers indentured servants, laborers (that included small children), and slaves.

This "free enterprise" was explicitly stated by French and English writers. Adam Smith (1776) wrote of it in his *Wealth of Nations*. At that time it became well known as the "Laissez faire" policy. That is, no restrictions or regulations on people's business-enterprising efforts.

From time to time in the U.S. the government has effected

changes that have prevented the worst of inequalities. Our government has often accepted its Constitutional responsibility to "...promote the general welfare." However, it has usually failed in placing restrictions on exploitative private enterprises.

Raskin speaks of the economy as political because he says, "In all modern political systems governments play the key role in setting economic arrangements" (p.142). Governments have been far less than perfect in providing the kind of conditions which are equitable for all the people; and some governments are not in control at all. In some countries governments have allowed the economy to be controlled by a few wealthy people who have exploited the masses for the economic benefit of the few. The economy is often the most powerful system in society, in many cases controlling government and in other cases creating government to its liking. Parenti noted:

> ...throughout most of the seventeenth, eighteenth, and clearly nineteenth centuries, leading...economists understood and openly stated as did John Locke in 1690 that "government was created for the protection of property"; and Adam Smith in 1776 that civil authority "is in reality instituted for the defense of the rich against the poor, or of those who have some property against those who have none at all" (p.2).

Many of the ruling rich would see the role of government in much the same way today. The "rule of law" protects their contracts, provides stability for their investments, their private property and their money values. They get financial assistance in crises, a Federal Reserve System which operates in the interest of banks and industry, and a guaranteed collateral system which shifts business risks from industry to the state. The public police and military protect them. Government provides roads and seaports; it manufactures currency which is controlled primarily by the largest banking interest; it provides a climate for investment which uses the state as a guarantee collateral system so that the burden of loss shifts from the private firm to the state; it provides through public taxation, education, fire protection, museums and various services while some of the wealthiest corporations often pay no taxes and usually receive many types of exemptions and subsidies; and it makes it possible for business to exploit, for tremendous profits, natural resources, lands, timber, and the health and medical needs of people. Government sets import quotas to benefit private concerns; and it subsidizes wealthy agro-business (e.g., tobacco, peanuts, and sugar). Again "socialism for the rich."

What corporate powers do not want is governmental interference in industries' control over labor, capital, prices, and profits. They want no responsibility for promoting equity for the "common good." They have the lobbying power to almost totally control government. These powerful industries not only control the U.S. government, they are able also to control the governments of a number of other countries governments.

Rights of Workers

Labor and trade union strength s rarely to that of employer/capitalist strength and since 1980 thc *labor movements* have become almost powerless. Capitalistic economic systems *have* assumed that managerial ability, profit-making talent, knowledge of the business world, and manipulative and exploitative abilities should be *rewarded* with wealth and material resources. This system does not even *allow for* those who labor in the production of wealth to be fairly rewarded. It seems that all of these approaches are seen by most people as reasonable and legitimate. But are they? To an increasing number of fair-minded people, this system is not only unfair, it is one of the chief causes of violence and war because entire nations as well as individuals are manipulated and made powerless.

People's live are so much in the hands of the economic system that it seems necessary for the public to gain been understanding of the economic power which controls them. *It is well* known that wealth gives power.

John Kenneth Galbraith (1983), in his book on *The Anatomy of Power*, analyzes power with reference to how and why people acquisite to power from others, how one achieves power, how those who achieve the power different from those who are subject to the power, and how the economy functions as the strongest arm of power. He speaks of

> "Conditioned power" as a primary force. One of the most amazing yet discouraging realities in the world is the ease with which economic powers can convince masses of people that economic inequities are fair and good for them and their country. Yet, the resulting poverty, lack of opportunities, poor education and many other accompanying difficulties promote violence and war. When people know the real facts they can make wise decisions based on what is good form them and people in their situation, but when the facts are clouded over, deceptions are so convincing, and people are not adept at searching out facts, they can easily be led to willingly accept a subservient position...the purposes for which power is being sought will often be extensively and thoughtfully hidden by artful misstatement (p.9).

Thus, in a major way, they control the lives of the workers. This is violence. Nobel Peace Prize recipient (1980), Adolfo Perez Esquivel (1983) stated: "No one has the right to create economy at the expense of the world's poor." But it is done,

Challenges-Opportunities of the Future

Every citizen has a challenge to help build an egalitarian economy for the future. The economic challenge is part of a momentous opportunity to change the direction of the future.

There are many alternatives to present -day inequitable economic practices which could be tried, and there are various ways to promote greater economic human well-being. Finding ways and means is not the greatest hurdle. The biggest problem is agreeing on which ways to try. Making needed peaceful reconstructions in economic systems is a tremendously difficult undertaking.

These difficult reforms need to involve the entire world. Since the world have become a neighbourhood and since economic affairs in one country affect people elsewhere, all citizens should take responsibility to cooperatively share in the reforms. Each person in cooperation with other individuals and groups, can make a difference (e.g, we can work through relevant agencies and institutions within the United Nations in order to facilitate the needed economic and ecological reforms). The European in Union seems to be an example of economic cooperative progress.

However, I agree with my friend, Ralph Ward, who has broad experiences in the field of business, that

> While, challenges and opportunities, are worldwide, we in America must start in our one country, our own state, our own city, own neighbourhood. Our tremendous infrastructure, especially our extensive means of communication places us in a unique position to lead these reforms globally (in comments concerning economic issues).

The following are among the challenges facing society. They are **difficult** but they can be rewarding opportunities. **We can be successful**.

1. *Study discuss and cooperate.* We should study all points of view of the many complex issues involved. We should engage people in discussion gather real statistics, encourage group-to-group and culture - to - culture discourse, and try to discover what is really equitable. Most of these issues are controversial and no one has all the answers. Therefore, much study, communication, research, and deliberation are needed.

2. *Transform society toward participatory economic democracy.* Such study, discussion, and cooperation at the grass-roots can lead to a democracy in which all participate and are in basic control. We can provide for this improved process of control.

In the founding of the U.S. Government a big step toward democracy was established. However, at that time slavery was legal and women were not allowed to vote. A basic principle of democracy should be that all people have a part in making decisions which are important to their lives. Employees and employers should work together on decisions on the running of a business and on the distribution of returns, Chapter Fifteen discusses the need for fostering fuller participatory democracy.

3. *Regulate income and wealth when and where needed to promote equity.* "We know that a peaceful world cannot long exist one-third rich and two-thirds hungry," said Jimmy Carter. We should place tight restrictions on the amount of income any individual or family can receive and the amount of wealth any person can own. It is not fair just, or ethical and it is violence against humanity for a relatively few to control other people's labor and Earth's resources causing millions to toil in poverty while providing luxury for the few. At present, the "American Dream" of riches for everyone who works for it is one of the biggest and cruelest of myths.

I once had firsthand experience with this type of back-breaking labor. One summer holiday season during World War II while I was teaching in a small town in northern California, I went with some women field workers of the town to work in the fields and in an apple dryer. I immediately acquired an empathy for the workers. I went to the wealthy owner and urged him to consider the feelings and needs on the workers, some of whom were from the mid-west who had lost their homes in the "Dust Bowl." His reply was that the "Japs" received no more before they were shipped out, and they did a better job. Such unfeeling cruelty is a shameful commentary on the immaturity of too many people. Government should, at least, raise the level of minimum wages.

It is important that we, as citizens, protect the poor and the middle class from the income-tax schemes that are proposed by congressmen who are being lobbied by the rich for tax reductions. The "flat tax" is one of the proposals that would abolish the policy of tax according to ability to pay. Such a policy would make the income tax inequality even worse than now and the wealth gap wider. Another proposal would change the income tax to a "consumption tax" which would tax practically all the income of lower and middle-income people because they buy consumer goods with practically all their income while the rich use only a small amount of their money on survival consumption.

Industry should not be allowed to promote strike breaking to prevent protests against working conditions. Wage, price, and profit controls can be set through citizen-government cooperation. A ethic of cooperation and sharing in ownership, production distribution, and consumption is also in order. Employers and laborers could more often share the profits and risks of business. Discrimination against women and minorities should be prohibited.

Stop unnecessary subsidies. It is also important that we stop the practice of giving away government assets to private companies, (e.g., lands, forests, and mineral rights). There should be prohibitions against monopolies, hostile takeovers, and such like.

I agree with those who recommend guaranteeing everyone enough employment/income for a simple shelter, minimum food, and medical care. This would be no more expensive than the kind of bureaucratic welfare system we now maintain. If humanitarian employment were provided with encouragement, education, and therapy when needed, the homeless, depressed, and misled people, as well as the temporarily unemployed, could be restored to dignity.

4. *Provide nonprofit banking and utilities.* Society could provide equitable banking services available for all with no treatment for any group or individual. Not-for -profit banking should be available, especially for poor people. Bob Kuttner (1982) said, "Rather than trust the market to steer capital, leaving small business and housing starved for credit, a government agency should set investment priorities." He said further that we should "get rid of tax incentives that now channel investment to unproductive activities like corporate mergers, real-estate speculation...." (p.28).

The people, through a fully democratic government should control prices of those necessities that individuals can not provide for themselves such as utilities, water, telephone, energy, railroad and transit systems, retirement insurance, and especially medical and health care. Employment should be available for everyone who can work. Although outright support (welfare) is necessary in some cases, meaningful important work (and sometimes training for work) is more profitable and satisfying for everyone concerned.

5. *Regulate financing of political campaigns.* All campaigns for political office should be open to poor people as well as to the rich. This is not possible at present. Political campaign spending should be greatly reduced by regulation. Large gifts from special interests, industry and the rich should be prohibited. Equal-time campaigning should be provided on public broadcasting and regulated with equal time on other broadcasting.

6. *Use technology to benefit life and Earth.* Technological benefits should be shared. Technological advances that have come from various sources should be directed toward making a better life for everyone as well as for business. For example: improve solar energy and use it more extensively; develop systems to eliminate as much as possible, the mindless drudgery jobs; facilitate more efficient communication networking and fact-finding processes; and protect and revitalize the environment.

The present prevailing philosophy seems to be that technology and the "marketplace" can solve all economic, and many other, problems without any change in the system's status quo. It has not closed economic gaps; it has increased them. The usual pattern is that employees are dismissed, wages remain the same, and excess profits go to owners and managers. **Workers should receive an equitable share of the earnings they help to create.**

Servan-Schreiber (1980) sees science and technology as having almost limitless possibilities in nearly all areas with potential for solving world problems such as food, health, resources, poverty, and information. But this is contingent upon cooperation and sharing of scientific information and technology. He says that it is now reasonable to invent a new society (paraphrased p. 273). Certainly almost unbelievable discoveries and break-throughs have occurred in recent years. They have changed most of what we thought about the world, but it has not done what it could or should in helping meet people's needs. There is tremendous potential for bringing abundant well-being to the world of only human qualities of self-otherness can bring equity to all.

7. *Minimize competition* Competition has become an inseparable part of life in the United States and in many other parts of the world. It has become extensively ingrained in the ideals, value systems, human relationships, and practices. Paul Wachtel (1989) says, "Competition is almost our official state religion" (p.284). (See the Index for other parts of this book that discuss competition)

8. *Provide for FLEP (Family Life Education for Peace).* Teenage child-bearing is a very serious economic problem. It is a psychological, health, and educational disorder. It needs serious consideration-not just condemnation and abandonment of young women and children. They must be cared for and educated. Throughout this book emphasis has been placed upon crucial needs for FLEP. Children need it to understand more about family/friend relationships and their own physical/sexual bodily development. Young people need it to help them relate constructively to the opposite sex, take responsibility for their sexual behavior, and understand their psychological/sexual needs. They need knowledge concerning marriage couple partnerships. and parenting practices. Adult education can also provide couple/ relationships enrichment programs. Such preventive education programs avoid injury to many lives and are also cost effective.

9. *Provide vocational and consumer education.* Educational programs and job training needs to be set up in a number of creative ways to help all groups that have had special difficulties to become self-reliant. Although inadequacies have existed in past special programs, many people have been helped by them. Consumer education should be included in all education.

According to an article in *Newsweek* (1982, April 19) the various types of help that the poor have received since the beginning of Lyndon B. Johnson's "War on Poverty," have made it possible for many to overcome problems and rise out of their poverty status. For example, the elderly poor dropped from 18% in 1966 to 13% in 1980. The drop for black males was from 17%

to 9%. Head Start is an example of humanitarian success.

Consumer education can be useful in helping people become more knowledgeable concerning nutritional needs of their families; more efficient in their purchasing practices; and more knowledgeable concerning services available to them such as the Legal Aid Society, The State Banking and Finance Department, the Small Claims Court, and the Attorney General's Office.

For a society to operate with freedom and equity, its people must be educated to respect the needs and rights of others and cooperate with them for the good of all. This means living frugally. Consider G.K. Chesterton's conclusion: "There are two ways to get enough. One is to continue to accumulate more and more. The other is to desire less" (Larson p.132).

10. *Encourage living not just having.* During most of homo sapiens existence in Earth, production has been the ultimate good and happiness was practically equated with consumption Eric From (1976) wrote: "The trinity unlimited production, absolute freedom, and unrestricted happiness formed the new religion,..." (p.2). it seems obvious to many people that this great new religion has failed. **Economic wealth does not equate with well-being and happiness**. It seems possible that more people are beginning to relinquish the vision of great economic affluence for all people. In the first place the tremendous growth in population and the presence of human greed have caused larger gaps between rich and poor with more poverty and starvation rather than an abundance for all.

Many people have learned that material prosperity does not —in and of itself—bring happiness. They recognize that happiness is a product of self-other productive living, not a goal to be sought for us own sake, especially if that means gaining maximum pleasure through economic affluence.

The most important *part* of this failure of consumer religion is the psychological effect *upon people* the whole psyche becomes bound around *psychological effect upon people. The whole psyche becomes bound around and within consumerism*. There seems to be no aspect of one's life which is not affected. Commodities purchased have become symbols of may aspects of people's lives. Social class, numerous privileges, and various forms of acceptance an rejection are on the basis of purchases and power in the economic system. A large part of one's status, and even one's ascribed worth and dignity are assessed on the basis of wealth, type of house, car. Cloths, and other possessions. There is tremendous pressure to acquire wealth. This part of what Jean-Christopher Agnew (1983) called. "...taw-dry spectacle of consumer culture" (p.75). Probably no culture today is free from the captive power of consumerism. Living in the milieu, it is most difficult, if not impossible, to live free of this elitist, manipulative system, and see clearly alternative values in living simply, yet meaningfully and providing general equity for everyone, rather than equating "having with being."

Perhaps most people need some shifts in values and ways of thinking, more enriching relationships, greater joys in learning and growing personally, more appreciation for the beautiful, more caring for the needy, more expressions of appreciation to those whom we love, greater closeness to nature, and since much of what we buy we neither need or really enjoy, let us analyze our desires more carefully. In summary, most of us need to live more and have less.

11. *Implement equitable economic global interdependence.* Along with individual interdependence and responsibility to each other, there is a crucial need for worldwide international responsibility, interdependence. cooperation, equity, and a better world economic system. Oh yes! There is a world economic system - a very unfair one. It has no central organization, no worldwide planning, or democratic participation. It is controlled by the industrialized nations, their transnational corporations (TNC), banks, and within many countries a business, political and/or military oligarchy. Together they exploit the countries and peoples and share the proceeds.

An example of this injustice is the TNC's control of many farming areas in less-developed countries. Lands, formerly maintained by native peoples for subsistence farming, are used by these corporations to grow crops for export such as coffee, bananas, cocoa, coconut, pineapple, sugar, and tea, while natives work for less than subsistence wages and hence, can not meet their own needs. We, as consumers of these products in industrialized countries, also reap benefits from poor people labors. This is far from fair trade.

Therefore, we should protect underdeveloped countries. This includes not allowing industries to exploit the weak trading positions of third-world countries, or capitalize on laborers. Many people throughout the world have only a choice of laboring long hours health-destroying work or living in appalling poverty while their corporate employers reap large profits from their work.. Such conditions may be a slightly better choice than starvation, but not much better.

We should also recognize that, in spite of the big problems, some TNCS are beginning to recognize their responsibility to care deeply for the people whereever they are, to produce that are truly needed, and not to damage the Earth and its atmosphere.

It is crucial that laborers throughout the world receive full employment with an income adequate for healthy living. If this is not accomplished, workers here in the U.S. will continue to lose jobs to Third World peoples and those peoples will benefit little or not at all. More growth is not the answer to full employment, but equity is part of the answer.

James Robertson (1989) wrote:

> Our long-term task, therefore, is to design international rules and institutions and practices that will reflect the reality of a one-world economy...and will systematically encourage enabling and conserving ways of economic life in every part of the world (p.3).

12. *Protect and revitalize Earth and its environment.* International cooperation and economic practices should include **protection of the environment and the reduction of population growth**. The public should require the restoration, maintenance, and protection of the planet's biosphere. This

cannot be done with the present rate of population growth and environmental destruction.

By whom and how land and natural resources should be owned, used, and controlled, has always been a controversial economic/political issue. A number of primitive societies have assumed that land was never to owned, but used and cared for by all. This principle applies to part of the land in the U.S. (especially the parks). On the other hand most countries have histories of violence to acquire other people's lands. The U.S. is no exception. Europeans began their stay on this beautiful land by taking it from the native peoples. They were driven into desolate places or cramped quarters; African people were captured, brought here and put into slavery; the West was taken by military force and various islands beyond our shores were made U.S. territories and so it has been throughout history. It is the present hope of many people that humanity is moving beyond these unfair cruel practices.

In Summary

Human beings have always had to rely on their own efforts to survive. Uncertainty of their success in this endeavor has provoked fears. It seems that cooperation within and among groups has always been a strong factor in gaining and maintaining physical survival on the Earth. Fear and the temptation to take advantage of others possessions have brought greed and cruelty to the fore.

Although they have not always responded constructively, people have surely known that cooperation among themselves is best for everyone. In this present era, there are many needs for survival that people can not provide for themselves individuality. They have created economies and governments that make it possible for them to combine their forces and accomplish much that they could not do alone.

Economic systems can be equitable and most of everyone's needs can be met. Presently there are enough renewable resources in the world for all living people to survive comfortably (not rich). But unless we control the population growth, resources will not be adequate. And unless we share, we destroy ourselves. As Servan -Schreiber says, "In a closed world, the battle for advantage is a battle against everyone else" (pp.273,274), Gandhi said, "There is enough for everyone's need, but not enough for everyone's greed." In his 1995 book, Reason to Believe, Mario Cuomo presents an excellent overall view of the present economic/political situation in the U.S. and shows how crucial it is for all of us to cooperate in a national community, meeting everyone's basic needs and curbing the damaging practices. I highly recommend the book.

Equity with moderate income for all could help to promote meaningful life, well-being, and peace. Inequity, with affluence for a few and poverty for many, promotes violence. If peace includes, as I have said, feelings of security trust, freedom from fears, then the necessities of life have a great deal to do with peace. When we fail to cooperate and abuse others rights, we are being greedy and destructive; and when people are deprived of their needs, they may feel inadequate, discouraged, resentful, hostile, and can easily become not only victims , but also villains.

We can leave behind our exploitation, greed, and cruelty and rise to self-otherness where we care for and share with other. We must, of course start from where we are. We can change ourselves and we can work with others. When enough people think seriously about these matters, change can be assured. There is a new economic frontier out there to challenge all of our creativity.

This chapter closes with a statement by my husband Carroll Cannon:

> Free enterprise, in order to be human, must be responsible enterprise; responsible to the principles of integrity, equity and justice. The free enterprise system, totally free, and ungoverned by the principle of justice, unleashes the forces go greed that form systems of exploitation and deprivation. However, governed by the principle of justice and balanced with commitment to the common good as well as individual

good, free enterprise ca generate motivation, foster creativity, and bring equity and human progress (in a statement to me).

Chapter-7

MILITARISM

Chapter-7

We have guided missiles and misguided men.

-Martin Luther King Jr.

Discussion in this chapter on militarism includes its primary and secondary roots, its manifestations, effects upon human development, families, governments, and resources, and some challenges to overcome militarism and move toward global peace and security.

Militarism: A Dominant/Violent Mood

It was high -pitched *militaristic mood* which Mark Twain portrayed in his "The War Prayer" at the beginning of the U.S Civil War. It resembles that mood of the 1991 Persian Gulf War. The setting and the actual events are very different, as the weaponry and their capacities for global destruction are eons apart. But the spirit of militarism, the glamour of patriotic songs and flags, the apparent surge of appetite for violence, and the almost neurotic atmosphere have the same tone. *Read this and listen*!

> It was a time of great and exalting excitement. The country was up in arms, the war was on, in every breast burned the holy fire of priotism: the drums were beating, the bands playing, the toy pistols popping, the bunched firecrackers hissing and spluttering; on every hand and far down the receding and fading spread of roofs and balconies a fluttering wilderness of flags flashed in the sun...in the churches the pastors preached devotion to flag and country, and invoked the God of Battles, beseeching His aid in our good cause in outpourings of fervid eloquence which moved every listener. In many places from the smallest child's toys, to junior's TV shows, to the male "Rambo" and models of modern weaponry; to the flag-carrying mobs, to the love affair with the "freedom

fighters" or "American heroes" of Desert Storm to the infatuation with space wars. Surly-eyed military leaders grit their teeth and plan their destructive strategy while: militaristic preachers call it a moral war; President Bush spoke of a "just" war; Saddam Hussein asked his people to pray five times daily for their "holy war"; magnets of the oil/ industrial/military complex smile and bask in their good fortunes; the many outcries of peacemakers are ignored; warnings of the wise are shunned; the innocent stand numb, feel fearful, and helpless; and the leisure-lovers ignore it all.

After the Gulf war, as the parades moved down the streets of cities and towns with their massive tanks, enormous armaments, and happy military men (and a few women) waved to the cheering crowds who displayed their flying flags, balloons, and yellow ribbons, there was no apparent recognition of the thousands of people who were killed, maimed, or left homeless in Iraq. There was no indication that there could have been a better way to resolve conflict than to draw a line in the sand, give no heed to ideas from the other side, and then **bomb! Bomb! Bomb!**

In his *Search for Sources of Violence*, Rollo May (1972) spoke of *ecstasy* and *violence*—the attractive, alluring, and fascinating elements in violence—the "lust for destruction" (pp.172-177).

As we recognize widespread shameful militarism, we must understand that most people are not psychically violent toward others. However, in view of the militaristic mood, large numbers seem to be culturally or emotionally conditioned to follow rather unquestioningly the militaristic spirit of the times. It was announced on NBC News one morning (February 26, 1991) that President's Bush's approval rating went up to 90% during the Gulf War.

Militarism according to A. Merriam-Webster (1986), is an "exaltation of military virtues and ideals" and /or "a predominance of military class or its ideals" (p-753). It is a belief in the military as a legitimate and sane means of resolving conflict and stopping violence. It is a spirit of admiration for things military, an unquestioning acceptance of military endeavors, and a psychic fascination with, or craving for, military violence.

Roots of Militarism

Why do people go to war? Why this nationalized worldwide violence? why this militarism and militarization? Should we conclude that military men are immersed in a sea of bloody fantasies; national leaders blind with the wish for omnipotence; greedy entrepreneurs wishing to exploit; submissive masses unthinkingly following along, the cautious paralyzed by fear, and a sizable number drunk with the wine of violence? Why have not human beings looked themselves in the face and asked: "Why are we doing this? Why do we fear, hate, and abuse each other, Why do people not understand that retaliation only promotes more violence? Why can we not promote equity among all people of this one home for all of us? Why do we use our talents, imaginations, and skills to create more and more deadly instruments to protect and/or kill each other? Why have people allowed themselves to obey the commands of violent leaders or to initiate violent behaviors? Who promotes these practices? Whose violence is it? Who are the enemies? Who and/or what is responsible for all this injustice, the insanity, this violent craving?"

We know that we do not know the full answer to all of these questions. This much I think we know: the military is a structure of the national state. As such it not only provides security, it also causes violence. Militarism arises more directly from people's personalities. We should look at these causes more carefully.

Personality Qualities and Behaviors

The most basic causes of militarism come from one or more of a cluster of feelings such as fear, hostility and inferiority and/or teaching and experiences. Much of this is a product of child-rearing practices and cultural conditioning. These feelings and experiences from a syndrome of attitudes, beliefs, values, character-qualities, and bahaviors. This syndrome fosters militarizing. We know also that these forces foster a cycle of violent cause and effects.

Militarism is among the many expressions of a syndrome of *dominant/violent personality qualities.* This syndrome is uncompromising in attitudes nonthinking in beliefs, belligerent in values, and aggressive in bahaviors. The militaristic manifestations are symptoms of the psychic causes and become secondary roots of other violence. Lyndon B. Johnston once said, "The guns and the bombs the rockets and the warships, all are symbols of human failure." (As quoted by Jeanne Larson and Madge Micheels-Cyrus, 1986, p.6).

There are three types of expressions of this millitaristic personality syndrome. The first two arise from dominant/violent psychic feelings within people. One of these tends to express psychic feelings in an aggressive manner, and can easily become domineering violent leaders. The other type tends to express their hostilities in a submissive manner. Both types have psyches that prompt them to be prejudiced, bigoted, and to approve of destructive policies, violent activities, as well as of cruel wars. Both have experienced unloving, degrading, hurtful early-life relationships that have caused them to develop those self-only orientations to life. These people have deep-seated fears, hostilities, inferiority feelings, and defenses. They have projected onto themselves and others the repressed hatreds which they should justly feel for their abusers. These feelings prevent the growth of esteem, confidence, integrity in themselves, and empathy with other people.

Children subjected to such humiliation may kneel to such harsh authorities and become inwardly hostile, unthinking puppets of violent leaders. Such followers fulfill dictators' desires for obedient lower-level military men. With what might appear to be same type experiences, some people stubbornly strongly resist the domineering behaviors of their elders and with more display of hostility lead in violent behaviors. These feelings and behaviors are usually supported or encouraged by unjust inequitable socio-economic conditions. Militarism is an easy means of release or outlet for these types of hostilities. Both of these two types of people need deep psychological consciousness-raising and healing.

A third type is not inwardly hostile. They have learned to be that way through direct teaching or examples in their families. School, communities, and/or peer groups. They have been taught attitudes, values, customs, and behaviors, and have acused them to believe that their particular group's way of seeing things, or behaving, is superior to other people's. Hence, such militarists believe in the use of violence and war, not because they are basically hostile and personally violent.. but because they have mistakenly accepted the belief that violence and war are moral and that the military has very special virtues. They do not know the facts or understand reality. They are *misinformed*. Hence, they need a higher level of awareness and a change in their belief systems.

Causes, effects, characteristics and various expressions of these three branches of the human taproots of violence were explained in Chapter Five. A simple diagram shows three branches of causation. Most people are a mixtures of these three types.

It is not commonly recognized that militarism is the result

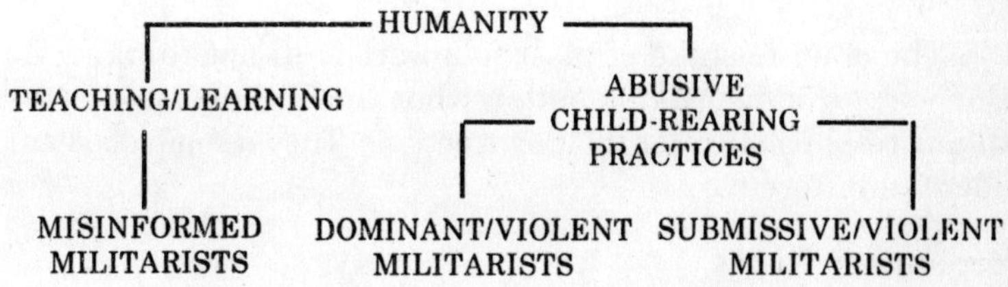

Figure **Human Origins of Militarism/Violence**

of these three basic tendencies that have been conditioned into people's personalities. Instead, only the symptons of underlying psychic emotions are examined. Although most psychic conditioning is done in early life, some is promoted in later years.

Americans have sometimes been appalled at how the Germans could have been brainwashed to the extent that they followed the cruelty of Nazism. Now, too many Americans, as well as other peoples have become brainwashed and have allowed the cultivation of their more hostile attitudes and violent inclinations to become more and more aggressive and violent. Some are prejudiced bigots who look upon other groups as inferior, and some are simply following orders and./or popular sentiments. This is frightening. It sounds too similar to the conditions under Hitler or Stalin.

Benjamin Ferencz (1988), who was a civilian prosecutor for the United States in the Nurenberg war crimes trials, tells of his experience with the Nazi leaders who were on trial. He concluded that if one has "...the distorted conviction that a person of a certain race, opinion, or belief is inferior, his extermination seems logical and even desirable."

Too often people follow blindly. As George Kennan said;

> ...like the victims of some sort of hypnotism, like men in a dream, like lemmings heading for the sea, like the children of Hamlin marching quoted by Ruth Adams and Susan Cullen, 1981, p.vii).

The chief mistake of most followers is in not thinking for themselves, not speaking out on what they believe, and in not taking responsibility for their own actions. They remain obedient, silent, indifferent.

Secondary Roots

Societal structures. As noted earlier, there are many cycles of causes and effects of violence. It could be argued as to "which comes first, the chicken or the egg." It may be arbitrary to consider the human psyche as the primary cause and all other causes as secondary, but that is the way I think it is. Hence I consider other causes as secondary roots or symptoms of the more basic human cause. Some of the senior secondary roots can cause cycles of violence. They are both cause and effect of the dominant /violent syndrome and the militaristic mood, direct violence, and militarizing. Government, the economy, education, and the environment are given special emphasis. These systems and others including the media, religion, culture and tradition, all can have defects that promote militarism and violence and other components that plant seeds of peace.

The military-industrial complex has been profiting from the production and sales of weapons to countries, groups, and individuals; it has great influence on all aspects of government and public opinion; and it exerts great power throughout the world. Industry also uses commercialization to exploit the militaristic mood of the people which in turn promotes militarizing.

Television toy guns, and war games. Many investigators of this issue express strong beliefs that in recent years. TV, guns, and war toys have been strong promoters of moods of militarism, the acceptance of militarizing, and many forms for cruelty and violence. Pervasive on children's television are cartoons with scenes and themes of war, fighting, bullying, and conflicts being resolved only through violence. Television and marketing strategies of large corporations are having an increasingly native effect on children.

TV programs and commercials are coordinated with war toy that children are urged to purchase. Such approaches encourage militaristic violent attitudes and behaviors. Regulations, that had been rather helpful in partially controlling violence on television and coordinated toy-marketing, were removed during the Reagan Administration. These deregulations set progress back in this field. Corporations are now marketing their cruelty, not only in the U.S. but also around the world.

War toys teach children that war is just a game, that killing is the big guy thing to do, that various other groups of people are evil enemies (the "bad guys"), that various other groups of people are evil enemies (the "bad guys"), that violence and power are synonymous, and that violence is the appropriate way to deal with conflicts.

"There is so much bad in the best of us, and so much good in the worst of us, that it hardly behooves any of us to condemn the rest of us." This adage has more truth in it than present attitudes seem to recognize. Contrary to this belief, is the prominent attitude that most children are now learning. They see many example that lead them to believe that the world is divided into two types-the "good guys" and the "bad guys". Furthermore they assume it is okay for us, the "good guys," to kill the "bad guys." This message is clearly depicted on television in the most graphic cruel ways. But the real pain of the enemy can not be experienced or understood. Strong, courageous, macho, or handsome-type heroes are made to appear glamorous and the bad guys or creatures are gruesome and evil. Older children note that the U.S. invades Granada, Iraq, and Panama; so they are the evil ones. We are the good ones was we are just and right in punishing the evil ones. So, we can be happy when we win. At all ages, children see too few expressions of: tolerance; encouragement for reforms; efforts to solve problems without violence; assistance for mutual maturation; refusal to retaliate; and understanding of the causes behind the behaviors of the "bad guys" and attempts to remove the basic causes.

Nancy Carlson -Paige and Diane Levin (1987) found that violence on television is also changing the way kids play. They discovered that children often do not distinguish between pretending to hurt someone and actually hurting them. And when they do hurt another child they often fail to realize it or not take the responsibility for it. The children who are influenced by TV violence are usually not in charge of their play (i.e., being imaginative and inventive), as would be normal, but rather are aggressive and aimlessly imitative of what they have seen on TV.

Guns and war games. Many children and men seem to be completely captivated by these. War games for men have become a terrible fascination for groups of men across the country who put on their camouflage fatigues and shoot each other with paint-filled guns. Howard Kohn (1988, March/April) suggests that it may be that these games tell us "...that there is something about war already loved too much by too many of us"

Love of real guns has taken us to war within our borders. Whether or not individuals have a U.S. Constitutional right to bear arms remains debatable, since there have been a number of conflicting court decisions on the question. It seems most difficult to change the situation, even in the face of horrifying results. Not only have individual criminals, racist groups, and drug gangs become a constant horror to the public, attitudes toward guns have promoted militarism and murders by the millions. Still, many otherwise respectable people insist on allowing guns to be available to everyone. It is a disgrace to our society.

Even though it is widely recognized that direct violence is often a cause of more and greater violence, it is also sometimes argued that war and personal violence can also bring peace. Violence may at times deter violence temporarily, but it does not produce conditions in which peaceful cooperative living can prosper. Violence usually causes violence in retaliation. It may restrain underlying hostilities that otherwise could emerge at any time as physical or psychological destruction. The Serb-Bosnian-Croatian War is an example of violent conflicts erupting after many years of repressed hostilities generated primarily by foreign invaders and passed down form generation to generated. Disputes can not be resolved through mass killings or individual murders. **Violence and wars become secondary roots of more violence and they do not bring real peace**.

Violent regional conflicts and wars, and other types of violence have greatly increased in recent years. There are several causes for this increase in addition to the fact that violence causes more violence. These include:

- violence has been made increasingly more glamorized by television, films, per groups, and hostile leaders;
- weapons for war and violence are more available, massive,

brutal and destructive than are fists, rocks, bows and arrows;

• an increase in a "hard-nosed" belief that humiliation, punishment, and execution are better deterrents to misconduct than are room efforts and teaching;

• there are more people to consume resources, get in each other's way, and kill each other; and

• information about violence is more widely communicated and hence there are more models for violence.

Even though there has probably been an increase of violence in recent years, there has always been violence. Although there have been some peaceful caring tribes and groups throughout recorded history, violence has been rather pervasive. Ambassador Samuel Lewis (1993, September 17) said:

> A conflict-ridden world has always been there out around the fringes. Internal conflicts, tribal conflicts, ethnic conflicts, bitter religious conflicts, and the old-fashioned warlordism that Somalia illustrates...[there is a] continuity of brutality and a strain of cruelty and near barbarism that runs throughout recorded history...The world had never been at peace and probably never will be.

I am not as pessimistic as was Lewis when the spoke those words. I hope, and prefer to think, that the world can, and will some day be at peace. Since various tribes seem to have lived very peacefully together and most people today are reasonably cooperative, there seems to be no doubt that people could live equitably together. We could make the changes recommended in this book. When we observe the tremendous scientific and technological accomplishments, we know that people are intelligent, capable, and creative enough to move beyond the present state of militarism. A few specific suggestions will be made later in this chapter.

Manifestations of Militarism

There are many manifestations or expressions of the militaristic violence promoting syndrome. Some of these are listed here.

Militaristic Vocabulary

There are hundreds of words which tend to exchange abstraction for the reality of killing people and destroying countries (e.g.., the words "collateral damage" is used instead of human deaths or "counter-value attacks" rather than incinerating cities, or "Peacekeepers" instead of MX missiles). Such aberrations desensitize people to the horrors of war. Carol Cohn (1987, June) wrote, "This language has enormous destructive power, but without the emotional fallout that would result of it were clear one was talking about plans for mass murder, mangled bodies, human suffering' (P.17).

Condoning Violence to Resolve Conflicts

A study of 1,400 American males ages 16-64 by investigators M.D. Blumenthal, R.L. Kahn, F.M. Andrews, and K.B. Head (1972) indicated that violence is widely regarded as instrumental by American men. Two thirds of the men would justify shooting in situations which require social control (e.g., they felt that shooting was a good way to handle campus disturbances). Militaristic people not only tend to approve of the use of violence as a means of resolving conflicts, they may often use violence themselves.

Militarizing Resources, People and Conflict

Militaristic thinking and feelings give birth to both the equipping and preparing of military forces for war and to giving a military character or emphasis to the problem. Militaristic imaginings can easily be transformed into military hardware and the exploitation of resources and people. Hence, with a heightened militaristic mood, there is a militarizing of the conflict itself. Use of peaceful conflict resolution and reform are ignored while people become more hostile, more weapons are constructed, dangers of terrorism increase; and neighborhood violence is compounded.

Illogical Thinking

Throughout this book, I have urged that people learn how to think and become self-directing. One purpose of this chapter is to encourage self-thinking and action concerning militarism. Other writers have considered militarism to be illogical, foolish insame, as well as violent. This sentiment was expressed by Dag Hammarskjold, former Secretary General of the United Nations, when he said,

> War has always seemed to me "the ultimate insanity." Violence and war as the maximum demonstration of man's capacity for inhumanity to man were against my religious beliefs, my sense of morality, and my common sense (as quoted by Larson, et al., 1986, p.35)

Fredrick the Great was surely right when he said: "if my soldiers began to think, not one would remain in the ranks."

The continued existence of atomic weapons and the multiplication of biological and chemical weaponry are other examples of militaristic thinking. The tremendous killing-power of these and the so called "conventional weapons" threaten every life and the future of the world. Still very little is done to destroy these weapons, prevent the making of more, change underlying harmful human psychic qualities, and prevent the development of such qualities through uninformed parenting practices. This is not constructive thinking.

The magnitude of the dangers, the folly of the reasoning, and the enormity of the direct and indirect violence which is resulting from present world wide militarism is morally shocking and goes almost beyond comprehension.

Military-Industrial Controls

Controls that the military-industrial complex has gained over governments. Earth's resources, and people's lives is a very harmful manifestation of militarism. The following facts were selected and abbreviated from Ruth Leger Sivard's 1987 report:

- More wars were fought in the 1980's than in any previous

decade in history, Four -fifths of the deaths in those wars were civilian. Most of the war deaths of three centuries have occurred in the 20th. This modern century in which we live will account for over 90 percent of the deaths in wars since 1700.

The world's annual military expenditure, at about two million dollars a minute, equals the income of 2.6 billion people in the 44 poorest nations.

More than half the governments of Third World countries are now military controlled. Such leadership has usually been autocratic, often inept and chaotic.

The fuel consumed by the Pentagon in a single year would run the entire U.S. public transit system for 22 years.

In 1987, among 142 leading countries of the world, the U.S. ranked first in armaments production; but it ranked 5th literacy rate, 7th in public education expenditures per capita, 8th in public health expenditures per capita, 18th in percent of women in total university enrollment, and 18th in infant mortality rate. (excerpted and paraphrased from throughout the report).

The Defense Monitor (1986, November 3) notes other manifestations of militarization:

> The long established tradition of civilian control over the military is loading...preparing for war in peacetime has become big business...Political Action Committee (PAC) contributions from twenty largest defense contractors have increased by 225% since the early eighties.

In addition to the excessive influence of the military - industrial complex on government and people, many other effects of militarizing endangers democracy and freedom within many countries. For example, dangerous secretive underground power is in the hands of non-elected peoples and an horrendous deficit deprives people of their basic needs and endangers our grandchildren.

The connections between militarism and social, economic and political suffering are appalling. As human welfare is **being** undermined an while conflicts between countries, gangs, and ethnic groups increase, there is a continuation of an obsessive, single-minded emphasis on violent forces to resolve issues, reduce crime, and satisfy greedy ambitions.

In less developed countries, the expansion of their military has deprived their people of economic equity and human justice. Limited public funds, have often gone for military instead of for upgrading education, protecting infants lives, providing food, shelter safe water, and protection from diseases. This condition exists in nearly all countries because of governmental and public support of the military/industrial complex with its arms trade (both legal and illegal).

When we think about the millions of people who are hungry, trying to exist on a tiny piece of earth, living in a refugee camp, or worse still completely homeless, sick, and/or jobless, and we then recognize that the billions spent on military could provide adequate food, water, education, health, and housing for all of these people, we can not help but wonder when humans will become humane.

Former U.S. President Dwight D. Eisenhower apparently saw dangers such of these, and although he was not able to reduce his nation's armaments, he gave many warnings and statements regarding the dangers and follies of militarization. He said "The problem in defense is how far you can go without destroying from within what you are trying to defend from without" (As quoted by B.B. Ferencz, 1988, p.35).

But some will argue that above all we must be prepared to defend ourselves against an evil aggressive nation. They reason that if we are not prepared, we could be over-run as other countries have been. I understand this fear, It would be justified if there were no other kinds of preparation. However, we should face those fears with creative thinking, and cooperatively devise nonviolent international and domestic preventive plans which could make war unnecessary and unwanted as soon as possible.

All too often wars are undertaken for very inhumane reasons, such as:

- to resolve claims over territories or to gain territory over which it can expert power and hence, build a more powerful empire; to align developing countries on the sides of stronger powers;

- to gain economic control over other people's resources such as oil minerals, fertile soil, and cheap labor;
- to secure profits for the military - industrial complex which sells weapons of destruction to all sides;
- to gain influence for a particular ideclogy or to force it upon another people (e.g., communism vs capitalism., Catholic vs, Protestant, one ethnic group vs. another , and conservative vs, liberal political views),

Frequently wars are rationalized to gain public approval of the violence, but often they are not real causes.

Effects of Militarism and war on Families

The chief purpose of this book has been to show the role of families in causing violence and/or promoting peace in the world through their relationships and child-rearing practices. I want now to stress the effects of militarism on families. Because this militarism is caused primarily by people who may have been harmed in their early years, very often by family members, there is a cycle of cause and effect.

As a result of public funding of the military, society has neglected its people's needs for food, housing, health care, education, and employment. The financial deficit has also obligated our children for generations to come The Earth has been destructively polluted, and our young people's minds are being contaminated by appear from to violent behavior.

Even in peacetime, families have had extra burdens from one or more family members being attached to the military. There seems to be no hard evidence that military children and spouses experience more psychological damage including than do other families. They do have special problems and stresses including the absence of the military aparent; mobility of families that require frequent adjustments to different communities, schools, neighbourhoods, and cultural patterns; adjustments to separation and reunion. A more serious difficulty is the authoritarian personalities cultivated by the military. The military structure is based upon the principle of absolute power. Obedience without question is the rule of order- an hierarchical system in which the underlings take orders from their superiors and give orders to their subordinates. This system is not compatible with democratic, egalitarian, peaceful ways of living,. But these tendencies are maintained in military life.

The military man's family may suffer from the authoritarian patterns of the military in other ways. The father may want his wife and his children to give the same type of nonthinking obedience that he experiences in the military. If he has accepted the submissive role from his own dominant/violent childhood, he may simply abdicate his responsibility in parenting, leaving it for the mother to provide. Whatever his parenting tendencies, if he is away from home most of the time, there may be great inconsistencies in his family's environment. In some cases children fail to develop their own inner directive power, their sense of responsibility and creative competence.

Wars, being a maximum form of violence, are particularly damaging to shatter hopes, dreams, and urgently needed resources for future survival and can result in poverty, homelessness and starvation. When the lives of loved ones are taken, people can experience much greater emotional pain. Children are sometimes abandoned and thousands become refugees. Families also suffer when one or more family members are away in war of when they come home traumatized from their wrenching experiences.

Can we even half imagine the cruel treatment and devastating tragedies of the indigenous peoples as they were being driven on foot from their ancestral homes in North Carolina to barren Oklahoma? I read with emotion of this terrible "Trial of Tears" in my first Oklahoma history book. My history teacher said it was a "trial of blood." There are many "trails of blood" throughout history.

The U.S. has experienced no war on our soil since the Civil War, yet we have war victims -not only those who are in the heat of the battles, but also wives, children, and mother who remain at home while fathers, brother, sons -an now even mothers and daughters go to war. (Among my very first memories was one of sensing my mother's worry about my old brother who was in the European conflict during World War I).

Even though we understood the fears behind it, in 1941 our hearts went out to Japanese families when we saw crowded train-loads of them being chipped to barren locations after having been uprooted from their comfortable homes in our California town. These innocent families suffered physically, emotionally, and economically.

Effects of direct violence and wars continue in this and in other countries. For example, Vietnam families are still trying to put their lives back together from unbelievable terrors. On this side, thousands of veterans of a most violent person-to-person war in Vietnam, are still in agony from Post-Traumatic Stress Disorder (PTSD).

Numerous studies were done to find the effects of war and their evacuation on children during and after World war II in England. They found many and varied types of harmful effects, a few of which were permanently damaging. (Researchers include: Anna Freud and Dorothy Burlingham (1942). directors of nurseries with children evacuated from war zones in England during World War II ; Ruth Inglis (1989) interviewed former evacuees and related her own memories as a refugee from North China in 1940; and J. Lousie Despert (1942) with several studies.)

We can, and we should, provide information and psychological encouragement that will help all people understand the folly and cruelty of retaliatory thinking. We should teach the simple but profound truth from Ghandi: "An eye for an eye makes the hole world blind." The teaching of this principle by parents and educators could help to move the world beyond retaliation and the scourge of war and reverse the cycle of violence into a cycle of peace.

The military mood, people's fascination with guns, violence on television, and the massive sale of toy guns and other military items have presented families with very difficult problems. It is true that the love and care provided in the home can counteract many harmful forces from the larger society, but some intrusions not families live may be most difficult and complex for families to manage.

In order to minimize the harmful effects from violent encounters in the future there should be more research on the nature of peoples psyches, the effects of violence on personality, and psychological development of children: children need to be made aware of the real dangers and how they may take precautions.

Our Challenge: Plant Seeds of Peace

Whose responsibility is it to build peace? Since we the people are the chief causes of violence, it is we who should take the responsibility to foster peace. The challenge is great to transform the present militaristic mood into a mood for peace, and to reduce the military and promote human well-being. It may not be too late if enough of us put forth the needed effort, but we can no do it by "rolling with the time." We may or may not have helped to create the militaristic/militarizing crisis we are in, but we can all do something to cope with that crisis and be challenged to plant seeds of peace. The well-known statement by Margaret Mead should be remembered in these days of urgent need for change. "Never doubts that a small group of thoughtful, committed citizens can change the world. Indeed, it's the only thing that ever has."

There is no attempt here to list all approaches to coping with this crisis, but perhaps some examples will be helpful.

Become Involved Personally

As we look with horror at militarism and its manifestations in its various forms of direct violence, we should remember that most people are not personally violent. Most people love and work for their families and give care and assistance to their neighbours when needed. They want peace and are willing to "live and let live" and occasionally to "help live". Our chief problem concerning public policies and practices is that we too easily follow without question the dictates of leaders of governments, a system of economy, or a cultural tradition that no longer promotes the well-being of people (in some cases they never did). We have not learned well enough how to think clearly and equitably and act from our own convictions. But let us be grateful to all those people, in the past and present. Who have given a large measure of their lives to making the world a better place to live.

We need also to remember that al component parts of the world have changed so radically that there is constant need for study, discussions, transformations, an changes. This is especially true of how we cooperate with each other and cope with resolving our conflicts.

Peace workers need to be as diligent as they were while the "Cold War" was still raging. Many dangers remain, some regional conflicts have become worse. and solutions without the military seem difficult. Therefore, our dedicated efforts are greatly needed. The process of change is worthy of our serious study, research, consideration, our involved dialogue, and our persistent efforts. Although wars have sometimes apparently been necessary let us work to make the unnecessary.

Self-growth. Let us examine our own feelings and attitudes toward violence, Lilitarism, and war. Do we need to develop our psyches to become more peace-promoting? If we need to do so, we can. We can develop greater empathy, concern, and love for other human beings (see Chapter Six for some suggestions). We can help to alleviate pain in others and abhor the killing of precious lives. We can refuse to do things which tend to desensitize ourselves to the suffering of others. such as watching TV and film that belittle people, emphasize the "good-guy/bad-guy" ideology, or resolve conflict through violence. We can transform our ways of thinking through conversation with peace loving peoples, reading humanitarian literature, and practice what we know. We can act and live as if we all really live on one small planet, which we do, and as if we really are one united caring human family, which we now are not.

Enrich relationships. Since international relations begin with personal relationships. People everywhere can contribute globally by first learning to live in peace with companions, family, friends, neighbors, and teach others to do likewise. We can be models for our children and they can learn to love, live peacefully prevent violence, and lead the world to peace.

We can develop attitudes, knowledge, and skills in constructive human relationships, conflict-resolution and problem-solving.

Nurture children toward self-otherness. if our world is to escape destruction from irresponsible blunders of misinformed people and the hostility of dominant/violent (militaristic) nations and groups. children must be nurtured to develop self-other (equity-peace) personalities, and be educated to become peace-promoting. The most effective war and crime prevention measures are unconditional love, nurturing, respecting, teaching and redirection, without insults, humiliation or competition.

We should also remember that healthy play is vitally important to the maturation of children, if it is not violence producing.

Reform Society's Systems

It is vry crucial for us to examine social structures. It is important that we understand the extent to which they contribute to militarism, militarizing, and other forms of violence. Reforms should be made in these societal structures of we are to reduce the level of violence both within countries and between nations.

It is recognized that all societies build their systems and maintain controls on the principles and values held by the controlling groups. This, of course, is based upon power. It is therefore urged that people get and keep democratic controls to promote the well-being of all people, not for the material profit for only the few.

Therefore we must demand that controls be placed on guns,

toy industries, and violence on television. There are a number of organizations in the U.S. that have been very active against the manufacture and sale of war toys, violence on TV, private possessions of guns, and for strict federal controls. We can do well to promote their cause. Some encouragement has come since a few cities, including Stockton and Los Angeles have passed gun prohibitions within city limits.

Create and/or strengthen international systems. Some societal systems are quite extensively under the control of international organizations (e.g. international air traffic and refugee programs). According to its Charter the United Nations was created "...to save succeeding generations from the scourge of war which twice in our lifetime has brought untold sorrow to mankind...."

> Founders of the United Nations recognized a close relationship between "conditions of stability and well-being" and peace. In Article 55 of the United Nations Charter they wrote:
>
> With a view to the creation of conditions of stability and well-being which are necessary for peaceful and friendly relations among nations based on respect for the principles of equal rights and self-determinations of peoples, the United Nations shall promote:
>
> a. higher standards of living, full employment, and conditions of economic and social progress and development;
>
> b. solutions of international economic, social, health, and related problems; and international cultural and educational cooperation; and
>
> c. universal respect for, and observance of, human rights and fundamental freedoms for all without distinction as to race, sex, language, or religion (p.30).

Reforms in all social, economic, and political structures are crucially needed in all countries, and among countries, for these conditions to exist. Hence, we should be moving toward the strengthening (in some cases the establishment) of international systems which can resolve such problems as: making and keeping peace and the reduction of armaments in all parts of the world; providing security in human rights, freedom for poverty, medical and health care, and provision for employment and for renewable sources of energy; insurance of equity in world trade and economics; population control and restoration and protection of the environment; care of refugees and victims of natural and human disaster; provision for laws, courts, justice and order, and self-determination for all peoples; equality for women, minorities, and the poor; and last but very important, universal adequate education including family relationships, and parenting. The United Nations has agencies, organizations, commissions, and committees now functioning in all of these areas. However, problem situation exists; these problems are international in scope and orientation, whereas the power to deal with them remains with the various nations.

Improve educational systems. Most of what is said in the chapter on education is applicable here. Special emphasis should also be given to ending the "plague of war." Preventive measures, as well as reforms, are necessary. Education should help children at all ages to learn how to think clearly for themselves; gain knowledge abut principles of democratic governance and citizens' participation: understand the United Nations and its work; learn principles of family life education for peace; and gain skills in nonviolent solutions to problems, conflict resolution, and crises coping.

There are times when people need to oppose the actions of their governments. Democracy requires our best thinking and action on what we believe to be right, not our blind obedience. I agree with that Banjamin Frencz (1988) wrote in this regard:

> True loyalty does not demand blind obedience. "My country right or wrong" is a prescription for national decay. As the Germans under Hitler learned, it could be recipe for disaster. Citizenship and true patriotism carry a duty to encourage your country when it is right and to help it when it has gone astray (pp.21,22).

Education should be genuinely honest regarding facts of our mottled national history. Yes, we need to be grateful and praise, as we usually do, our present and past strengths and greatness. However, we should also acknowledge our weaknesses, and our universal human immaturity. We should also provide the same information about other nations and peoples with whom we have conflicts. Awareness could help all sides understand each others less than perfect history, their potentials for greatness, and help them mature beyond hostilities.

It is very crucial that both children and adults learn to negotiate with respect. Bullying, belittling, condemning, and drawing lines in the sand are not conducive to effective conflict resolution. Feelings and points of view of the other party should be sought. Opinions and justifications for actions of both sides should be carefully examined. Use equity as an important guide in deliberations and decision making; find as many ways as possible to be fair to all concerned; create condition in which all people can meet their basic human needs; and discourage greed, exploitation, unfair practices, and trade inequities, all of which promote hostilities and ill-will.

People should stop thinking of military power as an option for resolving problems. There is always a better way. The idea situation, of course, is to anticipate and recognize the difficulty and work on its solution before it reaches the violent stage. But usual practice is to start building weapons to use when the violent clash occurs, making little or no effort to reach a solution by other means. The Charter of the United Nations, Article 33 requires that all peaceful solutions to an international conflict by exhausted before other actions are taken. It states: " first of all, seek a solution by negotiation, enquiry, mediation, conciliation, arbitration, judicial settlement; resort to regional agencies or arrangements, or other peaceful means of their own choice." This was not done in the case of the Gulf crisis. Citizens have the responsibility to require this of their governments. Governments are now in the process of trying to help negotiations in the Bosnian struggle. There is hope that this will succeed.

Control the Military - Industrial Complex

The people's government, not the military and the corporations, should be in control of regulating the production and deployment of whatever instruments of force are needed to enforce peace. To accomplish this, people must study and become knowledgeable of relevant facts, think clearly, discuss at length, elect wise representatives, and act as world citizens must do to insure our freedom and control our global institutions. Most of us have not been educated to do this. But unless we do , dictators, military leader, and armaments-producing industry will continue to exploit and destroy lives and resource.

One of our greatest tasks is to speak out "loud and clear," nonviolently and caringly, but firmly and unequivocally about the dangers, the folly, and the violence toward people and Earth which results from militarism and militarizing.

We can all be a part of a continuing movement to insist upon a multilateral freeze on development, testing, production, and deployment of nuclear weapons, and limitations on other. It is especially important to let our government leaders know how we feel. I like the way Ferencz puts this:

> The U.S. military purse is controlled by the Congress, and Congress is controlled by the people. It is up to us, the informed voters, to stop robbing the hungry and the poor to feed an insatiable war machine (pp. 120, 121).

We can all press members of Congress to support efforts to reduce military spending, stop selling arms to other countries, and increase efforts to resolve conflicts anywhere in the world.

The peace movement has been working toward the tremendous task of converting human and other resource and society's wealth from military production to civilian needs. This may seem like an insurmountable problem. Michael Renner (1990) says it is not. He affirms: "The major barriers are not technical but political, ranging from the power and agendas of vested interests to the widespread misconception that military spending makes good economic sense" (p.155). He says, "The myth of military-led prosperity has obscured the fact that civilian spending creates significantly more jobs" (p.156).

Is it too much to expect of human beings that they can and will act equitably and responsibly toward other human beings? Are we simply indulging in words fantasy when we say that living in this small world community in peace will require people to be responsible to act fairly, not exploitatively, toward each other? I think it is the starkest of necessities. This world has become a small community and people need to act like respectful caring neighbours toward each other. Part of the reality is that equity for others is also in our own self-interest. We should listen to the words of former ambassador Charles Yost (1980):

> If we can be persuaded that self-interest now demands much more sophistication borbearing, and harmonious accommodations with nature and with our fellow men [humans] of all colors and creeds than has been necessary in the past, there is no reason why we and our civilization should not go on to develop the almost magical capacities science promises. I, however, we persist in defining self-interest and national interest in terms relevant to more primitive eras, but incompatible with our own, we risk creating a world in which, not some instant generation, but our own grandchildren will become an endangered species (pp.343-344).

People should heed the advice of former President John F. Kennedy when he said:

> Let us examine our attitude toward peace itself. Too many of us think it is impossible. Too many think it unreal. But that is a dangerous, defeatist belief. It leads to the conclusion that was in inevitable, that mankind is doomed, that we are gripped by forces we cannot control (in Larson, p.213).

Not so: we can be in control; peace is entirely possible. Equitable peace has existed for some groups of people, and to a certain extent, in some countries. Human beings have usually been able to accomplish what they have envisioned as being very important. Images of a bright future can dispel hopelessness and despair, and build courage and determination. In the past, too many dreams and visions have awakened to reality as military inventions and instruments of war -war which General Douglas MacArthur called "a Frankenstein" which contains he "germ of double suicide." He saw the urgency for actualizing our imaginations when he urged the "abolition of war." He wrote:

> Abolition of war is no longer an ethical question to pondered solely be learned philosophers and ecclesiastic, but a hard core one for the decisions of the masses whose survival is the issue. Many will tell you with mockery and ridicule that the abolition of war can only be a dream that is the vague imagining of a visionary. But we must go on or we will go under! We must have new thoughts, new ideas, new concepts, we must beak out of the straitjacked of the past. We must have sufficient imaginations and courage to translate the universal wish for peace—which is rapidly becoming a universal necessity—into actuality (quoted by B. Ferencz. 1988, p.41)

Activities of peace-loving hard working people give us hope. Conferences, magazine and newspaper articles, occasional television programs, and peace activists' efforts have alerted people to the present situation. Ruth Leger Sivard (1987) who, for 26 years, published an annual edition of facts on "World Military and Social Expenditures." expressed hope that there may be some progress toward "...reducing the size of the world's burden and its dangers." It is encouraging to note that she saw change especially in "...thc remarkable growth of effort by public interest groups and concerned individuals to lay out the facts and bring sanity to the political process (p.5).

Greater public concern and effort should be focused on cause an effect of dominance/violence tendencies and all of their manifestations. We should, certainly, do what we can do directly reduce armaments and reform structures, but unless there is a transformation of people, changes in child-rearing practices, and improvements in family relationships, wars and crime will continue and increase. More and better peace education, especially in FLEP (family life education for peace), can gives us hope and courage. In conclusion I encourage us all to think of the precious lives of our children and grandchildren, Let us help to make this beautiful planet a safe place for them to grow and live cooperatively together. **Let us move from universal militarism, to global peace and security.**

Chapter-8

Education as a Force for Peace and/or Violence

Chapter-8

Only the educated are free.
-Epictetus: Discourses II.i.

Human history becomes more and more
A race between education and catastrophe.
-H.G. Wells (1931)

Education can be a freeing, uplifting, joyful, and empowering process. It is unfortunate that not all educated people are free. Much depends upon how *education* and *free* are defined; what *kinds* of formal and informal education are received; and what other forces interrelate with the educational process.

In this chapter consideration is given to; meanings and components of education for peace; forces in culture and societal systems that educate; stumbling blocks to peace-promoting education; suggestions for change; and fostering a more peace-promoting education.

Education : What and Why?

Although I agree with both Epictetus and Wells, I have concluded that not all education helps to prevent catastrophe or loosens the chains of bondage. In truth some forms of education can enslave the self and destroy people. Since education implies learning, people can learn that which is constructive to self and /or others or they can learn that which will cause violence, even destruction. **Hence, the future may be determined be a race between education for self-otherness and education for self-onlyness** (i.e., a race between education for peace and education for violence). Rodrigo Carazo, past president of Costa Rica and leading founder of the United Nations University for Peace in Costa Rica, told us (in 1986): "It is often said that if we want peace, we must prepare for war. but NO! if we want peace we must educate for peace." Throughout time there have been forces that sway people in the direction of becoming peaceful and others that teach ways of living and being that foster hostility, inequity, and violence. From birth to death educational processes are ongoing. We can, and must, work for the race to be won by education for peace. We may be able to win that race sooner than we think possible, if we educate for peace.

Education for peace means: a teaching -learning process in which the learner acquires knowledge of the world of realities; cultivates self-thinking self-directing competencies; acquires caring loving attitudes; examines and incorporates a set of equitable values to live by; learns constructive behaviors, envisions a better future; and gains skills for a life-long process of maximizing fulfillment of life's potentials for love, joy and service. This is a bit like hiking up a trail on a mountain. Every curve and every new height gives new vistas of the world of which we are a part. Among other things, education can mean; opening passages to worlds of the past; deepening awareness of the infinite complexities of the physical/natural universe; gaining empathy for distant peoples; and acquiring abilities to be a responsible citizen of family, community, country, and world.

Throughout the ages, humanity has been successful in learning many things that have brought "civilization" to its present state. Homo sapiens have learned to : think creatively, write their thoughts and read them, solve problems, keep records of their past, plan for their future, write inspiring literature, make music, and learn and teach millions of tremendous facts, skills, and amazing technologies. It is marvelous that people can pass all of this knowledge on from generation to generation. Methods of teaching have leaped forward since my childhood. There are problems, but people are intelligent enough to solve them.

It is unfortunate that formal education has too often meant a guide book on how to make money or training only for special kinds of occupations a fulfillment of social expectations; a place to have fun; a period in life from which to escape as soon as possible; or a way to study a very limited number of subjects such as reading, writing, and arithmetic. Motivations is often very strongly oriented toward selfish materialism (the bottom line being money). Such education concentrates (skills for a male dominated economically centered, cruelly competitive world. Mathematics, science, technology, sports, and history (primarily on a chronology of wars and conquests) are given priority. As Erich From (1976) emphasized this type education encouraged on orientation toward just having, rather than **being and becoming**. Since so much of our society is very materialistic, educational programs often instill this orientation into students; the results is neglect of full maturation and the reaching of potentials.

What worries we most is that much learning in schools and in families pushes children into nonthinking obedience. It prepares them to be submissive followers-self degrading puppets of whomever urges them to follow, be it parent, teacher, charismatic leader, dictator, cult follower, or gang member. This kind of blindly obedient are not competent citizens of a humanitarian democracy.

Education comes, not only from formal school systems, but also from many informal sources where children are encouraged to explore, satisfy their natural curiosity, grow in knowledge, build life's meanings, and discover joy in learning. Teachers can facilitate, motivate, and teach through example and attitudes as well as by words and pictures.

Peace-promoting education means not only freedom from ignorance and misinformation but also freedom to be, to become, and to contribute to the well-being of all living things. This may sound idealistic. Certainly no one possesses, or perhaps is capable of possessing, all truth or perfect self-otherness, but these are realistic goals toward which to work if life on Earth is to survive and peace is to become a permanent, encompassing reality.

Education for peace, no matter how realistic, is very controversial because it can result in transforming cultures and customs, social institutions, economic and political structures, and changing personal feelings, behaviors, habits of relating to others, ways of thinking, and value systems. This can mean a transformation or growth of self, which is most difficult for most of us.

What Betty Reardon (1988) wrote about *Peace Education Curriculum* can be said of education in general. She wrote:

> Stated most succinctly, the general purpose of peace education, as I understand it, is to promote the development of an authentic planetary consciousness that will enable us to function as global citizens and to transform the present human condition by changing the social structures and the patterns of thought that have created it (p.x).

She goes on to state that it will not be easy to make such needed transformations because, there are "...counter trends of greater violence, factionalism, alienation, and degradation of all life forms" (p.x). She says this is a challenge to education to transform itself, transcend the negative forces, and thus encourage reform. When major changes have taken place in any society, education has played an indirect role.

All education should lead toward development of peace-promoting personal qualities in learners–self-otherness. Family Life Education for Peace (FLEP) is a fundamental part of this education, because it promotes self-otherness from birth onward. FLEP helps families and formal education to perform their tasks.

Education can help foster the well-being of families and encourage peace-promoting elements in other social systems. For example, freedom and participatory democracy can be learned in schools where these principles are utilize. Education systems can also help to eliminate exploitation in the economy, prejudices, cultural superstitions, and mores which harm people.

Culture as Educator

People learn from all segments of their culture. In informal ways culture is absorbed from every moments experiences. While children are small, they very largely accept what they experience around them in behaviors, practices, and attitudes. These forces have tremendous power to educate. People learn from parents, family, peers, and from other human relationships in play and in work; they accept traditions, ways of thinking, beliefs, values, attitudes, life goals, and other people's behavior patterns that they see expressed around them. They learn from nature, written an spoken words, the media, religion and other social institutions, recreation of various types, and in many formal and informal situations and experiences. Learning sites include, not only formal schools, but also homes, television, religious institutions, community centers, work places, organizations, and play grounds.

What people learn may be true or false and skills and behaviors learned may be helpful or harmful to self and /or society. Everything that is learned, from whatever source, contributes to the development of the inner psyche and the complex system of interacting qualities, behavior patterns, ways of thinking, and attitudes which make up an individual person, who becomes self-other , self-only, or (as is usually the case) some combination of the two.

For better or worse, people absorb large amounts of their culture while they are young. In alter years, it is their responsibility to examine an evaluate concepts which they encounter. Children need help in learning to look critically at their culture and measure it suing facts, reasoning power, and values that they are learning from day to day. They should learn not to be culture-blind to fuller truths. This means holding on to every aspect of the culture until finding something that is truly better for self and others. Cultural traditions should not be thrown away without very careful consideration. On the other hand everything should be questioned. The Buddha expressed this very well:

> Do not put faith in tradition, even though they have been accepted for long generations and in many countries. Do not believe a thing because many repeat it. Do not accept a thing on the authority of one or another of the Sages of old, nor on the ground that a statement is found in the books. Never believe anything because probability is in its favor. Do not believe in that which you yourselves have imagined, thinking that a God has inspired it. Believe nothing merely on the authority of your teachers or of the priests. After examination, believe that which you have tested for

> yourselves and found reasonable, which is in conformity with your well-being and that of others (as quoted by Roger Walsh, 1984, p.49).

A number of elements of culture were mentioned in Chapter 3. As powerful forces for violence and peace television, peers, and play are given further consideration in this chapter. They are powerful teachers of both peace and violence.

The Media

When television was in its infancy, Edward R. Murrow said of it:

> This instrument can teach, it can illuminate. Yes, and it can even inspire But it can do so only to the extent that humans are willing to use it to those ends (as often quoted on Public Television).

This statement is still true, but we recognize that it is presently being used for other ends. It educates for violence as well as for peace. It can seldom educate beyond its creators and controller's attitudes and values. When its creators are self-other oriented it can be at its best. Public Television has been creating many constructive educational programs. The adult population can raise its level of knowledge by watching selected educational programs.

It is crucial that improvements be made in television. For example, more family life education on television could make a significnt contribution to marriage enrichment, family harmony, and parenting competence. Violence could be eliminated from programs and constructive skills could be taught to young people.

However, not only is the content of most television loaded with violence, commercialism, and sexism, it also negates the person's participation in any other activity, and even worse, evidence indicates that it retards educability. Time spent in television reduces time for family interaction, school work, development of self-directing creative projects. Television fosters follow-the-leader tendencies and dependency. Marie Winn (1985) wrote:

> Children need to acquire fundamental skills in communication —to learn to read, write, and express themselves flexibly and clearly—in order to function as social creatures. The television experience does not further verbal development because it does not require any verbal participation on the child's part, merely passive intake (p.7).

Even though pre-school children are the largest viewing audience, there is considerable evidence to indicate that because of their immaturity, they are harmed more than older people by watching television. Winn says that "...there is a similarity of experience about all television watching. .Certain specific psycological mechanisms of the eyes, ears, and brain respond to the Samuli emanating from the television screen regardless of the cognitive content of the programs." She emphasizes that there is a great difference between adult and child viewing.

> As the adult watches television, his [or her] own present and past relationships, experiences, dreams, and fantasies come in to play, transforming the material he sees, whatever its origin or purpose, into something reflecting his own particular inner needs. Children's life experiences are limited....To a certain extent children's early television experiences will serve to dehumanize, to mechanize, to make less real the realities and relationships they encounter in life. For them, real events will always carry subtle echoes of the television world (pp. 10-11).

Children often seem to be in a real trance as they watch television. Parents speak of their children as being "mesmerized," in a stupor, deaf to outside sounds, and there seems to be no evidence that they are mentally alert. There seems to be a "Sensory overkill."

Various research studies, including those by the National Assessment of Educational Progress (NAEP) (sponsored by the federal government's National Institute of Education), provide some indications of a negative relationship between television viewing and school achievement including educational skills, and clear thinking.

Other types of the media (e.g., newspaper, books, journals, the Internet) can educate for violence, peace or for both. They all need careful selection and good judgement.

The media, as both educator for peace or violence and as deterrent to education, are only two of the issues surrounding the media. Another alarming situation is the power which transnational corporations have over the media. As Carlota Lopes da Silva (1987) said: "The control of information is a major barrier to peace" (p.1). Educators should be aware of this and other social issues and be sure that students, especially on the university level, discuss, study, and debate them.

Peers

From the time children start making friends outside the family, peers are very influential forceful teachers. Young people learn from and mimic behaviors of their peers because: there is fear of ridicule, loss of status, and friendship; there may be a need for role models; there is deep understanding among peers and friendship among them can give fun, strength and security However, tremendous problems can arise if children become attached to a group that has tendencies toward violence.

If children are nurtured toward self-otherness from infancy onward, they can have the capacity to think independently, to make decisions according to their own best values, and can recognize and refuse harmful behaviors when they are suggested by others. Therefore, education for self-otherness is the best help in selecting peer friends and the greatest defense against harmful peer influences.

Play

Play is essential to children's development. From a very early age play becomes a large part of children's lives. It is a vital learning tool for children play patterns and play materials are determined by culture, but play of some type seems to be central to development. From these activities children can learn much.

- Healthy play helps children come to understand and

learn how to constructively express vital feelings such as respect/disrespect, confidence /timidity, courage/fear, empathy/anger. love/hate and internal conflicts, that they experience in their day to day lives.

- By replaying experiences, children become able to distinguish between fantasy and reality and learn more about what the world is all about.
- Through playing through complex situations they can develop creative and problem-solving skills. They learn how to gain important information, think creatively, and develop intellectual and cognitive concepts.
- By being physically active in play, children learn how to manipulate things and develop muscle use, coordination, and strength.
- In imitation of healthy living and dramatic play children can rehearse adult roles, internalize their meanings, and learn to accept the roles they are expected to take later.
- In cooperative play children can become more empathetic with others, learn how to formulate values, principles, and guides for their behavior, and use of psychological skills.
- As children and adults develop these competencies, they gain self-esteem, self-control. and self-direction. They take steps toward autonomy and self-otherness.

Play can also help child-care gives nurture better. By watching children as they get deeply involved in pay adults can learn much about their feelings, thinking, and needs.

In their 1990 book Nancy Carlsson-Paige and Diane Leve also emphasized that parents can :learn from children's play and playthings...the issues they need to work on...the content and quality of their play determines what they will learn" (p.3). They say that "...parents need to find ways to influence their children's involvement" (p.4). They give valuable information and suggestion for ways to compensate for the harmful effects of violent television and war toys. Some of these are summarize in the following.

- Healthy play requires many opportunities, places, time, and materials (not just manufactured toys). It is important that they have toys that can help meet their needs.
- Provide toys which encourage cooperation, sharing, empathy and growth for others as well as self, rather than toys which glorify war, fighting, violence, and which desensitize children to pain and killing of others.
- Avoid violent television and war toys as long as it can be done without creating too many negative feelings in children. Limits, negotiations, and compromise are sometimes in order.
- Toys should be removed if they are used to be destructive or hurtful. Reject Nintendo which allows no room for imagination or dramatic play, and also those toys that can be used only for imitation of TV scenes or mutilation of human body parts.
- Without condemnation of children and their ideas, discuss their feelings and those of their make-believe characters.
- Share your information, ideas, ways of thinking, values, and dialogue with children; and teach them how and why to think for themselves based upon principles such as equity and concern for humanity.
- Find ways, when needed, to direct play to creative, thought-provoking avenues.
- Discuss with children their television programs and their imitations of them. Relate statements to their level of understanding.
- Provide other interesting activities. For example, let them share cooking, shopping, gardening, and other tasks, and compliment them on the work they do.
- Encourage cooperation and interdependence and be

patient because these things are difficult to learn. Avoid competition as much as possible and let them share in decisions which affect them.

Play and fun can be tremendous assets to parents and teachers for releasing tensions for everyone and creating a climate of good will with children. Play usually plants seeds of peace but it can foster violence. It can be an asset or a liability in the educative process.

Great effort should be placed on fostering cooperative play and recreation and avoiding competitive violent sports. This issue is discussed in Chapter 3.

Components of Education that Promote Peace

Educators, parents, and students should make every effort to include, as nearly as possible, all vital areas of constructive education in students programs. There are many more areas of education that can be examined here. I have chosen the following to discuss as components of education that encourage peace: *General education, Locating and using factual information, Learning to think, Developing self otherness, Formulating values for self-direction, and Education for social action.*

General Education

Peace-promoting education should include a well-rounded general education. This means gaining knowledge skills, attitudes, and behaviors from all studies appropriate for meeting individual needs. Very important are : the arts, history, literature, music and the sciences - biological, physical, and social (this includes FLEP). Education should integrate these fields of study, give them a global perspective, and a human maturation approach.

It is important to recognize that all fields of knowledge influence human life. Each constructive area of education can promote peace, but each can be taught in ways to promote violence. For example, economics can be taught to include the urgency of equity in business, in taxation, and in income; or economics can be taught as exploitative economic procedures (i.e., the "I win, you lose" type) that hampers cooperation, and human well-being.

Present educational curricula and their learning environments need to be analyzed with the sure of peace promoting criteria. Those conditions, curricula, activities, teaching and surroundings which are conducive to ill-will, inequity, competition, violence, and physical or emotional ill-health should be eliminated. Those conditions that foster peace and maturation should be strengthened and expanded.

In my opinion, most public education in the U.S has been effective and certainly should not be throw out without substituting something better. Many educational practices, areas of study, courses, and materials have been tried for years and have been found to be relevant and growth promoting. However, they are not necessarily helpful just because they have been used traditionally. New offerings and materials may need to be added, even though they are not in the traditional programs (e.g., FLEP)

This is also true of disciplinary practices; punishment as a means of promoting desirable behavior and violence for resolving conflict are practices that have been tried throughout time, but research has found them to be damaging and ineffective in self-directing constructive character building. For each age group and situation, old ways should be evaluated and new possibilities considered. We can them save throw out, or reform education accordingly.

Locating and Using Factual Information

Knowledge is necessary as raw material for constructing meanings, and for making judgments and decisions. It is important, therefore, to learn how to search out facts. Students can learn how to examine research findings, analyze theories, evaluate traditional cultural patterns, challenge beliefs and to employ thinking processes to determine as far as possible what is truth and what is false. As facts are found, they can be used as appropriate.

The search for truth appears to have had its beginning in the long-forgotten past and hopefully will continue as long as Earth sustains life. For what they thought was truth, Socrates struggled and died, Epictetus was driven from Rome. Plato and Aristotle debated, honest loving parents have taught their children, and dogmatically-minded bigots have waged war. It is the responsibility of all of us to find and live by as much truth as we can find and be tolerant with, and listen to, those who disagree with us.

In addition to formal education, where do we get our information? The word informed is an important one. We are dependent upon the media to become informed. We learn from the written word, from television, from radio, from direct communication with other people, and from our own observations and integration of everything. Thus, we need more self-other people to be involved in writing articles, letters, books, speaking out on television, radio, in groups, and with friends.

In the United States we are fortunate to be free to express our beliefs and be willing to listen to others. We do not exercise that freedom as much as we should; if we do not locate facts, think for ourselves, and participate as citizens, others will take that freedom from us.

If of course, confusing because there are so many facts, and false precepts posing as truth, that we tend to get lost in the maze of it all. It is easy to decide that there are no reliable truths, or that all things are true if we choose to believe them. There is a tendency to confuse freedom of thought (which we want for everyone) with the idea that in the realm of ideas whatever is believed is true. In the physical world we know that theories are not necessarily true- the belief that the world was flat did not make it so. But in the realm of social issues, it is too often assumed that their are no truths, Not so-truths are there whether we find them or not. Certainly, we can rarely, if ever, be sure that what we think to be fact is absolutely true. But this should not deter us from forever searching for truth and acting upon the best evidence we can find, and respect others rights to do the same. It should also be recognized that for many questions there are no easy "right" or "wrong" answers. Rather, because of the complexity, and the many facets involved, the most creative thinking will bring forth several possible alternatives. Then, we should act upon what we think is the best alternative.

People are by nature seekers of knwoledge. A brief observation of a child under three years of age can convince one of that fact. Babies are born with no understanding of their surroundings. They immediately start reaching out to investigate and experience everything. They are curious. They ant to handle, explore question, and examine. They throw themselves into every experience, patiently inspect, and sometimes try to tear things apart to make sense of them. It is amazing how much they learn in two or three years, but it is alarming to see how adults often frustrate that learning drive in the very early years by hampering their investigation. Formal education often continues to suppress children's desire to investigate and search out facts and acquire an understanding of their environment. As a result children can become defensive, unimaginative, timid, dull, evasive, inwardly hostile, and/or violence prone.

Therefore, parents, teachers, and everyone else should learn how to encourage the force to grow and inspire the love of learning. They must do more than just hand out facts to be memorized. Children need encouragement to locate and use facts to meet their needs, to answer their own questions, and to empower themselves to become self-directing, without harming others.

Learning to Think

Education's most important task is to teach people how to think for themselves and become self-directing people. According to John Holt (1964) teaching and textbooks often espouse "...the cause of making children grow up into the kind of people we want them to be, thinking whatever we want them to think" (p.212).

Children have been encouraged to be fearful, obey without

question, and be either docile or domineering. Children are often praised for unquestioning acceptance of what they are told, and receive disapproval for individual thinking and exploratory behaviors. Approval is given for obedience, conformity, suggestibility, and docility rather than on investigation, questioning, thinking through situations, and learning to become self-directing. Children become "answer-grabbers." "teacher-pleasers," and nonthinking followers.

Adolf Hitler said, "What good fortune for those in power that people do not think." In his reign of terror there where millions who were indeed, nonthinking obedient followers. No doubt, there were many willing followers who were also emotionally hostile terrorists and thus willing followers. Many were those who were fearful and disliked the cruelty, but being weak and seeing no way to oppose, they followed. The difference between these followers and millions of nonthinkers and non-actors today all over the world is not in kind of people but in the kind of situations and the kind of leaders.

If the world is to avoid such dictatorships and other human exploiters, and if there is to be an advance in democracy, human rights, freedom, and eventually peace on earth, greater educational emphasis must be placed upon individual thinking ability and self-direction. When children are not taught at an early age how to think, they continue throughout life to be victims of other people's dictates, indoctrination, and conditioning influences. Such nonthinkers can be led like lemmings to their own destruction. Or they can be led or motivated to injure others.

An example of such victimization has been noted in modern-day religious cults. Most of the following members of these alarming cults have not developed the powers of thinking for themselves, resisting brainwashing, and avoiding authoritative persuasion. It is critical that educational systems teach children how to be self-esteemed, confident, and able to think critically and reason rationally, always in the search for greater truth.

Therefore, one of the most important tasks/responsibilities of child caregivers and educators is to **teach children how to**

think, not just what to think. They need skill in "inferential reasoning" which Marie Winn (1985) defined as the ability

> ...to draw conclusions, form **judgments**, and interpret and create new ideas out of what one reads; it is the crucial factor that underpins meaningful reading in literature, history, science, and other subjects (P.85).

Teachers should set up conditions under which constructive thinking take place. This encourages children to feel free to question if something does not make sense to them. Teachers can provide experiences that arouse children's curiosity and calls forth reasoning, judgment, attention, intelligence, interest, concentration, and involvement.

Albert Schweitzer (1953) said, "With the spirit of the age I am in complete disagreement, because it is filled with disdain for thinking" (p.170). He attributed people's mistrust in thinking partially to influences which rob them of confidence in themselves and their own thinking: He added:

> They [people] lose all feeling for truth, and all sense of need for it as well, finding themselves quite comfortable in a life without thought driven now here, now there, from one opinion to another (p.173).

Schweitzer said that it was his own thinking which led him

> ...to the ethical and affirmative position of reverence for Life...I therefore stand and work in the world as one who aims at making men less shallow and morally better by making them think (p.170).

hence, Schwetizer, through his thinking, formulated a system of values which guided his life's decisions. He was also able to help others develop their own thinking abilities. Like Schweitzer, we can think for ourselves and become our own authorities. Of course it is important to consider others' views and to be open to change as more truth is discovered, but not because others think we should.

We can then, as Kenneth Boulding (1965) suggests; "Contribute to the noosphere" i.e, the world of knowledge). What we think influences what we do, and everything we do influences others' thinking and behavior, whether we are aware of it or not. Let us then, accept our opportunities and responsibilities to think and contribute our thinking in discussion or in whatever ways are available to us. Boulding advises:

> It is good *for all of us to stop* occasionally and *inquire in what* direction the content of *our minds is changing*, and what the *processes* are by which this changed takes *place.* [*and*] ...through the information outflow which we make toward *others. In* conversation, *writing*, and the ordinary activity for daily life we are constantly communicating with others, and as a result of these communications their images of the world change (p.194).

He contends that we can "..come to have new knowledge which no one had before. This process is often regarded as the privilege of a few how are engaged in professionals research." This is not the case. Probably more common than outright creations in the realm of discoveries and inventions is in the creation of new concepts, the formulation of new combinations and dimensions of concepts, and the clarification of ideas which can influence change.

Educators need to believe that *every one of us can, and do, make a difference in the world.* All human begins should be encouraged to pursue constructive change. It is too easy to see the terrible destructive forces around us, recognize the fearful dangers, feel the hurtful pressures, and become discouraged. Many way want to give up hope because many greedy people, especially in high places cause destruction and violence to people and the planetr. It is crucial that people's enormous potential for constructive transformation be developed. The resultant life-giving healing forces could diminish the dangers, promote human well-being and lead to universal human cooperation and peace. There is still hope for humanity. Hope, not fear, promotes creativity, progress, reform, and joy in living. We can guide *change by* means of conscious purposes created by rational thinking. We can have a *better* world. Reevaluation and reorganization using rational empathetic *thinking* may be education's greatest responsibility. Teachers and parents need to understand and cooperate in these processes.

The how-to-think process. This process includes the following:

1. Elements involved inconstructive thinking include: concentration analysis logic, objectivity, interpretation, imagination, evaluation, reasoning, judgment, synthesis, and intellectualization.

2. Basic psychic forces that begin developing at a very early-age are interacting influences in the thinking/learning processes. They provide criteria for judgments, guidelines for goals, and basic background for thinking. These include: *feelings, beliefs, emotions, attitudes and memories of personal experiences.*

3. How to think peacefully is also dependent upon ability to integrate personal qualities into the thinking process. his means *thinking* honesty *critically, empathetically, equitably, lovingly, compassionately*, and *independently*.

4. Intellectualization is the process of giving rational form, content or reason to something. In this context, I am referring especially to applying thought, understanding, knowledge, and insight into feelings beliefs, attitudes, values, and partially forgotten experience. An example of a need for intellectualizing is when children have been psychologically or physically abused, they may feel great fear, guilt, and humiliation as though they are to blame, or/and they may repress all memory of the condition and express their hostility toward themselves or someone else. They usually need help in intellectually recognizing that the guilt lies with the abuser, not with themselves, fully feeling the hurt, and accepting it as a real situation with which they can cope when they have the needed assistance and encouragement. This is where significant others, including teachers, can be of help.

5. Thinking with integrity is a basic principle in a peace-promoting thinking process. By this I mean basing conclusions upon what one honestly thinks is true based upon one's investigations and convictions, not upon what other people may expect.

When working with students, teachers should encourage them to *question* and *argue* points of view so that their conclusions will be their own. Students and teachers can question each other as to the evidence (such as research, experiences, observations) to support their thinking. Teachers may ask: what values are your ideas based upon? what effect will various alternatives have upon the situation, yourself, or others? Do aspects within the arguments seem illogical? is more thought needed before reaching a conclusion?

Imaging is another thinking process that is especially important for creating alternatives that foster peace. It is the ability to create images. Elise Boulding (1988) calls it "Image literacy." She writes that imaging "involves the individuals ability to combine the materials of inner and outer experience worlds, drawn from all the senses, to shape new patterns of 'reality' (p.86). Based upon the worked of Fred Polak (1972) and the workshop format of Warren Ziegler (1982, 1987a, 1987b), she has developed a detailed system of "social imaging" which ,makes use of imagination in a disciplined way. It is a way of visualizing alternative possibilities for something other than the present situation that could better meet needs and resolve problems. Imaging can help people approach problems (from personal through international) and bring about concrete possibilities for transformation of self and society. This process assists both individuals and groups to see relationships beyond the obvious reality. Encouraging the development of imagination should be a basic goal in education. Students can be taught to imagine solutions to many types of situation such as how could schools, homes, television, and even the world be better?

Other activities can be used in conjunction with imaging. For example; brainsforming in small groups, drawing pictures of their ideas, writing letters to community leaders and legislators and role-playing win-win solutions.

All of these approaches influence the thinking process and are very important to helping children become self-directing peace-promoting people.

Developing Self-Otherness

In preceding chapters, considerable detail was given to the meaning of self-otherness, qualities of self-other oriented people, conditions conducive to the development of these qualities, and progressive steps and principles that lead toward self-otherness.

Because peace and freedom can exist best among self-other oriented people, education at all levels should find many ways to promote the development of student's self-otherness. Procedures, relationships, and activities in the schools should help children build feelings of self-esteem and love for others. Education can enlarge people's conviction that they are worthy, unique, strong, and capable of being and becoming that which is best for them to be and become. It can reinforce people's confidence that with their inherited potentials and the resoruces (in family, school, and communicative available to them they can formulate their own set of values, beliefs, skills attitudes, ethical qualities, and social responsibilities. These students, in turn will promote equity, equality, altruism, and integrity in society.

Education should avoid practices and conditions that cause students to feel ashamed or insecure, in their efforts to function on their present levels of learning. Everyone needs respect acceptance, and appreciation regardless of their level of functioning Education can help each student check his/her progress in moving toward levels of achievement that are appropriate for her/him. Students need motivation, encouragement, and help, but competing, brainwashing stereotyping, threatening, condemning, shaming comparisons with others, and punishment, should be avoided as they seriously impede development and teach self-onlyness.

People begin developing their psychic forces and their unique personal qualities at a very early age. Modifications are made as life goes on, and education can provide opportunities for this process. Growth and change is what education is all about.

Teachers are faced with great burdens and tremendous educational challenges with children who enter school having feelings of unworthiness and qualities of self-onlyness. Many times they have not been adequately loved and cared for and/or have been abused in their early years. Hence, they need special encouragement, respect care, and motivation. Teachers are often not prepared to help such children and may condemn or punish them. Teachers need competence in teaching children how to manage their feelings healthfully, and how to facilitate their own growth. This is most difficult, especially with the heavy teaching load many teachers have to carry.

If, when children reach formal school age, they are already developing well toward their goal of self-otherness, they can continue this maturation process if teaching is oriented toward peace-promoting, not violence-causing incentives. However, studies indicate that most children's self-esteem decreases rather than increases as they progress through school . This is disappointing. Education for social responsibility and self-otherness can help prevent this crisis.

However some principles which are important to the development of the full range of components of self-otherness, are beginning to be given more emphasis. Somewhat more attention is also being given to countering those forces in society, in schools, and within the family which cause hostility and violence to develop and which inhibit the ability to love. More teachers are avoiding condemnation and threats and giving encouragement, explanation, and acceptance which promotes honest constructive behaviors and reduces defensiveness, destructiveness, competition, retaliation, and self incrimination. We are also learning more about how to help students understand and deal with feelings such as fear, anger, hostility, and discouragement. Furthermore, we recognize that emotions need educating fully as much as does the intelligence and the relationships. But much more research and dialogue is needed in acquiring teaching skills in this area of education.

Education can enlarge its teaching for self-otherness and restrict experiences that cause self-onlyness. Adults in the future will not then, with Jan Rye Kinghorn (1986), have to say in condemnation of former teacher:

you helped me extend my hands with incredible machines.
my eyes with telescopes and microscopes.
my ears with telephones, radios, and sonar,
my brain with computers,
but you did not help me extend
My heart, love, concern
to the entire human family.
you, teacher, gave me half a loaf (p.9).

Let us confirm the statement made by Former Secretary General of the United Nations, the late U. Thant, in a speech in Toronto in 1966:

> The law of love and compassion for all living creatures is a gain a doctrine to which we are all too ready to pay lip service. However, if it is to become reality, it requires a process of education, a veritable mental renaissance. Once it has become reality, national as well as international problems will fall into perspective and become easier to solve. Wars and conflict, too, will then become a thing of the past, because wars begin in the minds of men, and in those minds love and compassion would have built the defenses of peace (as quoted by Robert Muller, 1982, p.7,8).

Society in general should urge educational institutions to provide the kind of education that fosters the development of self-esteem love care cooperation, and other qualities that are a part of a self-other orientation to life.

Formulating Values for Self-Direction

Values as criteria for decisions. It was noted earlier that values are important besides for behavior. They are people's codes of conduct. Therefore, it is important that people formulate a clear set of values, Educational systems play a large role in fostering the formation of students' values. At every level of education students, value-making is influenced by teachers, peers, programs, and various activities.

It should be emphasized that education cannot be "value-free" as a popular notionaffirms. Everything is taught from a value frame of reference and in my opinion, should be. Value building is important in education because children need help in learning how to decide on values for themselves. Even when teachers chief goal to help students develop their own critical creative thinking and value-clarification powers, values are implied and taught. It is true that certain controversial an sensitive ideas can be avoided in discussion, by their very omission makes a value statement. Also, since teaching is very much a matter of learning by example, teachers necessarily teach many of their own values by being whom they are. Since teachers cannot prevent the teaching of values of some kind, they should think carefully as to what kind of values they really believe and want made available for children to consider? Values should not be dictated but discussed and given consideration among students and teachers.

It is vital that students learn to formulate their own values, but they need help to use their thinking in this continuing formulating process. It is most crucial that students be taught how to search out various types of facts, ideas, and opinions, to clarify and evaluate them, and to rely on their sharpened judgment to choose appropriate alternatives rather than relying entirely on prescribed formulas. However, we must recognize that not only logical thinking, but also value criteria must be determined. Families, peers, schools, and society are very influential. However, early in life each individual needs to become more and more skilled in how to make their final decisions.

Examples of criteria that are self-other oriented include: love and respect for all life, desire for equity for all people, a love for learning which will continue throughout life a better interrelated world without violence, and one's self as a respected self-other person.

Materialistic values have been allowed to dictate many goals of education. This has often left society floundering for solutions to social and psychological problems—problems that influence people most seriously in their daily lives. Interpersonal relationships skills and issues of responsibility are often neglected. The resulting frustration and confusion has led to conflict violence, and in its worst manifestations, to war.

More attention is often given to the technical pieces of education than to values. Vito Perrone (1990) give examples:

> There is, it seems, more concern about whether children learn the mechanics of reading and writing than grow to love deeply reading and visiting; learn about democratic practices than have practice in democracy; engage in competition rather than learn the power of cooperation and collaborative thought; see the world narrowly, as simple and ordered rather than broad, complex and uncertain; come to accept the vested authority that exists around them in organizational structures and text rather than challenge such authority, bringing a healthy skepticism to the world...(p.22).

Some common values are important to make education relevant to the times in which we live. In order for education to have significance for the present and for the future, we must have a clear idea of where we are and where we want to go based on our values. One reason "history often repeats itself" is that people usually do not analyze the past to determine what has been constructive and what destructive, and they become victims of change rather than creators of their futures.

Most of us value democracy. Educational systems need to become more successful in teaching and practicing skills in democratic cooperative decision-making. Both equality of all rights, opportunities, and grass roots participatory democracy are still unfinished issues for most people and for education.

It is time to reevaluate our values. Societies throughout the world have not worked hard enough (either nationally or internationally) to cooperatively formulate common values for the common good. Hence, conflict, chaos, and war over ideologies still prevail. One of society's biggest tasks is to cooperatively come to a consensus on some basic human values upon which to base education, social structures, and international relations. This does not mean, as Elise Boulding says,

...that you or I should decide what the world should be like and then try to get other people to do what we think is necessary. Our own experience and insight are important, but they can only develop further as we dialogue with others and learn to work with others (p.xxi).

I should like to think of this period as an age of transition when we are moving from some harmful "moral values" (e.g., punishment and competition) which do not meet people's needs, to other values that encourage self-otherenss (e.g., empathy, equity, and helpfulenss). It may be that as we have moved along that unmarked trial to higher values we have sometimes lost our way. Perhaps there are justifiable hopes for building a better road clearly marked with human values. This we shall learn as we work together on the important issues involved.

Education For Social Action

Another important component of education that promotes peace could be called *social-educational action.* Self-otherness implies social responsibility. This means personal participation in the world outside the home, school, and work, in economic, political, and social, affairs. It can result in feelings of empowerment, dispelling feelings of alienation, indifference, and hopelessness. Such participation can: enlarge students knowledge of social systems and their role in causing violence and peace in the world; build confidence in their abilities to make a difference in the world; promote maturation of their personal lives; contribute to transformation of social structures; and give them some satisfactions of their need to contribute to a cause larger than themselves. William Glasser (1969) say,

> Students who are taught social responsibility in school, who learn in a living situation to think of ways to help each other solve their problems both as individuals and as groups, are better able to help solve, or at least to cope with, the larger problems of society. We must get more students involved with each other in an educational system that seems important enough to them so that they will work to learn to think, to solve problems, and to become socially responsible

(p.76).

Surveys indicate that voting-age young people are very skeptical of their ability to make any difference in the way the world is toady. Many also hold out very little hope for the world. Hence, it is understandable that their voting rates are very low. Taking part in discussing important world issues and then going out and participating in action to advance their point of view empowers them and encourages further participation. Therefore, if we expect to live in a democracy, we must educate our children to participate in democratic procedures both in and out of school, not just listen to teachers talk about democracy and patriotism.

Since extensive curriculum guidelines are not within the scope of this writing, the following suggestions for activities may be in order here:

- Help students develop greater empathy and conflict resolution skills by getting them to take the perspective of people with opposing views, recognizing points of agreement as well as points of difference and being willing to make changes if greater truths are gleaned. This helps them to take less dogmatic stands and to participate more willingly. Both real examples and role-playing can be used.
- Promote cooperative relationships *through many* different regular school activities, by getting children to help each other, by studying real and fictional role models, and role playing.
- Encourage students to discuss ideas with friends and family and formulate a project which will change some sector of their community, including the school community.
- Write letters to editors, congressmen, and community leaders. This common idea is much more effective than most people seem to realize and should be used more extensively.
- Participate in model UN programs and action clubs.
- Encourage young people to explore together issues that are relevant to their own lives. In this way they can more easily understand the roots of violence and the seeds of peace within

societal structures. For example, when teaching about the dangers of drugs, parents and teachers can also encourage thinking and discussion about why these conditions exist and what might be done to change them. Shelly Berman (1990) says:

...I've realized that helping young people develop a sense of social responsibility means opening a conversation... We cannot impose attitudes and understandings. Instead, we must beign a dialogue by listening carefully to young people's ideas and questions. Not only do they need to feel herd and validated in order to grow into meaningful adult roles in society; but we, too, need to learn from them what their real issues are in order to facilitate their growth most effectively (p.7).

- Allow children to organize and carry out projects such as tree-planting cleaning up the school ground or a park, formulate rules, guidelines, and a set of in-common values for the classroom or entire school, organize a drive to collect money to relieve hunger. Such projects help children feel they can make a difference.
- Set up a program in which students visit and even volunteer their time in various social service programs. This will help them learn about what is being done for people, and how they may be of service. Such programs are applicable at various ages.
- Solve part of the summer problem of idleness of children by setting up a children's peace campaign which children, school personnel, and community people cooperate. One such camp, was organized by Millee Livingston (1987) at Auburn, California. She reported that:

Activities were designed to create an atmosphere of mutual respect and of appreciation for nature; to discover the biological interdependence of all living things and to extend this understanding to global interdependence; and to present alternatives for children. Other than war, as a solution for disputes (p.19).

A word of caution: project objectives should not be too complex, large, or distant, because they lead to failure and thus to discouragement and insecurity.

A function of education is to help students become knowledgeable about the total "web of life" on this planet and to see in that total functioning a particular place for themselves in contributing and promoting peaceful living.

Other Ways to Upgrade Education

This section includes many ideas from John Holt's (1964) classic little book. *How children Fail. He gives* a bit of his educational philosophy and points to a number of ways schools fail in teaching children and how hey could better meet children's needs. Holt saw "educational failures" which are impediments to children's development and stifling to their drives to learn.

Understand how children feel and think. Children are very sensitive, easily damaged, and their true feelings are often hidden under various masks they learn to wear to cope with adults who fail to understand them. Teachers should be very diligent in gaining understanding of, appreciation for, and empathy with the feelings of children. Warm, caring, empathetic, knowledgeable, close relationships with teachers are very important components of education. Future teachers need opportunities for close association with children, together with help in gaining insight into their feelings and behavoir. Therefore, this learning should be an important part of teacher education programs.

Holt seems to have a deep understanding and sensitivity to the feelings of children. He said children fail primarily because "...they become afraid, bored, and confused. " He continued.

They are afraid, above all else, of failing, of disappointing or displeasing the many anxious adults around them, whose limitless hopes and expectations for them hang over their heads like a cloud.

They are bored because the things they are given and told to do in school are so trival, so dull, and make such limited and narrow demands on the wide spectrum of their intelligence, capabilities, and talents.

They are confused because most of the torrent of words that pour over them in school makes little or no sense. It often flatly contradicts other things they have been told, and hardly ever has any relation to what they really know to the rough model of reality that they carry around in their minds (p.16).

Children are sometimes disallowed to be honest about their own feelings, like/dislikes, and what they think. Teachers often fail to "listen sympathetically and honestly." School should be a place where students are accepted as they are and can feel free to express their own feelings and thoughts, without rebuke or condemnation; where it is okay to make mistakes and learn from them; take part in formulating rules, making decisions, giving suggestions, and evaluating procedures and results.

Make education relevant to students needs and interests. Teachers quell initiative and investigative learning by handing out too many facts, rules, symbols, and ideas which have little meaning or relevance to children's needs. Present knowledge, or interests. Students should gather facts in response to a need for them in order to make a decision, clarify an issue, resolve a conflict, or solve a problem. Rules should be cooperatively made by students and teachers for the good of all. Symbols and ideas should be clear and relevant to students' real lives. William Glasser (1969) gave an example of unrelated teaching. When he was working with a group of fifth graders in a special session, the children they had been learning the Roman numerals. He asked them what use there was for knowing the Roman numerals. They could think of nothing except that they are sometimes used to number chapters. He then asked if they were used in Rome. Some thought, yes, this would be a good reason for learning them. Glasser reports that: "This seemingly good idea did not last long...because one had been to Rome the previous summer. He told the class that, all the time he had been there, he had ever seen a Roman numeral" (p.55). Glasser says we should try to break down the "wide disparity between school materials and the outside world". Until this day I can recite in the proper order, the names of the Oklahoma Territorial Governors that I was required to memorize. The only reason I have *ever* found to use them was to illustrate the fruitfulness of learning irrelevant materials. I could have learned another meaningful poem which I loved doing.

Teaching is often coercive. Classrooms, and experiences within them, should be set up in such a way that students can pursue their interests, develop their abilities, learn "naturally" and "grow" in knowledge, in the love of learning. In this way students can go on to "deal realistically, imaginatively, and constructively with whatever new experience life throws...[their]way" (Holt, pp. 220-222)

Minimize formulas devices and recipes. There is too much "cookbooking" that is, the use off.

> ...formulas, devices, or recipes dimly remembered and never understood...it is numbo Jumbo, and the notion that if a child repeats a meaningless statement or process enough times it will become meaningful is as absurd as the notion that if a parrot imrattes human speech long enough it will know what it is talking about (Fomt. Pp. 147-150)

There is too much "answer directing" (i.e., emphasis placed on getting the "right" answer rather than on understanding the why, the procedures, and the background. Too much stress is placed or immediate success and too much shame in failure (wrong answers), rather than on patience and persistence in the pursuit of understanding.

"Disconnected hunks" of subject matter are hander out rather than giving tasks that are "interesting and demanding." This handicaps students from seeing the world as one system with many sub-systems. They may need help in relating issues, events and processes holistically and in making interconnections between world crises, social, economic, political practices, and their family relationships and personal growth. Much of the curriculum need to have a systems-dynamics orientation. On upper levels of education, more interdisciplinary courses could be offered to meet this need. The interdisciplinary course, following the general outline of this book. Which I developed and taught and San Dieggo State University, is an example.

Cope constructively with problem behavior. Problem behavior is too often countered with condemnation, put-downs, retribution, and even physical punishment. It is unfortunate that "spanking" seems to be growing in popularity in schools Antisocial, disruptive, or violent behavior should not be condoned. However, misbehavior can be met with empathy, respect, explanation , acceptance of the person (not the behavior), and constructive approaches and efforts to get at more basic roots of the situation with confidence that he/she can succeed in changing behavior. If a climate of warmth, affirmation, trust, cooperation, and good communication is maintained, problem behavior will occur less frequently. Children will help each other with problems if they have positive self-esteems and the atmosphere is relaxed and comfortable; and if there is a feeling of community within the group. Punishment ad retaliatory measures may relieve an immediate crisis, but they will cause rebellion, send hurt feelings underground with resulting nonthinking submission or domineering attitudes. In the long run, the situation is aggravated by showing approval for condemnation and violence as a way of solving problems.

Teachers must have fewer students and more help if they are to effectively cope with the misconduct crisis. Jim LaBates (1987) wrote an article on "the perils of assembly -line education." He argued: "Mass production may have worked for Henry Ford, but it doesn't work in education. We can't put our children on assembly lines and expect them to grow as individuals" (p.5).

Urge that education be given higher priority in society. More research needs to be done to discover how schools can better facilitate learning in students. Most teachers have done remarkably well with limited support, resources, and background in coping techniques.

Teacher certainly could do a better job if education were given a higher priority by the public and if societal structures would better support their efforts. The possibilities are almost limitless, but it cannot all be accomplished by teachers who are overloaded with work, lack adequate materials, have too many students, and have sometimes been given inadequate preparation.

As citizens we should make sure that there is universal education that it is of peace-promoting quality (provides seeds for peace, not roots of violence); that it is well supported and upgraded; and that formal education is available for everyone regardless of sex, race, culture, religion, or abilities. In urging education for all. Robert Muller points out that adult literacy rates, range all the way from 98-100 percent in the most literate countries to a low of 3 percent for women in some of the least literate countries. The quantity and quality of education now being received varies widely both from region to region in the U.S. and from country to country.

Foster cooperation, eliminate competition through education. One of the most damaging common practices in education is the extensive use of competition. The issue of competition is discussed quite extensively in Chapter 12; additional points here will relate the issue to education.

Everyone concerned is harmed by competition but cooperation brings many rewards, especially for children. In most competitive situations, most people lose and one or a few win. The few how win may tend to form elitist attitudes toward themselves and degrade other who lose. Those who lose tend to have difficulty maintaining or gaining self-esteem which is so necessary for their total well-being. This is especially true when these patterns of win and defeat occur repeatedly. There is also a tendency for jealousies, hostilities, discouragements, prejudice, and discrimination to develop among children as a result of competition.

Instead of competition, teachers can use, and teach children how to cooperate. Cooperation elicit is better learning, higher self-esteem, kinder social relations, fuller sense of responsibility, greater group productivity and a more peaceful atmosphere. Children can grow best by making improvements in themselves as they need it, not in competition with others. They can better accept other regardless of their level of maturity or competence. Self-improvement is more stimulating, encouraging and productive than either winning or losing.

Alfie Kohn (1986) in his book. No Contest makes many valid arguments against the pervasive practice of competition. He wrote:

> A child's performance should never be compared with that of someone else (including a sibling; a classmate, or onesel as a child) in order to motivate her [the child] to do better. Affection and approval should not be made contingent on a child's performance... we should be particularly alert to the subtle and insidious ways in which we encourage our children to tie their feelings of self-worth to winning; so long as we need them to be the best in their class. They will get the message and require the same of themselves. The result, as we have seen, is not excellence but anxiety, self-doubt, hostility and a decline in intrinsic motivation among other things (p.185)

Kohn continues to urge that children be taught in explicit terms...about the myths of competition and the respects in which cooperation offer a healthier alternative...Let us show our children both how and why to cooperate" (pp. 185-186).

The practice of giving children letter grades is a form of competition the results of which are very damaging. Glasser says, "Grades...have become a substitute for learning, the symbolic, replacement for knowledge" (p.61). Grades were created to measure children's progress and to stimulate students to learn more, but they do neither.

Avoid sexism and racism in schools. Chapter 12 gives considerable emphasis to sexism as an example of prejudice and a source of violence it should be added that sexism, as well as racism are still serious problems in education. White male students are still given greater opportunities, encouragement, financial assistance, greater motivation, and opportunities for advancement.

Include Family Life Education for peace (FLEP). One of the most serious omissions in education at all levels is in the field of family life education. As stated in various ways throughout this book, peace and the well-being of all people are dependent upon children being taught to become emotionally and physically healthy, loving, cooperative, creatively, thinking, self-directing (i.e. self-other people).

There are some excellent child/family education programs from pre-school through university. However only a small number of children and young people are exposed to them. Subject matter is determined by age and needs of students. In the early years it is centered primarily on family relationships and self-development.

During the later junior high school years, there are continued opportunities and special challenges for helping youngsters feel comfortable with their families, their changing bodies, relationships with the opposite sex, responsible behavior, greater independent thinking and acting (especially in relationships with their peer groups) and how they relate to family values and rules.

By high schools students, are ready for solid courses in preparation for marriage and parenting. Such a preparation for marriage course should include; meanings of love, infatuation, and intimacy; dating practices and responsibilities hopes for their own future families with reality considerations as to whether or not to marry, live together, or remain single principles and practices for equality and equity between the sexes; roles, rules, and relationships in the family; and couple and family egalitarian communication, decision-making, conflict-resolution, and crisis - coping skills. The child development curriculum should include : the psisychological and psychological development of children; competencies in, and experience with care of them; and discussion of choices regarding having children. At every age, children and young people need to have planned experiences with babies and young children. Tremendous learning comes from these experiences.

Beginning college courses are similar, but more advanced

than the high school classes. Upper level classes should include in depth study of the various topics and issues in the FLEP curriculum. Students need to become familier (through contact) with community services for families and they need to understand related social and political issues. Students also need much deeper understanding of the psychology of human development toward self-otherness and human relationships. Very crucial is the educating of future FLEP teachers.

There are adult and continuing education programs in marriage enrichment and child guidance available in many places, and communities are becoming more creative in providing useful learning experiences. One of the most satisfying experiences of my teaching occurred after my retirement with a San Diego State University continuing education class of senior citizen couples. They reported great enrichment in their marriage relationships (We called the class "Staying afloat on golden pond.")

Teacher education should become more relevant. Teacher's have a great responsibility since *teaching is probably* the second most difficult task in the world next to *parenting.* It *holds* tremendous challenge and opportunity to be of service. Teacher's certainly could do a better job of teaching if education were a higher *priority in society.* The possibilities are almost limitless but it cannot be accomplished *by teachers* who are overloaded with work and have too many students and inadequate financial assistance. Industry would not think of operating with such limitations.

Note the words of Aronowitz and Giroux (1985):

> If the crisis in schooling is to be addressed adequately we will need to construct a public philosophy that points to new approaches for the education of existing and future teachers. At the core of such an approach would be a commitment to developing forms of knowledge, pedagogy, evaluation, and research that promote critical literacy and civic courage. From this starting point federal education policy would use its financial and political resources to promote absolute commitment to public schools as sites of learning. of social

> interaction, and of human emancipation. Within this theoretical context can be developed policy recommendations that encourage research and education that view teachers are intellectuals and moral leaders rather than mere technicians; students as critical thinkers and active citizens rather than simply future participants in the industrial - military order; and schools as centers of critical literacy and civic courage rather than merely training sites for occupational positions is the corporate order (p.206).

Educating for peace is a responsibility for all of us. We are all teachers of peace and/or violence whether we recognize it or not; so perhaps we should make greater efforts to be teachers for peace.

Let teachers, administrators, parents, and students work together on what each sees as the purposes, policies, and goals of education as a whole as well as of certain specific areas. Thy can look squarely at the beliefs and values upon which these are based, and they can formulate their own policy statements. From the consensus reached, curriculum, scope and sequence, learning experiences, an teaching materials drawn from many sources including the many published materials available. Peter Martorella's 1976 book on social studies is a good example.

In concluding this chapter, I quote form the 1986 commencement speeches of Teachers College President and Dean. The told graduates that the highest callings they should answer to as they embark on their careers are "Commitment an caring." These principles continue to be guiding forces at Teachers College where dedication to improving excellence in teaching and in educational systems include a graduate-degree program in peace education, President P.Michael Timpane said that graduates need "...to be rooted in a community of value and interest and to share with that community and others a commitment to social welfare."

Dean Judith Berman Brandenberg, vice President for academic affairs, said

> We sacrifice because we have a chance to make a difference,

> to do important work, and to serve society in critical ways. To care. As educators, psychologists and health professionals, we have chosen professions that can make a difference—professions where neutrality and indifference are unacceptable and where we must take sides. We must take the side of our clients, patients and students…As members of the TC community we are joined together by our commitment to care (p.1).

May we *care* enough for life and planet to *commit* ourselves to their welfare through education. Let us remember Rodrigo Carazo's words, "if we want peace we must educate for peace."

Chapter-9

Undermining Nonviolence: The Coming Role Of New Police Technologies

Steve Wright

Chapter-9

IN THE DECADES which have followed Gandhi's elaboration of nonviolent forms of social resistance, innovations in both the techniques and instruments of socio-political control have developed which threaten the functional viability of some of the practical applications of Gandhi's teachings and other more recent nonviolent tactics. What is presented below is a series of snapshots covering the state of the developments in new repression technologies, their role, function, and implications for future nonviolent actions. Evidence is presented both to explain how certain police and paramilitary tactics can undermine peaceful nonviolent actions and how a creative approach can take such possibilities into account and therefore maintain the principle and the power of nonviolent action. The paper concludes with an analysis of what can be done for expanding our awareness and for actually dealing with the threats that new tools of repression pose to the ethos of nonviolent techniques of social resistance. In particular a case is made for increasing nonviolent actions against the production and export of the technology of political control at the site of their manufacture. Such actions can forge a direct link of contact and solidarity to highlight the implications of local work by white-collar mercenaries in the so-called liberal democracies.

The New Technologies of Political Control

To illustrate some of the threats posed by what might be lumped together as advances in state repression technologies, it is worth exploring both what is meant by such terminology and what might be called the state of the art. The arsenals of repression now comprise the following categories:

Area denial technologies include razor wire used to seal off selected zones; surveillance, telephone and fax-tapping networks used to track dissidents; computerised communication; command and control systems linked to data banks and remote terminals (in security vehicles, border checkpoints etc); automatic vehicle recognition and tracking equipment; riot technology including whips, shotguns, incapacitating and less lethal weapons such as water cannon, sten grenades, multi-shot riot guns, plastic bullets, chemical irritants, electrified shields and 50,000 volt shock prods; jelly fish venom injector weapons; sound, light and electromagnetic zapping technologies; pre-fragmented exploding ammunition, dum dum bullets; internal security and public order vehicles; helicopter mounted crowd monitoring equipment; stroboscopic cameras which can photograph every participant in a demonstration in a matter of seconds; identity recognition systems; silenced sub-machine guns and assassination rifles; precision infrared and laser night sights; automated execution systems image intensifiers prison and restraining technologies, leg irons and thumb cuffs, blunt trauma inducing drugs; and interrogation and torture technologies. Apart from this hardware, there are also numerous standard operating procedures which from the software component of the trade. For example, the riot and counter-insurgency training. "low -intensity conflict" advisory support and technical support provided in various counter terror manuals, including the business of teaching scientific methods of interrogation, torture, execution, and the more brutal forms of human destruction supplied to authoritarian regimes.

The role and function of this equipment is to enhance the operation capacities of state security, paramilitary and policing agencies, by both speeding up processes of mass socio-political control and making them much more efficient in targetting those who might think of further questioning the prevalent status quo. The number of companies which make up the police industrial complex supplying such wares has grown substantially over the last decade or so. When the Richardson Institute first started to monitor the companies trading in state security supplies, less than 60 were identified.[1] More recently TRACES has uncovered nearly 3,000 and the list is still growing.[2] With an increasing number of ethnic and national conflicts emerging, it seems probable that many government will actively seek technological panaceas to destabilizing internal strife.

Undermining Nonviolence

Many of these new instruments provide a flexible but not always less than lethal coercive response to combat nonviolent actions. A design criterion has been to mask the real impact of their effects so that the media do not get an accurate picture of the level of coercion being deployed. Different pain thresholds can be built into the variety of the so-called less lethal weapons deployed. In practice, this means that quite severe punishment can be meted out to activists both directly at demonstrations etc and less visibly via sustained harassment and tracking following surveillance operations to single particular individuals out. There is also some evidence, from studies of the anti-Vietnam war demonstrations and from the conflict in Northern Ireland, that nonviolent episodes could be much more easily pushed into violent confrontations once new police technologies were either in evidence or actively deployed.

Work undertaken at the Richardson Institute, for example, showed that the so-called "less-lethal weapons" could produce a long-term series of dysfunctional effects that further destabilized this conflict.[3] Not all of the effects of these weapons are intended. For example, it was noted in the early 1970s that each new introduction of less-lethal weapons in Northern Ireland was more severe in its effect than the system it augmented or replaced and was associated with an upsurge in the overall political death count.[4] Further empirical work suggested that because these riot systems were being deployed within the context of a phased set of counter-insurgency tactics, the resistance they bred led to a successive deployment of each subsequent and more violent phase of the low-intensity conflict programme. In effect, they bred the dissent they were designed to "fix."[5] Quite odd patterns of weapon deployment emerged when the statistics of munitions fired were analysed over longer periods of time. For example, fairly constant levels of munitions were used as if the supply itself was the greatest determinant of usage (see Fig. 1).

A new form of multivirate time series analysis was evolved to track the effects of deployments of these weapons and tactics.[6] What emerged was a complex set of causal influences which locked the participants into their own violent behaviour. During the periods where this conflict broke down, variables, indicating violent behaviour of the various participants was most influenced by their own previous behaviour.

Paradoxically, whilst these weapons were meant to provide a new series of flexible reasonses, their ultimate effect was to programme their targets into traditional anti-state activities and procedures.

The Threat to Nonviolent Resistance and Social Defence

The challenge, now that these technologies are being subject to substantial vertical and horizontal proliferation, is to restructure new forms of dissent in ways which are less centralised and less easily targetted.

Many of these systems will undermine the efficacy of nonviolent forms of social resistance. The weapons described above have been designed to mask their violence and they form a bridge between doing nothing and opening fire with live rounds. Gassing and firing rubber bullets relatively innocuous on TV screens but provoke unmistakable terror on the ground. Furthermore, the weapons and the indoctrination which goes with them (the weapons can kill but are presented as non-lethal), mean they are far easier for state security forces to actually use on crowds.

Not all of the new control technologies are mono-functional. There are gray areas where what might be a legitimate technology in one state can be used oppressively in a different set of political circumstances. Computer systems, for example, or the traffic monitoring systems which are used in China were able to take photographs of the students in Tiananmen Square. These pictures were subsequently broadcast with a demand for identification together with a telephone number to ring for an anonymous reward.

What can happen during such extreme circumstances is that people spontaneously develop countermeasures. For example, in Iran during the days of the Shah, demonstrators burnt his picture in front of the myriad spy cameras in the plazas around Teheran which directly fed into his palace-with a depressing effect on his morale. A more recent example is that of communications monitoring after the Tiananmen Square massacre-the authorities closely watched telephones and telexes but messages passed through the University Computer networks reached a world audience apparently without interference.

Future Prospects

Whilst such examples provide inspiration against a depressing backcloth of rising ethnic and nationalistic violence, spontaneous actions, no matter how heroic, can be a pure substitute for advanced preparation based on adequate Research & Development.

Such work may inevitably be seen as subversion in almost every existing political context, barring one. Yet any government with full confidence could provide its people with powerful programmes of noncooperation. However, few governments (with the honourable exception of a previous Dutch coalition), have had the vision to actually recognise the need for R & D in supporting NVDA as part of a rehearsed strategy of social defence. The ambitious proposals put forward by the Dutch Commission on Nonviolent Conflict Resolution and Social Defence were controversial and yet in financial terms quite modest. For about the price of just one modern weapon system and a fraction of a percentage of the overall defence budget, the proposal set about exploring "the possibility of social defence in the face of advanced repression by states." Obviously such techniques can just as easily be used against a government at home as against any external attacker and for a variety of internal reasons the full study was never undertaken. And a government, providing formal support for such research to make social resistance more effective, must either have confidence in their own democratic credentials or rely once again on apathy. The coalition which supported this study collapsed and the rest is history but the vision was a brave one.

There are numerous zones of vulnerability and areas of resistance which with imagination and determination could yield new forms of political resistance which are not easy prey to such technologies.

In recent years, several related conferences have taken place to exchange information on the increasingly powerful innovations in the new technologies of political control (TN in the Netherlands; CILIP in West Germany; and RSSC, CAAT, AIIMSP & Lobster in the UK). The initiative of groups such as TNI, CILIP, and State Research and others to create an informal anti-state repression alliance and network in the early 1980s proved a useful beginning. Conferences like these have led to an extremely useful, albeit informal, exchanges of sources and approaches for consolidating the material available to researchers in this field. Such forms of international cooperation are likely to become even more important in the future.

Indeed many of the people involved in his commission will have experiences which are instructive and creative in avoiding state structures of domination. The plea here is to consider the advantages of collating and sharing methodologies to circumvent advanced state repression. State agencies worldwide are currently orchestrating their research efforts to produce even more efficient means and mechanisms of socio-political control. Multinational corporations and conglomerates have now spread the production of internal state security supplies in to new spheres of influence. A destructive side-effect of this process is the increasing militarisation of the public sector. Countervailing research is necessary even to discover the level and extent of government and commercial involvement in manufacturing and supplying repressive techniques and technologies.

Tracking the suppliers and manufactures of repressive technology and publishing what emerges is one powerful and nonviolent way of providing solidarity to those being targetted elsewhere. Many of these companies are harboured in the liberal democracies or are subsidiaries of quite well-known companies. With the growing trend for people to consider ethical investments, such companies are vulnerable to criticism - particularly if it affects their investments. A company TRACES–has been set up n Manchester, UK, with precisely this objective Using a sophisticated inter-relational database, it can track wares back to source and provide a higher profile for companies which would prefer this area of thier work to remain entirely secret. Media enquiries can be despatched tc the doors of directors to ask searching questions and set in trail political lobbying which can effectively halt the trade.

In the long run, however, detailed and determined research into countering new technologies of political control will become imperative. Initially this may simply mean organising structures of social resistance in new ways to retain effectiveness whilst avoiding the traps of a coercive police and paramilitary intelligence and infrastructure. Inevitably such work will be considered to be a form of subversive Research & Development but it can be argued that such a nonviolent undermining of coercive state structures is the raison d'etre of peace research, even our moral duty.

All these systems and technologies have basic flaws which permit their effects to be countermanded, if sufficient skill and determination are applied. If nonviolent forms of social resistance based on community rather than state are to continue to evolve, the threat posed by these technologies needs to be seriously addressed. As Johan Galtung has emphasized, "the social scientist should have at his disposal concepts and insights that enable him to construct worlds that have never existed, societies nobody dreamt of, and even indicate the condition that may lead to the."[7]

To reiterate what has been said above, the use of modern repression technologies might make future resistance to either external attack or tyrannical internal control even more dangerous and difficult, if nonviolent approaches are to survive as the chosen principles of opposition. Without a grater measure of prior preparation, planning, and afore thought to deal with advanced technologies or repression, such principles may be doomed to turn into their opposite. Future research should address the challenge of understanding the hidden as well as the direct consequences associated with the use of repressive technologies. Such knowledge may potentially be applied to the development of relatively nonviolent counter-measures which did not merely reinforce, service, or sustain the programmes of repression which are opposed. The role of new police technologies in undermining nonviolence is no longer a future -related matter. Through a process of decision and technological drift, as well as aggressive marketing strategies by the police industrial complex, such technologies are being integrated into state control systems now. Future strategies and tactics to obviate their effects are urgently required, if nonviolent social resistance strategies are to have more than an academic or ethical focus. This challenge must be a key objective of the collective efforts of peace researchers working in this field over the next twenty-five years, if the poverty-repression-militarisation cycle is to be broken.

Notes and References

1. Steve Wright, "The New Technology of Repression," in M. Hoefnagels, edu. Repression and Repressive Violence (Amsterdam: Swets & Zeitlinger, 1977). Pp.133-65.
2. For further details on this, see different papers presented at the Human Rights & Development Commission at the IPRA General Conference held at Groningn in 1990.
3. For a detailed technical description of such weapons, see Steve Wright, "Public Order Technology: 'Less-lethal weapons," In Civil Rights, Public Opinion, and the State, Working Papers in European Criminology, No.8, Rolsten B. & Tomlinsonm;. (eds.), 1987. ISBN) 9511708 1 3.
4. See Steve Wright, "New Police Technologies -An Exploration of the Social Implications and Unforeseen Impacts of Some Recent Developments," The Journal of

Peace Research, Vol. XV, No.4, 1978, pp. 305-22.

5. Steve Wright, "A Multi-Variate Time Series Analysis of the Northern Irish Conflict 1969-76," in Alexander and Gleason, eds., Bahavioural and Quantitative Perspectives on Terrorism (Permagon, 1981).

6. This work was further elaborated as part of a doctoral thesis: Steve Wright, New Police Technologies nd Sub-State Conflict Control (University of Lancaster, 1987).

7. Johan Galtung, Theory and Methods of Social Research (Oslo, 1967), pp.461-62.

STRUCTURE OF RIOT WEAPON USE

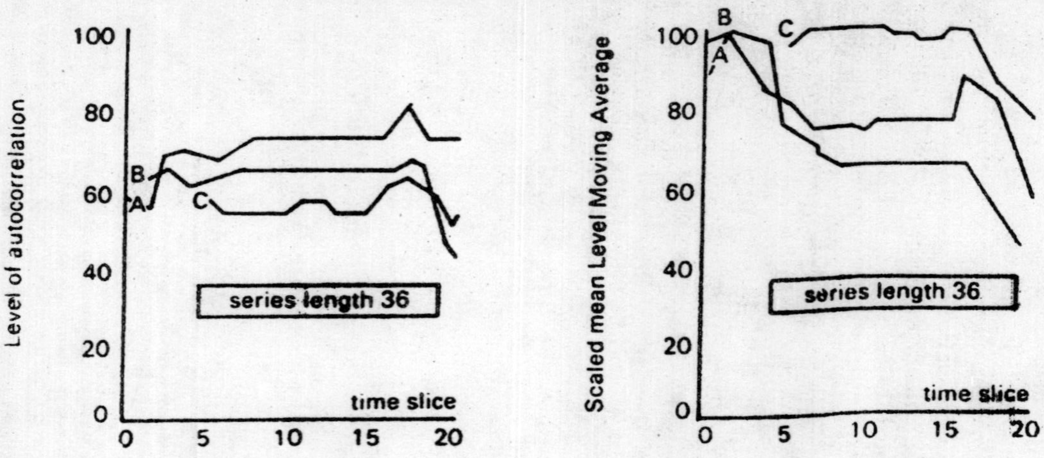

KEY: A=CS cartridges fired
B=CS grenades fired
C=rebber bullets fired

Figure 1

Chapter-10

Exercises In Nonviolent Action

Theodore Herman

Chapter-10

THE PURPOSE of this paper is to offer a few exercises for training oneself or other people in nonviolent action. Exercises such as these, whether performed for the occasion or reported as having actually happened, make us aware of how much we can learn from personal experience once we begin looking. In order to reveal some of the varieties of nonviolence, we will offer a definition of the word, and then a conceptual framework that has helped me to make that definition and to go beyond it in learning.

The word itself has many meanings, even to the same person. This, however, is not unusual, because many words have different meanings and are constantly acquiring new ones. Just as the words "peace," "war," "love," and the like are used to mark different conditions, the word "nonviolence" is also used quite broadly, especially in its religious and ethical context.[1]

The definition from which we can work today (and that covers most of the ideas found in the literature to date) is as follows:

> Nonviolence is both an attitude and a course of action that leads both an individual and a group of people to resist tyranny and injustice other than by physical force, and to build a community of caring by the reconciliation of adversaries. It also has a positive meaning as people strive to remove the causes of violent conflict, both human and environmental.

Whether the action is confrontational or constructive, the effort is always to devise new ways of thinking and acting in order to achieve a more peaceful world. Whether the emphasis on action rules out the Daoist teaching of *wu wei*, the action of no action-can be left to those who wish to explore this ancient East Asian teaching.[2] A less being meaning of nonviolence would reveal its use to suppress dissent, a condition all to familiar to people in many parts of the world. In any case, nonviolence provides a rich field for research into a given society's values, institutions and techniques, while its propagation as a benevolent force becomes a creative option for people everywhere.

To arrive at that definition I have found the simple conceptual framework set out below quite helpful to generate ideas, identify attitudes, and indicate relationships. The training exercise will illustrate some of them with specific actions that can be carried out anywhere.

Ideally the exercises should involve a group of no more than twenty people, as different as possible in physical characteristics, and conducted in a room that permits free movement. Whether you are involved or not, you should try to identify with the actors and the action, one of the basic steps in understanding nonviolence in any form.

There is no guarantee that such exercises will convert a non-believer to nonviolence with the first encounter. It would be far better to do some nonviolent activity along with someone already involved, and backed up with appropriate readings, as ,for example, Colman McCarthy does.[3] But let us see what we can learn.

A Framework for the Meanings of Nonviolence [4]

Personal or Individual	*Group*
1. Personal transformation or psycho-spiritual change	4. Nonviolent struggle and Civilian-based defence
2. Pacifism or non-retaliation in kind	5. Conflict resolution
3. Reconciliation with an adversary	6. Removing thecauses of violent conflict
	7. Developing a sound relationship with the earth

It is easy to make connections between most of these forms, although there does not seem to be any necessary numerical order of influence. For example, most people who practise #2 or #3 would have experienced#1, while #5 would probably reflect some aspects of #3. A national international policy for #7, protection for the environment, would involve #5 and #6. In short, the flows can move in any direction and involve several forms together, leading to a more unified way of life.

Also, these forms are not walled off in exclusive categories. For example, non-cooperation and civil disobedience are just as important under #3 as under #4, even though they might be justified differently. And anyone who experiences a strong change in personal outlook, as in #1, stands a good chance of moving through the other six forms from the personal to a global outlook. Obvious examples are William Penn, Leo Tolstoy, Gandhi, and Martin Luther King., Jr., but many other outstanding people could also be listed.5 Each began at one point and grew to include all the others.

Exercises in Training for Various Forms of Nonviolence

1. Personal transformation or psycho-spiritual change

1.1 Sit quietly together for inner control.

1.2 Stand in a circle for touchy-feely exercises with partners who differ in appearance. Leave your jewelery, watches, and money beneath your chair.

Expresses a sense of common humanity and trust in working and rejoicing together to overcome one's negative stereotypes.6

1.3 Marks in contrasting colours, five items in the daily newspaper that reflect violence, and five for nonviolence. Explain your choices.

Widen one's range of experience in recognizing both of these aspects of human behaviour.

1.4 In your regular life over the next few days, perform some different action of nonviolent intent, write the story briefly, and report to the group at its next meeting (this could be a regular activity).

Encourages each person to observe and to act.

Provides discipline in organizing and explaining to others.

2. Pacifism or non-retaliation in Kind

2.1. Who in the group has been discriminated against for some reason other than his/her actions or behaviour?

How did you respond?

Reveals the practice of negative stereotyping and the long remembered hurt.

Your responses may have given you and the other person a valuable lesson for the future. What has the lesson?

2.2 in a spot of hard body contact or a contest of intense rivalry, salute your rival's good actions as soon and as often as possible.

Gives respect to both persons in place of fear and avoidance.

3. Reconciliation with an adversary

3.1 Describe an important confrontation that you have had with another person, the outcome, and how it might have been improved for the benefit of "both" parties Ask for suggestions from others present.

Show the importance of listening and of putting one self in the other's place.

Draws on the helpfulness of all those present by emphasizing the common needs of human beings.

3.2 Listen to a short tape of an actual experiment in reconciliation by T. Herman at the Hegins, pa., Pigeon Shoot, 2 September 1991.

Reconciliation comes from making explicit our common aims and needs rather than our differences.

4. Nonviolent struggle and civilian based defence

4.1 Designing a scenario for nonviolent struggle (review the attached scenario on nonviolent struggler at Elizabethtown College , 23 October 1990).

Shows eight steps in organizing and conducting such an activity. Involves uniting the particiapnts, conducting negotiations, diplaying power, and settling for a modest gain.

4.2 Notice of France's halting of nuclear weapons tests in the South Pacific after strong opposition by Greenpeace.[7]

Shows strong commitment at great personal risk.

Demonstrates the importance of good publicity far and wide.

5. Conflict resolution

5.1 Perform a skit or simulation of a confrontation wit solutions to be proposed by those present. Example: A faculty member takes his family to a campus football or ice hockey game and wonders how to counter the jeering and profanity launched at the officials and opponents by the people around them. What would you advise him to do?

6. Removing the causes of violent conflict

6.1. Ask for suggestions on how to avoid the violence, both systemic and overt, that is so common in the US today. Brings together people of various views and backgrounds in a common search for nonviolent solutions, should be used to emphasize that one party's insistence on its own solution or on a perfect plan, at whatever scale, always leads to frustration and hence to more violence. The results depends on a sound process of mutual respect and willingness to change.

6.2 Share examples from literature, biograhpy, religion and the arts that move those present to deepen their commitment ot peace and justice via nonviolence.

Creates appreciation for the importance of human values expressed via the emotions, and encourages local expression in such media. Accepts the contributions of all present, with explanations, if necessary, for common

Notes and References

1. Theodore terman, "A Conceptual Framework of Nonviolence for Peace Research, "*International Journal fo Group Tensions*, Vol. 21, No.1 (spring 1991).
2. Liu Xiaogan, "Wuwei (Non Action) : From Laozi to Huainanzi, "*Taoist Resources*, Vol. 3, No.1 (July 1991), pp. 41-56.
3. Personal acquaintance with Colman McCarthy, Director, Center for Teaching Peace, 4501 Van Ness Street NW, Washington, D.C. 20016.
4. See Theodore Herman, "A Conceptual Framework of Nonviolence for Peace Research."
5. Useful guides to such a warm-up exercise for small children and adults alike are given in "Sharing Space," *Bulletin of Children's Creative Response* to *Conflcit* (Nyack, N.Y.: Fellowship of Reconciliation, 1990).
6. *New York Times*, 9 April 1992.

PL